"With the intellectual depth of an academic peric
potency of investigative journalism, this project is
nuanced and potent writing. This radiates particularly trom tne authors' inquest
into the treatment of Black, Asian and Minority Ethnic (BAME) women in
prison. As somebody who has conducted their own review into the punitive
treatment of BAME individuals, I am in awe of their courage in uncovering
how some women are forced to repeat the same brutalising exchanges with
authority that defined the colonial era. Stunningly broad yet rigorously focused,
these authors ruthlessly expose the harm of a criminal justice system that
responds to complex histories of trauma with retribution rather than understanding. Expertly examining the intersection of violence, marginalisation and
racial disproportionality, this book is not just hugely enlightening. Rather, it is
essential, particularly for those who legislate on how women are treated by
a penal system that is in desperate need of reform."

– David Lammy, MP

"This book couldn't be more timely in exploring the invisible trauma of women
in prison, from childhood, to imprisonment and after serving their sentence. It
uncovers the multiple harms of the prison system – created by powerful men to
control men with less power, and in the end serving no one. All those in a position to bring about change – Ministers, MPs, Criminal justice leaders and staff
(including prison governors and all those working with women affected by the
Criminal Justice System) need to read this. The chapters draw together decades
of evidence of a brutal, racist, sexist and broken system. We should all be angry
that so little has changed despite this overwhelming evidence and the blueprint
for a new system in Baroness Jean Corston's 2007 report. But at its core this
book is about hope and about imagining the power of a new system built round
the evidence and the traumatic reality of the lives of those women and men
caught in the prison system. A government delivering such a new system would
have a great legacy, because, as Gandhi warned and one of the chapters notes,
'A nation's greatness is measured by how it treats its weakest members'."

– Kate Paradine, Chief Executive Women in Prison

"*Invisible Trauma* by Motz, Dennis and Aiyegbusi offers a valuable insight into
the experiences of women in the criminal justice system, highlighting underlying
causes of offending and the need to divert them from custody wherever possible.
It will make essential reading for all who are involved with this complex and
vulnerable population."

– The Rt Hon. The Lord Bradley, House of Lords, London

Invisible Trauma

There is an expectation that women will be nurturers and carers. Women who have been judged violent, destructive and criminal and who are detained in the criminal justice system can find themselves perceived through a distorted lens as unwomanly. This book explains how they become hypervisible in their difference, while the histories of trauma and suffering that are communicated through their offending and other risk behaviour remain hidden, and so are unseen.

Bringing together authors uniquely placed as experts in their fields, *Invisible Trauma* argues that it is essential to trace the traumatic roots of women's violence and criminality. Powerful intergenerational factors perpetuate the cycles of offending and trauma re-enactment that current sentencing practice overlooks. The authors present a psychoanalytically informed account of the development of violence and other offending, identifying pathways for change to address trauma within the lives of these women and their children, and also to create a responsive, effective and sensitive workforce.

Invisible Trauma highlights the role of emotional, social and cultural forces in traumatising women who come into contact with the criminal justice system and uncovers areas of their lives that are all too often hidden from view. It will be invaluable to those working in clinical and forensic psychology, mental health nursing, psychotherapy, social work, medical practice and women's health, as well as frontline practitioners in the criminal justice system, the health service and third sector organisations and for anyone with an interest in racism, equality and social justice.

Anna Motz is a Consultant Clinical and Forensic Psychologist with the Central and North West London NHS Foundation Trust working within Offender Care and a Psychoanalytic Psychotherapist with extensive experience of working with women with trauma and offending histories. She is the author of *The Psychology of Female Violence: Crimes Against the Body* and *Toxic Couples: The Psychology of Domestic Violence*, and the Editor of *Managing Self Harm: Psychological Perspectives*.

Maxine Dennis is a Consultant Clinical Psychologist and Psychoanalyst (British Psychoanalytic Society) and is Groups Lead in the Adult Department, Tavistock and Portman NHS Foundation Trust. She is also a Visiting Lecturer at the University of Essex Clinical Psychology Department where she organises and contributes to the teaching on diversity and psychotherapy. Currently she is Chair of the British Psychoanalytic Council Task Group on Ethnicity, Culture and Racism.

Anne Aiyegbusi is a Mental Health Nurse, Forensic Psychotherapist and Group Analyst. She manages a clinical network for personality disorder at West London NHS Trust and is a Director of Psychological Approaches CIC. Anne has extensive experience of working with women who have histories of self-harm, trauma and offending; and of working with racism in forensic and psychotherapeutic contexts. Anne is a member of the Board of Trustees at the Institute of Group Analysis where she is also a member of the Diversity in Training Group, prioritising issues of 'Power, Privilege and Position'.

Invisible Trauma

Women, Difference and the Criminal Justice System

Anna Motz, Maxine Dennis and Anne Aiyegbusi

Routledge
Taylor & Francis Group

LONDON AND NEW YORK

First published 2020
by Routledge
2 Park Square, Milton Park, Abingdon, Oxon OX14 4RN

and by Routledge
52 Vanderbilt Avenue, New York, NY 10017

Routledge is an imprint of the Taylor & Francis Group, an informa business

British Library Cataloguing-in-Publication Data
A catalogue record for this book is available from the British Library

Library of Congress Cataloging-in-Publication Data
A catalog record has been requested for this book

ISBN: 978-1-138-21865-9 (hbk)
ISBN: 978-1-138-21866-6 (pbk)
ISBN: 978-1-315-39000-0 (ebk)

Typeset in Times New Roman
by Swales & Willis, Exeter, Devon, UK

For Bert, and for the untold and unseen women who died in prison, and the people who championed them

Contents

Acknowledgements

Anne Aiyegbusi: Holding views and values that may fall outside of the existing mainstream is often to walk a difficult path. As is speaking truth about the invisible traumas underlying profound distress, especially when it includes behaviour easily perceived to be offensive to social norms. As such it can feel like a privilege and a blessing to work with like-minded colleagues. This was my experience of co-authoring this book with Anna Motz and Maxine Dennis, whose passion to make the world a better place for women who offend has been uplifting, helping to navigate such essentially traumatic and painful material. I would also like to thank a number of colleagues and friends who have supported and helped me over the years of my professional life, especially in regard to the emotional challenges involved in working with the trauma of racism and the care of women who offend, which in turn has enabled me to contribute to this book. They are: Gwen Adshead, Anthea Benjamin, Sally Bild, Julia Blazdell, Maureen Burke, Dennis Czech, Jenifer French, Suzanne Higgs, Susan Iles, Gillian Kelly, Gabriel Kirtchuck, Kingsley Norton, Julie Ann Owen, Gemma Trainor, Stuart Stevenson, Ray Travers and Estela Welldon. Many people have supported my professional development such that I have been able to co-write this book. I thank colleagues and friends over many years, institutions and countries for providing enduring intellectual stimulation, professional inspiration, emotional support, joy and laughter. Because of this I have been able to work and inquire at depth and hopefully through my writing contribute to sharing a wider understanding of women who often find themselves on the margins, alienated from the care and support they desperately need. It is the women I have met and had the privilege of working with in forensic mental health and criminal justice settings to whom I am most grateful. My life has been enriched and I am thankful.

Maxine Dennis: I would like to thank the various individuals and families I have worked with clinically and whose lives I have shared. Their experiences have helped me to formulate some of my thinking. I would also like to thank the various training institutions, supervisors and colleagues I have worked with over the years. In particular Fakhry Davids, Sue Levy, Frank Lowe, Joanne

Stubley, Philip Birch and my co-authors Anna Motz and Anne Aiyegbusi. Finally, I am indebted to my own family for their patience and support.

Anna Motz: I am most grateful for the openness and generosity of the women on both sides of the bars, who have spoken to me about their experiences and given permission for me to share their stories. I would like to thank Sarah Allen, Julia Blazdell, Kayleigh Holden, Rupi Johal, Caroline Logan and Vicki Mclean for their interest and encouragement in this project, to longstanding friends in the International Association for Forensic Psychotherapy, especially John Adlam, Gwen Adshead, Estela Welldon, Sandra Grant, Pam Kleinot, Celia Taylor, Tilman Kluttig, Bandy Lee and Jessica Yakeley, and to Joy Doal, Sister Enda, Sarah Gallagher and Deborah Hickman from Anawim who offer hope for the most vulnerable women in society. The generous support, thoughtfulness and enthusiasm that my late friend Mike Solomon offered was invaluable and he is much missed. Friends and colleagues who have helped me to write parts of this book were exceptional in their kindness, insight and patience, especially Sean Kelly and Dorian Singh, whose painstaking reading of multiple drafts of chapters have been invaluable. Sean has been a kindred spirit in this and other writing tasks and his enthusiasm, interest and care has never wavered. I greatly appreciate the support of Joanna Burrell, Ted Colman, Christian David, Herbert Edlis, Maggie Fishman, Charlotte Fox Weber, Chris Mawson, Sheila Redfern, Kate Thompson, Marian Wassner and especially Hannah, Joshua and Nigel Warburton. Thanks also to those who have read and commented on individual chapters including Erika de Filippo and, in particular, my courageous and insightful co-authors, Anne Aiyegbusi and Maxine Dennis. Finally, I thank fellow members of the Advisory Board for Female Offenders whose passion and dedication to improving the lives of women in the criminal justice system is inspirational. We especially want to thank Oliver Durose and David Lammy for their interest and support in this project. The Lammy Review of the urgent issue of racial discrimination in the criminal justice system has been a guiding light for our research.

We are grateful to our copy-editor Nicholas Fox, production editor Ellie Jarvis at Swales & Willis and editors Alec Selwyn and Joanne Forshaw at Taylor & Francis for their commitment to this book. We are grateful to Lea Getu for permission to publish her untitled poem, to HarperCollins for permission to reproduce Maya Angelou's poem 'Caged Bird', to Julie Bindell and Aeon publications for permission to quote her, and to Laura Seebohm of Changing Lives for permission to quote from the Changing Lives website.

About the authors

Anne Aiyegbusi manages a clinical network for personality disorder at the West London NHS Trust. She is also a director, consultant nurse, psychotherapist and group analyst at Psychological Approaches CIC. Her nursing experience spans all roles from 'ward to board' in the NHS but the greater part of her career was as a consultant nurse for women's secure services. Her experience of these services is extensive, including two high secure hospitals and an enhanced medium secure service. In addition to her clinical work as a nurse and psychotherapist, Anne has developed and delivered trauma informed leadership, training, reflective practice and supervision to support front-line practitioners in their therapeutic work with traumatised women with offending histories. Anne integrated trauma and attachment-theory-informed psychodynamic psychotherapy into her work as a nurse for many years. This informs her academic work including her PhD and contributions within numerous higher education affiliations. Her many national and international academic presentations and her publications reflect this paradigm. Anne has contributed to national strategy concerning women in secure services and women who self-harm. For many years she has worked in a consultancy capacity to services for women diagnosed with personality disorders, including those who have offended. Professionally, she is registered with the Nursing and Midwifery Council, the British Psychoanalytic Council and the United Kingdom Council for Psychotherapy. Anne is also a long-time member of the International Association for Forensic Psychotherapy where she is a past board member and secretary. Additionally, she is a member of the Institute of Group Analysis, Forensic Psychotherapy Society, Black and Asian Therapy Network, and Group Analytic Society International. Past publications include co-editing (with Jenifer Clarke-Moore) *Relationships with Offenders: Introduction to the Psychodynamics of Forensic Nursing* (Jessica Kingsley Press, 2008) and co-editing (with Gillian Kelly) *Professional and Therapeutic Boundaries in Forensic Mental Health Practice* (Jessica Kingsley Press, 2012). She has written and presented extensively about personality disorder, women's forensic services and racism. Anne's main professional interests and activities involve trauma, attachment theory and racism.

Maxine Dennis is a consultant clinical psychologist at the Tavistock Clinic as well as a psychoanalytic psychotherapist and psychoanalyst. She works with adults at the present time and has worked with adolescents and their families. She is a senior member of staff at the Trauma Service at the Tavistock Clinic. Her work with individuals who are described as having a personality disorder includes providing intensive psychotherapy and group psychotherapy. Her concerns centre not only around how these women end up incarcerated but also the transition out of prison and factors leading to recidivism. She has a long-standing interest in the development of these difficulties across the life span and works with such marginalised communities. Maxine's therapeutic work with individuals who have experienced trauma and abuse over many years is relevant to the experience of many of the histories of female offenders. In addition to long term work she is a trainer, supervisor and practitioner in brief models including brief psychodynamic therapy (BPT), interpersonal therapy (IPT) and dynamic interpersonal therapy (DIT). Currently she is the lead for Groups in the Tavistock Clinic, Adult Department. She has directed and been a staff member on a number of Group Relation Conferences in the United Kingdom. Maxine has published in the areas of clinical psychology, supervision and racism.

Anna Motz is a consultant clinical and forensic psychologist with extensive experience of assessing and treating women who have long-standing difficulties with violence against themselves and others. She was Clinical Lead for the Community Forensic Outpatient Service in Oxford, a dedicated forensic service for high-risk offenders with personality disorders, and is now Consultant Psychologist for Central and North West London NHS Trust, working within Offender Care. She is also a psychoanalytic psychotherapist and the author of *The Psychology of Female Violence: Crimes Against the Body* (Routledge, 2001, 2008), editor of *Managing Self Harm: Psychological Perspectives* (Routledge, 2009) and author of *Toxic Couples: The Psychology of Domestic Violence* (Routledge, 2014) and numerous papers on female violence, self-harm, shame and its role in violent enactments and destructive dynamics within intimate relationships. She is an independent consultant who has designed the Women and Personality Disorder BSc and MSc modules for the Institute of Mental Health, commissioned by NHS England and Her Majesty's Prison and Probation Service (HMPPS) and delivers these modules nationally. She has 28 years of experience of working within forensic services as a clinician and expert witness to the courts, and is a mentalisation-based therapy supervisor for the treatment of antisocial personality disorder, employed by the Anna Freud Centre, and offering supervision to the Irish Prison Service as well as forensic services across England and Wales.

Anna is a member of the Advisory Board for Female Offenders and an independent consultant to the National Crime Agency.

Chapter 1

Introduction

Anna Motz, Maxine Dennis and Anne Aiyegbusi

Invisible trauma: visible difference

Women's routes into the criminal justice system differ distinctly from men's. They generally do not commit violent offences, but when they do, their targets are their intimate partners or children, family members and their own bodies, rather than strangers. Men pose greater risk to members of the public than to intimates and are responsible for over 75% of violent crime according to the 2017 British Crime Survey. Despite these clear differences, female offenders are often sentenced without consideration of their social, personal and family circumstances, or the mainly non-violent nature of their offences, and they receive short custodial sentences in a prison system designed for men. As more women than men are primary carers for children, the impact of their imprisonment is significant and harmful; these short sentences disrupt the care of children, can jeopardise accommodation and do not enable the women to engage in treatment programmes that address their complex difficulties and help reduce the risk of their reoffending.

Against the backdrop of this general neglect of the meaning and origins of women's offending, and the injustice of social and legal responses to female offenders, the particular discrimination against women of Black, Asian and Minority Ethnic (BAME) backgrounds is a critical area that has for too long remained unexplored and unchallenged. Women and men from BAME backgrounds are over-represented in the criminal justice system (Ministry of Justice, 2016; Lammy, 2017). The brutalising experience of racial discrimination is well described by the African American poet Langston Hughes in his poem, 'Harlem', and speaks to the loss of hope and unmet promises that so many BAME women face in the United Kingdom, when he asks,

> What happens to a dream deferred?
> Does it dry up
> like a raisin in the sun?
> ... or does it explode?

In this final line Hughes suggests that this dream might ultimately explode, indicating the violence that continued oppression and humiliation can generate. The traumatic roots of this violence are all too often overlooked, and women of colour and those from ethnic minority backgrounds are viewed simply as bad or dangerous, or alternatively not seen at all. We hope to redress that inequity in this book through a psychological exploration of the manifestations and roots of racism, both conscious and unconscious.

We will focus on the experiences of women within the United Kingdom throughout this book, though we are aware that there are commonalities in other countries, particularly in the USA. We will also focus on initiatives within the United Kingdom that have been developed in response to this issue, namely the Women Offenders Personality Disorder Pathway and, more recently, the government initiative, the Female Offender Strategy, designed to review and revolutionise the sentencing and disposal of women who commit offences. We are all psychoanalytically informed therapists who will focus on psychological understanding of traumatic experiences and how they impact on the lives of women within secure mental health and criminal justice settings, as well as within the community.

Although we have different areas of specialisms, we share expertise in working with women with trauma histories, in specialist services, and a passion for understanding, exploring and treating the long-term impact of these destructive experiences. We are particularly interested in those aspects of the women's presentations and histories that are hidden or unseen; we want to reveal and attend to the invisible trauma that has shaped their lives.

Aims of the book

In this book we argue that it is essential to trace the traumatic roots of women's violence and offending. The trauma that these women have experienced in the past, and still battle, is not only overlooked in their sentencing and subsequent placement, but is also often re-enacted within custodial settings and in the community. There are powerful intergenerational factors that perpetuate these cycles of offending and trauma re-enactment that current sentencing practice overlooks. In her groundbreaking report of 2007, Baroness Corston revealed that women in the United Kingdom are imprisoned in environments designed for men, with disastrous consequences for them and their families (Corston, 2007). We present a psychoanalytically informed account of the development of violence and other offending and identify pathways for change to address trauma within the lives of these women and their children, and also to create a responsive, effective and sensitive workforce.

Women who are in a minority in terms of cultural, ethnic and religious difference, or their extreme psychological complexity, are at particular risk of being overlooked, misunderstood or harshly treated. BAME women are disproportionately represented in the criminal justice system and viewed as more dangerous than their white counterparts. Bias against women who do not fit cultural stereotypes of acceptability is widespread, and often occurs at an unconscious level. We seek to identify and deconstruct this process here.

Although certain aspects of these women's lives are under the spotlight, their histories are invisible. In an important sense they are the invisible women: the facts of their past lives and the oppression of their present circumstances is not seen, and their humanity, creativity and social connections are ignored, though their criminality is seen in full. As Ralph Ellison (2014) eloquently states in the opening to his 1952 novel, *Invisible Man*, 'I am invisible, understand, simply because people refuse to see me'. Ellison chronicles the experiences of a nameless black man in America who not only is unseen by others but also unable fully to see himself, caught up in a toxic mix of identity confusion, racial persecution and black nationalism, taking on board the projections of others. He faces an existential crisis, eventually resolved when he literally goes underground, illegally siphoning off power from the electricity board to light up his basement apartment. This metaphor, of stolen light that allows him to see his surroundings, and finally himself, while remaining invisible to others, has deep resonance for the women in the criminal justice system. They do not exist in isolation, but are shaped, structured, fleshed out, seen in some aspects but unseen in others, dependent on the beholding eye, that is all too often blinded by conscious and unconscious bias or focused on a shadow (see Chapter 3).

In this volume we focus on marginalised women, cast out of the mainstream by virtue of their religion, cultural background, sexuality, histories of trauma and neglect, geographical dislocation and experiences of extreme acts of violence, including sexual violence, as perpetrator, victim or both. We discuss the lived experiences of women who are mothers as well as the particular issues they face in the criminal justice system, and upon their re-entry into the community. We explore the tremendous and intergenerational harm of either being seen in a distorted light or rendered invisible. Using anonymised clinical material where consent has been obtained, we examine the experiences of women whose trauma is buried and whose otherness cannot be borne. Their deferred dreams, unrealised hopes and destroyed families may, in turn, lead to their explosive violence, as Hughes suggests, in reference to the oppressed men and women of Harlem. Like the dried raisin, turning syrupy sweet, the women's dreams and their disappointment can transform them from within, in ways that are hidden to the beholder. Their underlying anger and passionate sense of injustice goes unnoticed, as the blind eye can only see the pretty and feminine facade, not the festering rage within.

The role of women's anger as an instrumental force for change, not as an expression of pathology, is crucial. Women have agency and passion and can express protest directly at injustice, or when their capacity to tolerate frustration is stretched beyond reason. This is well illustrated in the uprising of women's protest movements in the United States this year:

Instead of recognizing female fury as the righteous spark that alters what we see, what we know, we are typically encouraged to focus on feminine 'peaceability': Mamie Till's grief, or Rosa Parks's stoicism and exhaustion in refusing to give up her seat on a Montgomery, Alabama, bus, the same year that Emmett Till was murdered. In fact, Parks was a fiery life-long organizer challenging sexual and racial violence, a defender of black men wrongly accused of sexual misconduct by white women, and an elected NAACP secretary who investigated the rape claims of black women against white men, including the brutal 1944 gang rape of the sharecropper Recy Taylor in Abbeville, Alabama.

(Traister, 2018)

The context in the United Kingdom[1]

* As of 15 June 2018, the women's prison population was 3,867, accounting for 4.7% of the prison population.
* Women have consistently accounted for around 5% of the total prison population since 2007.
* An estimated 24–31% of female offenders have dependent children.
* Over 60% of female offenders have experienced domestic violence.
* A higher proportion of women in custody are living with their dependent children prior to imprisonment than imprisoned fathers (60% vs 45%).
* Female prisoners are more than twice as likely as male prisoners to report needing help for mental health problems, 49% and 18% respectively.
* The reoffending rate for women released from a custodial sentence of fewer than 12 months during April–June 2016 was 71%.
* Evidence shows the imprisonment of mothers has a greater impact on the living arrangements of dependent children than the imprisonment of fathers, and that binge drinking and Class A drug use are risk factors more strongly associated with reoffending for women than they are for men. (Prison Reform Trust, 2017.)

The inefficacy of short-term custodial sentences is well described by the former Secretary of State for Justice, David Gauke, in his foreword to the Female Offender Strategy:

Seventy point seven of adult women and 62.9% of adult men released from custody between April to June 2016 following a short custodial sentence of less than 12 months reoffended within a year. There is persuasive evidence that short custodial sentences are less effective in reducing reoffending than community orders. Short sentences generate churn which is a major driver of instability in our prisons and they do not provide sufficient time for rehabilitative activity. The impact on women, many of whom are sentenced for non-violent, low level but persistent offences, often for short periods of time, is particularly significant. The prevalence of anxiety and self-harm incidents is greater than for male prisoners. As more female offenders are primary carers than their male counterparts, these sentences lead to a disproportionate impact on children and families and a failure to halt the intergenerational cycle of offending.

(Gauke, 2018: 3)

The treatment of foreign national women is a major source of disquiet, as these women are also over represented in the criminal justice system, and a significant proportion have been trafficked. Foreign national women represent 8% of the general population in England and Wales but over 12% of all women received into prison each year and nearly 19% of those remanded, according to the 2018 report on the treatment of foreign nationals, *Still No Way Out* (Swaine, Earle and Litchfield, 2018), are foreign nationals. The report describes the harsh treatment of foreign national women, and their often-hidden histories of sexual exploitation and violence. It identifies that between February 2013 and March 2017, 45 women were victims or potential victims of trafficking, facing prison for between one month and up to three years, despite having disclosed that they had been exploited. This report found that foreign national women, many of whom were accused or convicted of non-violent offences and who had in many cases been trafficked or coerced into offending, received inadequate legal representation, poor interpreting services and disproportionate punishment.

The trauma histories of criminalised women

The trauma histories of women in the criminal justice system are extensive and associated with alcohol and drug dependence, high-risk behaviours, prostitution, self-harm and physical and mental health disorders. Even in the general population, women are more likely as children to have suffered emotional abuse, emotional neglect, sexual abuse and to have observed within the household environment one or more of substance abuse, mental illness or their mother being treated violently. Studies have shown that women in general are 50% more likely than men to have a score of five or more adverse childhood experiences, contributing to increased risks of alcoholism, injecting drug use and suicide attempts.

> Understandably then, the female offender population – and especially the female prison population – contains some of the most disadvantaged, damaged and vulnerable people in our society. At once both prolific and persistent in their offending – and often repeatedly victimised by those who abuse and exploit them.

(Centre for Social Justice, 2018: 7)

Vilification of criminal women

Women who step out of the role of traditional femininity are 'doubly damned' (Lloyd, 1995): they are punished harshly within the criminal justice system and further condemned by wider society as evil, monstrous or otherwise depraved. Women who commit sexual offences against children, or those who kill, will be targeted for a particular brand of hatred and vilification that few men will be exposed to, even when their crimes are equally heinous. Women who commit such offences shatter dearly held stereotypes of femininity, and of motherhood; it is this violation, as much as their actual offences, that is seen as unforgiveable.

Women are often misrepresented when they appear in courts as offenders. The dual role of women as perpetrator and victim is almost impossible to bear in mind and women who offend are viewed either as passive victims, stripped of moral agency and reason, or as demonic creatures, devoid of humanity.

We examine the idealisation and denigration of womanhood in general, and criminal women in particular, describing the ways in which female offenders are both pathologised and demonised, further leading to punitive responses to female violence and sensationalistic, alarmist portrayals of women who offend. We describe how racism functions to continuously force black women to contain projections of wickedness and dangerousness, casting them in the role of perpetrator while blind to their current and generational histories of trauma.

As Helena Kennedy has described, the law is often harsh to women who are victims of crimes, let alone those who are perpetrators. This is especially the case with black women:

> Any review of our newspapers shows that the press and public want their victims packaged in an acceptable form. Drink, drugs, any kind of unconventional past, even ethnicity, can conspire to damn a woman as unworthy of the law's protection. The Times columnist Mary Ann Sieghart wrote that, when she was working on a tabloid paper, she was asked by the editor to do a feature on rape. She found an appalling story of a young woman who had been viciously raped but the story was binned when she explained that the victim was black.
>
> (Kennedy, 2018: 29)

Intersectionality: discrimination

The statistics relating to BAME women in the criminal justice system tell a grim story of discrimination, over-representation and misperception. In this way, women of difference are hypervisible while their underlying stories and hidden needs remain invisible. This is the central paradox to which we in this book repeatedly return, indicating the urgent need for radical reform of the way that marginalised women are treated within the criminal justice system.

The disadvantages all women face with the criminal justice system, such as experiencing a greater likelihood of imprisonment than men for first offences and non-violent offences, higher rates of remand and poorer outcomes on release, are compounded for BAME women. They make up 11.9% of the women's population in England and Wales, but 18% of the women's prison population. This represents a decline since 2012 when it was 22%, but it remains significantly disproportionate (Cox and Sacks-Jones, 2017).

Other statistics confirm the data collected by the Prison Reform Trust and David Lammy in his 2017 *Review* and are documented in the 2017 report *Double Disadvantage* by Cox and Sacks-Jones, indicating clear discrimination against black women in the criminal justice system:

If convicted, black women are 25% more likely than white women to receive a custodial sentence. There are broader consequences of this, as black women are particularly likely to be single mothers. More than half of black families in the UK are headed by a lone parent, compared with less than a quarter of white families and just over a tenth of Asian families. Despite the law's requirement that the welfare of children affected should be considered in sentencing, many women in the focus groups conducted by Agenda felt that their family circumstances had not been considered in their sentences. Proba-tion officers describe how increasing time constraints mean they are not able to gather a full picture of the women's family circumstances when preparing pre-sentence reports, despite the training that requires them to do so.

There is particularly marked disproportion in the experience of black women in the Crown Court for drugs offences. These defendants are 84% more likely than white women to be remanded in custody, despite no significant difference in conviction rates, and then more than twice as likely (127% more) to receive a custodial sentence than white women.

Although there is a surprising absence of data on the ethnicity of women in the criminal justice system, the report carried out by the Prison Reform Trust, *Counted Out*, revealed the following:[2]

> Women from minority ethnic groups face many of the same challenges as white British women compared to men within the criminal justice system, including exposure to domestic and/or sexual abuse, problematic substance use, and the probability that they have the primary care of dependent chil-dren … we know the ethnic origin of those in prison on any given date (the 'snapshot' figure) but not that of women received into prison over the course of a year (the reception figure). Nor is information published on the ethnicity of women who are recalled back to prison following release, or of women who are on community orders. However, even the currently limited range of published statistics and survey evidence lays bare real disparities:
>
> • Black women are more likely than other women to be remanded or sentenced to custody.

- Black women are more likely to be sole parents so their imprisonment has particular implications for children.
- Women from minority ethnic groups are more likely to plead not guilty in the Crown Court, leaving them open to potentially harsher sentencing.
- Women from minority ethnic groups feel less safe in custody and have less access to mental health support, according to surveys by HM Inspectorate of Prisons (HMIP).
- Women from minority ethnic groups experience racial and religious discrimination in prison from other prisoners and from staff, according to surveys by HMIP.
- Some women from minority ethnic groups are also foreign nationals and may be subject to immigration control and face language and cultural barriers.
- Asian and Muslim women may experience particularly acute stigma from their own communities.
- There are very few specialist organisations working with women from minority ethnic groups in the criminal justice system.

For every 100 white women given a custodial sentence for drug offences, 227 black women are sentenced to custody for the same offence.

(*Lammy Review*, 2017)

While emphasis has recently been placed upon the need for services to be gender responsive, there remains a significant lack of attention to the intersection of gender with race and ethnicity, as well as other sources of oppression and inequality.

Maternal imprisonment: invisible victims

Across England, Wales and Scotland, most female offenders are themselves mothers. They also often have no work outside the home, had problems at school, gaining few (if any) qualifications, rely on state benefits and have problem debts, and accommodation problems. Many will have experienced some form of abuse, have suffered psychological distress and have serious problems with alcohol and drug misuse. Furthermore, a good proportion grew up in local authority care as children – with some losing the care of their own children to the state, in a repetitive cycle.

(Centre for Social Justice, 2018: 7)

The impact of even a brief period of imprisonment on mothers and children is significant and destructive.

The destructive impact of maternal imprisonment on their children must be recognised. In her seminal report in 2007 urging prison reform for women,

Baroness Corston made this abundantly clear, urging that short sentences for women be replaced with sentencing to holistic 'one stop shops' in local community centres. Her report followed the suicide of six women in HMP Styal and identified three categories of vulnerabilities for women related to: domestic circumstances and problems such as domestic violence, childcare issues, being a single parent; personal circumstances such as mental illness, low self-esteem, eating disorders, substance misuse; socio-economic factors such as poverty, isolation and employment. She called for an urgent reform of the women's prison estate and the development of community based provision.

It is most regrettable that the resources required for this urgent reform have not yet been made available. Recent research has cited the destructive impact on children: children were overwhelmingly sad, missed their mothers, had no places in schools, had difficulties seeing their mothers – and women's prisons are far away and children are often stigmatised by the fact of their mothers' criminal status. Additionally, these children were emotionally harmed by the separation from their mother, often their primary caregivers.

In her moving and powerful research on the impact of maternal imprisonment on mothers and children, Baroness Corston found that 20,000 children a year are affected by maternal incarceration (up from 6,000 in 1995): only 5% of those children remain in their own homes, only 9% are cared for by their fathers and 14% of these children are placed in the care of the Local Authority.

In their research paper on the impact of short sentences on mothers, 'Short but Not Sweet', Baldwin and Epstein (2017) describe the short and long-term consequences of often unnecessary custodial sentencing. They recount the experience of one young mother who was sentenced to a community order, following a three-week remand period. A positive result perhaps, but even during the relatively short remand the woman was made homeless by her landlord and her son was taken into care. As a consequence, the young mother's substance misuse spiralled downwards and she ultimately returned to prison and never regained custody of her son. This is not an isolated case – the continued use of both short sentences and remand in relation to mothers who commit less serious non-violent crime will result in the continued devastation to ever more families. Research indicates that magistrates are often reluctant to remand on bail in relation to women due to a belief that women misusing substances (around 50% of female offenders) lead lives that are 'too chaotic' to facilitate compliance with bail conditions, or a hope that custody will offer those women support services.

The research on mothers in prison and the impact of separation, both on the children and on the mothers themselves, is powerful and points to the urgent need to reduce custodial sentencing of women dramatically, particularly when they have dependent children. An unintended consequence of sentencing mothers to prison is that this will increase the risk of intergenerational transmission of criminality, as the rates of antisocial behaviour and conduct disorder in the children from whom they separate will themselves increase (Kevin Browne, personal communication).

The pain of losing care of a child ranks high as one of the many wounds female prisoners may bear secretly. Laura Abbot (2019) undertook extensive research on the experiences of women who give birth whilst serving prison sentences and are not able to remain with their babies in a mother and baby unit. She describes this powerfully, in terms of the mother's wish to become invisible and mask her pain. 'Returning to prison post birth as a childless mother may lead a woman to want to be as invisible as possible, as if to numb her pain and merge herself into the background' (Abbot, 2019).

Women forcibly separated from their babies are targets for a perfect storm of grief and distress intermingled with the normal post-natal physical and emotional responses. In 2016, it was reported that a woman committed suicide shortly after returning to prison following the birth and subsequent removal of her baby five days previously (Parveen, 2016).

Shona Minson's research (2017) demonstrates that having a mother in prison negatively impacts on the child's relationship with her and can affect all areas of psychosocial functioning for the child, and can lead to stigmatisation, social isolation and discrimination. Minson, in collaboration with the Prison Reform Trust's Transforming Lives Programme, has been able to create resources for criminal justice professionals involved in sentencing decisions to enable them to understand the destructive impact on children of maternal imprisonment. This work has been instrumental in leading to training for probation officers that stresses the inclusion of maternal status in Pre-Sentence Reports, to enable magistrates and judges to take this into account when passing sentence.

On 18 June 2018 Lord Farmer's review into women and their family ties was released. This review was commissioned by the Ministry of Justice, following his earlier report into the family ties for male offenders. His report is entitled, *The Importance of Strengthening Female Offenders' Family and Other Relationships to Prevent Reoffending and Reduce Intergenerational Crime.* Over 500 women were interviewed and/or gave evidence to inform this report.

The importance of Lord Farmer's report rests on his recognition of the central place that relationships play in the lives of female offenders, the highly significant fact that over 50% of women in prison are mothers of children under the age of 18, and the clear, destructive impact of separation on both the women and their children. When their mothers go to prison only 5% of the children stay in their own home. The report emphasises the urgency of maintaining these ties, and enabling women and their children to have reliable, regular and meaningful contact even once the mothers are imprisoned. He highlights the link between the reduction in the women's rates of reoffending and contact with their children, the significant role of trauma in the lives of women who commit crimes, including high rates of domestic violence: over 60% of women in prison have experienced such abuse. Indeed, recent reports from HMP Drake Hall have highlighted the strong link between women presenting with acquired brain injury and a history of domestic violence: of the 173 women screened, 65% had signs of brain injury and 96% of these reported histories of domestic violence (Disabilities Trust and Royal Holloway, University of London, 2018).

As well as describing the trauma suffered by imprisoned mothers and their children, this book addresses the significant issue of self-harm by women in the criminal justice system, and how to respond to and understand its meanings, including its non-suicidal functioning. While exploring the ways in which self-harm can function to help women to cope with trauma, we acknowledge and discuss the stark fact of suicides in women's prisons and post-release, noting the grim statistics cited by the 2019 update on the Inquest briefing: 'Since the Corston Review was published in March 2007, there have been 106 deaths in women's prisons (to 10 May 2019). An additional 159 women have died after release from prison between 2010 and 2018' (Inquest, 2018, 2019).

The structure of the book

Throughout the book we offer clinical illustrations that are based on composites of women with whom we have worked, with potentially identifiable features anonymised and disguised, and from whom written consent for publication has been obtained wherever possible.

In Chapter 2, Anna Motz describes the roots of societal attitudes related to violent women, and particularly towards mothers who abuse their children, using examples from case law, media representations of violent women and anonymised clinical illustrations based on women she has both treated and assessed. She develops arguments and discussions that featured in her earlier work, both in *The Psychology of Female Violence* and in *Toxic Couples*. She outlines a model for understanding acts of violence by women within particular social and cultural contexts, rather than simply as manifestations of individual psychic imbalance, and describes psychotherapeutic work with mothers who have killed. She argues that to deny female violence is to deny female agency, as stated in 2001, and to ascribe violent actions to a pervasive disturbance of mind and a fundamentally deviant personality is another form of denial and caricature. In this case, the violent action is viewed as an uncontrollable expression of a characterological deficiency rather than, at times, a choice, freely made. At other times it is an unwanted re-enactment of an earlier trauma, but this time reconstructed in order that the former victim is now powerful, as she becomes a perpetrator of brutality, emotional, physical or sexual.

In Chapter 3, Maxine Dennis explores how intergenerational and transgenerational trauma in the criminal justice system and the negative internalisation of blackness has implications for a sense of self. She describes how the legacy of the trans-Atlantic slave trade and the mechanism of turning a blind eye leads to the denial of difference, and the devastating consequences of this. This phenomenon is linked to the demonisation of women of colour when they express anger, or a refusal to see them at all, by the non-seeing eye, portraying unconscious bias and hatred. A narrative within which her-story is defined externally and may not support the internal experience, the chasm which results from these diametrically opposed positions, is thus filled with overt and covert violence and the resultant damage supported by the idea of the empty category of 'races'. Those at the bottom of the 'race' hierarchy are afforded little value or care.

In Chapter 4, Anne Aiyegbusi also organises her description of racist phenomena in terms of the part played by the visual register and what it can do in the face of blackness. She describes how the generationally transmitted trauma of racist atrocities such as slavery and colonisation can become most graphically re-enacted in the criminal justice and forensic mental health systems where black girls and women are particularly vulnerable. She refers to the well documented and tragic death of Sarah Reed in London's Holloway Prison in 2016 as an example of how this occurs. The racist gaze is elucidated in this chapter, clarifying how it distorts and degrades black people who are at risk of internalising the accompanying projections. Where black girls and women have been unconsciously but conveniently cast in the roles of oversexed, invulnerable, criminal, unfit or violent mothers in order to maintain wider societal delusions of white purity, they are at risk when they become overwhelmed or distressed. The risk is that their vulnerability will not be seen and their distress not understood, while racist tropes serve to obscure and reshape their circumstances such that they are treated with disproportionate discipline and punishment, not the care, treatment or support they need.

In Chapter 5, Motz explores women's routes into prostitution and its links with exploitation, sexual trauma and stigma, offering a critique of the view that entering the sex trade is a choice women freely make, and instead seeing it as a form of structural violence and a strategy for survival in difficult circumstances. She traces the trajectories of women from abused child to prostituted woman.

In Chapter 6, Motz focuses on self-harm, one of the most serious issues in women's secure establishments, and one of the most eloquent forms of expression. She describes its communicative power and hopeful aspect, as well as its destructive potential, identifying current treatment and prevention strategies as well as analysing its unconscious meanings.

In Chapter 7, Motz then discusses and critiques the notion of psychopathy in women, and offers an alternative conceptualisation, 'the psychopathic state of mind.' Motz discusses the notion of the female psychopath with reference to current research on women and risk. She explores how female psychopathy can be understood through a personality trait approach. This chapter includes a critique of the construct of personality disorder and its application to women, especially those from an ethnic background where issues of difference and unconscious bias can play a significant role in contributing to assessments of 'dangerousness'.

In Chapter 8, Motz considers women deemed high risk within the criminal justice system, placed on Restricted Status within prisons or held in high secure hospitals under the category of Psychopathic Disorder, in relation to their deprivation of liberty and the potential for loss of hope. She also considers the sense of hopelessness that Indeterminate Public Protection Sentences can engender in women who have received them. She examines societal blindness in relation to violent women and how it alternates with hyper-acuity, exploring why certain women are perceived to be of the highest levels of dangerousness, suggesting that stereotyped notions of femininity can obscure the accurate assessment and treatment of female offenders. Motz discusses female terrorism and women who are serial murderers, and the media view of these relatively infrequent crimes.

The last three chapters in the book focus on organisational and individual defences against working with the women described, with particular attention to how cultural and ethnic difference impacts on the way these women are seen and treated. In Chapter 9, Motz explores the impact of working with violent women in terms of its 'intoxicating aspects' and relates this to the function of violence for the offender herself, as well as to the actual use of substances to achieve states of intoxication.

In Chapter 10, Aiyegbusi describes a cohort of severely traumatised women who may be found segregated, almost hidden within systems of secure care. The extreme treatment of their bodies, the current and historic abuse of all that is theirs and the impact they have on front-line workers tasked with caring for them typically threaten to overwhelm the entire system. Aiyegbusi draws on the work of Lucy Johnstone and the British Psychological Society in their *Power, Threat, Meaning Framework* (Johnston and Boyle, 2018) that offers a strong critique of the notion of personality disorder and suggests that the question to be asked of women who are often classified as such should be reframed as 'What happened to you?' rather than 'What is wrong with you?'. Her argument is one that supports the urgent need for trauma-informed services.

In Chapter 11, Dennis describes organisational defences against working with black women and girls, and analyses how these result in the creation of a toxic Other. She describes the institutional anxieties that underpin the strict hierarchical treatment of women prisoners, and which often follow lines of racial bias, with black women as prisoners and white women and men in role as prison officers. Drawing on clinical material, the chapter explores internal implications of trauma, internalised self-hatred and the development of identity in relation to her-story, in addition to exploring group functioning and implications for staff.

We warn the reader that this book may make difficult reading at times. It has also been difficult to write, as the brutality of the subject matter is hard to bear. We consider this to reflect the unbearable reality of the women's traumatic experiences, as victim and perpetrator, and the ways in which this evokes and uncovers our own hidden pain.

Finally, in the concluding chapter, 'Why the caged bird sings', the authors tie together the themes of the book and describe important recent developments in the United Kingdom including *The Farmer Review* (2019), *The Female Offender Strategy* (Ministry of Justice, 2018) and the ongoing work of the Women Offenders with Personality Disorder Pathway, and its psychological, trauma-informed and gender-specific focus. We outline the training needs for workers in this area, and the importance of reflective practice and analytically informed supervision, identifying areas of good practice and suggesting ways forward.

Although this book will not be able to explore in depth the full range of social and political issues that impact on women within the criminal justice system, we will highlight some of the recent developments and research that address central concerns facing marginalised women and explore the underlying psychological forces that can lead women to commit crimes, some of which involve serious violence. We focus on those women whose visible differences are emphasised at the expense of their invisible trauma. To return to Ellison, whose words encapsulate the pain of being unseen:

> I am invisible, understand, simply because people refuse to see me. Like the bodiless heads you see sometimes in circus sideshows, it is as though I have been surrounded by mirrors of hard, distorting glass. When they approach me, they see only my surroundings, themselves or figments of their imagination, indeed, everything and anything except me.
>
> (Ellison, 2014: 1)

Notes

1 From the Press Release for the Female Offender Strategy, published by the Ministry of Justice, 27 June 2018.
2 This report drew on Home Office data including that obtained through the Lammy Review, which identified pronounced disproportionality in the treatment of men and women from minority ethnic groups at the point of arrest, in relation to custodial remand and sentencing, and in prison discipline adjudications.

References

Abbot, L. (2019) Transition to motherhood and becoming a child-less mother in prison. In Foster, A. (ed.), *Mothers Accused and Abused: Addressing Complex Psychological Needs*. Oxon: Routledge.

Baldwin, L. and Epstein, R. (2017) *Short But Not Sweet: A Study of the Impact of Short Sentences on Mothers and Their Children*. Oakdale Trust. Leicester: De Montfort University.

Centre for Social Justice (2018) *A Woman-centred Approach: Freeing Vulnerable Women from the Revolving Door of Crime*. London: CSJ.

Coles, D., Roberts, R. and Cavcav, S. (2018) *Still Dying on the Inside*. London: Inquest.

Coles, D., Roberts, R. and Cavcav, S. (2019) *Still Dying on the Inside: Examining Deaths in Women's Prisons*. London: Inquest.

Corston, B. (2007) *A Report by Baroness Jean Corston of a Review of Women with Particular Vulnerabilities in the Criminal Justice System*. The Home Office.

Cox, J. and Sacks-Jones, K. (2017) *"Double Disadvantage" The Experiences of Black, Asian and Minority Ethnic Women in the Criminal Justice System*. London: Agenda Alliance for Women & Girls at Risk.

Disabilities Trust and Royal Holloway, University of London (2018) *Making the Link: Female Offending and Brain Injury*. Barrow: Cadbury and Pilgrim Trust.

Ellison, R. (2014, first published in 1952) *Invisible Man*. London: Penguin Essentials.

Farmer, M. (2019) *The Importance of Strengthening Female Offenders' Family and other Relationships to Prevent Reoffending and Reduce Intergenerational Crime*. London: Ministry of Justice. Available at: https://www.gov.uk/government/publications/farmer-review-for-women

Gauke, D. (2018) *Foreword to Female Offender Strategy*. London: Ministry of Justice. Available at: www.gov.uk/government/publications/female-offender-strategy

Johnstone, L. and Boyle, M. with Cromby, J., Dillon, J., Harper, D., Kinderman, P., Longden, E., Pilgrim, D. and Read, J. (2018) *The Power Threat Meaning Framework*. Leicester: British Psychological Society, 27–30.

Kennedy, H. (2018) Mothers and the law; Mythologies and stereotypes-a woman's lot?. In A. Foster (ed.), *Mothers Abused and Accused: Addressing Complex Psychological Needs*. Oxon: Routledge.

Lammy, D. (2017) *The Lammy Review: An Independent Review into the Treatment of, and Outcomes for, Black, Asian and Minority Ethnic Individuals in the Criminal Justice System*. London: Ministry of Justice. Available at: www.gov.uk/government/publications/lammy-review-final-report

Lloyd, A. (1995) *Doubly Deviant, Doubly Damned: Society's Treatment of Violent Women*. Harmondsworth: Penguin.

Ministry of Justice (2016) *Black, Asian and Minority Ethnic disproportionality in the Criminal justice system in England and Wales*. London: Ministry of Justice.

Ministry of Justice (2018) *Female Offender Strategy*. London: Ministry of Justice. Available at: https://www.gov.uk/government/publications/female-offender-strategy

Minson, S. (2017) Briefing Paper: The Impact of Maternal Imprisonment upon a Child's Wellbeing and Their Relationship with Their Mother: Findings from 'Who Cares? Analysing the Place of Children in Maternal Sentencing Decisions in England and Wales'. University of Oxford (November 8, 2017). Available at: https://ssrn.com/abstract=3067653 or doi:10.2139/ssrn.3067653

Parveen, N. (2016) Prison mmbudsman investigates death of new mother taken of suicide watch. *The Guardian* (February 9, 2016). Available at: https://www.theguardian.com/society/2016/feb/09/new-mother-killed-herself-prison-shortly-after-taken-off-suicide-watch

Prison Reform Trust (2017) *Counted Out: Black, Asian and Minority Ethnic Women in the Criminal Justice System*. London: Prison Reform Trust.

Swaine W., Earle, K. and Litchefield, Z. J. (2018) *Still No Way Out: Foreign National Women and Trafficked Women in the Criminal Justice System Summary Report*. London: Prison Reform Trust.

Traister, R. (2018) And You Thought Trump Voters Were Mad. American women are furious — and our politics and culture will never be the same. *New York Magazine*. Available at: www.thecut.com/2018/09/rebecca-traister-good-and-mad-book-excerpt.html

Chapter 2

Maternal violence

Ordinary and extraordinary

Anna Motz

Female violence in a social and developmental context

In this chapter I discuss female violence, and its denial, describing how the idealisation of women renders invisible their potential for aggression and re-enactment of trauma. This is particularly true for mothers, who are especially idealised and romanticised. The difficulty of seeing women, in their complexity, agency and capacity for violence, has implications for the assessment and treatment of all female offenders. Female violence can be hard to imagine, as the predominant myth is that women are victims not perpetrators, though there are exceptions – women who are fundamentally 'bad' or 'mad'. In this chapter I will describe the psychological motivations for violence in mothers, and the social pressures that increase its likelihood. Societal denial of maternal aggression rests on an idealised notion of motherhood and an unconscious disavowal of hostility towards mothers, or the possibility of their hatred of their young. I address the sense in which maternal abuse recapitulates past trauma and outline the crucial interaction between the mother's external world, including social forces that oppress her, and aspects of her inner world that also restrict and threaten her.[1]

I focus on maternal abuse, examining the more 'ordinary' aspects of violent behaviour by women, and the factors that contribute to their development. Women who are convicted of crimes against their children have often had histories of complex trauma and narcissistic mothering, (Motz, 2001, 2008), and have used the weaker bodies and minds of their children to recreate their own early maltreatment, in an unconscious effort to rid themselves of these awful memories.

Using the premise of forensic psychotherapy (Welldon, 1988), namely that there are unconscious meanings and reasons for violent acts, I argue that in most cases of maternal abuse, aside from sadistic sexual abuse, there is an unconscious wish to be understood and prevented from inflicting further harm. The ambivalent and often hateful relationship the women have with their children reflects their toxic and confusing feelings towards themselves, and towards their own harsh or preoccupied mothers.

How can we understand maternal re-enactments of past trauma? Are they expressions of female psychopathy or of intense psychic distress, often followed by guilt, remorse and fear in the mothers? While such acts of maternal cruelty can be labelled psychopathic, I suggest that this term is not fundamentally informative or helpful. Although the state of mind within which the mother enacts aggression or inflicts pain can have qualities of psychopathy, such as lack of remorse, enjoyment of another's pain, a wish for tremendous excitement and power, with little fear of consequences, this does not mean that she is fundamentally psychopathic. These acts occur within what I consider 'psychopathic states of mind'; transient and overwhelming experiences in which violent and cruel action overwhelms thinking and empathy (see Chapter 7).

Female violence unseen: the denial of female aggression

Despite evidence that women can and do commit acts of violence, against others, notably their intimate partners, their children and, less frequently, against members of the public, the denial of female violence remains an entrenched social prejudice. It is at its most powerful when women perpetrate violence against children, or in the form of sexual crimes. As Welldon powerfully showed in her seminal 1988 book, *Mother Madonna Whore: The Idealization and Denigration of Motherhood*, one destructive consequence of this idealised notion is that when women do act 'uncharacteristically' they are vilified because they have not only committed acts of aggression, but also because denigration is the flipside of idealisation. They have acted out of character of women and shattered a revered image of womankind.

Ann Lloyd (1995) suggests that violent women are 'doubly deviant and doubly damned' for both committing aggression against the person and against the idealised image of womanhood itself. Marina Warner offers a description of the particular brand of hatred reserved for Myra Hindley, the accomplice of Ian Brady who tortured and murdered seven children in Yorkshire, in the 1960s: 'The new demons of crimes against children still act in character as biological women, but they have disqualified themselves from the rank of mother, and the category of women altogether' (Warner, 1998).

The role of discrimination, poverty and the intergenerational transmission of trauma

As Welldon (1988) revealed, the intergenerational transmission of maternal violence can be traced across at least three generations of women. Practitioners who work with a woman who has both inflicted and endured harsh treatment need empathy, understanding and the capacity to hold in mind that this mother is both the victim and perpetrator of cruelty and neglect; this is the central aim of forensic psychotherapy.

Mothering also takes place within a social context, and the quality of care that a mother can offer in situations of extreme poverty and racial or sexual discrimination reflects this. Particularly harsh judgements are made in relation to black single mothers, who may be viewed as responsible for perceived violence or criminality in their children. The social world impacts on the internal world of mothers and their children.

Empirical research demonstrates unequivocally that social circumstances, including poverty, abuse, the experience of racial and social discrimination and previous trauma, can adversely impact on the quality of maternal mental health and the consequent capacity to attend to the needs of an infant (McDonnell & Valentino, 2016; Racine et al., 2018). Adverse childhood experiences (ACEs) impact across the lifespan, and the trajectories of women who have been abused in childhood can be affected adversely in ways that directly impact on motherhood, through for example a higher risk of entering into abusive relationships in adolescence, having unplanned pregnancies, suffering from mental health difficulties including psychosocial problems and personality disorder, and becoming dependent on alcohol and substances as a means of coping. One mediating factor leading to potential difficulties for affected women in parenting their children is depression, itself related to ACEs. As McDonnell and Valentino note, 'maternal ACEs predicted higher levels of prenatal depressive symptoms. Childhood maltreatment experiences, in particular, predicted higher postnatal depressive symptoms and a smaller reduction in depressive symptoms across the perinatal period' (p. 317).

Childhood experiences of trauma, abuse and neglect, as well as other adverse events, such as imprisonment of a parent or drug and alcohol misuse and intimate partner violence between parents, impact on parenting, and, in the most serious and tragic cases, contribute to infanticide or neonaticide, or, in less extreme instances, to neglect of the basic needs of vulnerable children.

The social context of maternal abuse interacts powerfully with intrapsychic disturbance, as cases of maternal killings reveal. Neonaticide, the killing of a baby in the first 24 hours of life, is a crime that is particularly difficult to detect, as many such mothers have concealed their pregnancies and the fact of childbirth. Infanticide, the maternal killing of a baby within the first year of life, is another crime whose true prevalence rate is unknown, as many of these murders happen without detection. Spinelli (2003) argues that infanticide is most often committed by young women from deprived backgrounds, where the birth of a baby would bring shame on them and their own families.

The conceptual basis for the crime of infanticide is predicated on notions of women being fundamentally disturbed by the hormonal changes brought about by pregnancy, childbirth and lactation, creating the likelihood of 'post-puerperal psychosis'; but I suggest that biological factors interact powerfully with psychosocial ones to create conditions in which a young mother may attempt to kill her own baby. For example, in 19th-century Mexico, infanticide was often not prosecuted as it was understood as an unfortunate, if necessary, means of preventing shame and protecting family honour (Jaffary, 2012). Research has indicated that infanticide rates increase with economic pressures (Gauthier et al., 2003). Hatters and Friedmann (2007) report that maternal infanticide studies in the general population found a predominance of unemployed mothers in their early 20s, and Brookman and Nolan (2006) found that many cases occurred in the context of child abuse, though some mothers had associated suicide attempts. Often they experienced psychiatric disorders (36% to 72%). In Japan, the infant victims frequently had physical anomalies.

The cases of murders by mothers in psychotic states are particularly tragic, and perhaps most easily understood by the general public, as killing out of madness is easier to imagine than a mother killing her newborn baby because of social circumstances, economic hardship or her own sense of powerlessness and fear; that is, a crime motivated by rational assessment. Mothers may therefore commit this act for rational reasons, through consideration of their desperate circumstances, alongside the terror of raising a child, rather than out of psychosis. Similarly, some suicides by pregnant women appear motivated more by social factors than by biological symptoms of depression.

Clinical illustration: infanticide interrupted

Tanya was a dual heritage 24-year-old woman who was adopted when she was 12 days old, and had been removed from her mother at birth. She had never known her biological mother, though she had unsuccessfully tried to find her when she was 14. Her sense of being unwanted pervaded every aspect of her life, and she described how she would tell people she had just met that her name was Tanya and that she was adopted.

Tanya was 24 when she gave birth to her first baby, a son she named Isaiah. She had little family support during her pregnancy, though she had a good relationship with Isaiah's father, Jesse, her partner of two years. During her pregnancy Tanya was diagnosed with gestational diabetes, and became highly anxious that she would lose the baby, becoming convinced that she was being punished for two previous terminations she had undertaken in her early 20s; these were unplanned pregnancies, unlike Isaiah's conception, for which she had longed.

During her pregnancy Tanya became increasingly preoccupied with a sense of something deathly inside of her, and a conviction that her baby wouldn't survive to term. She was tormented by guilt feelings that surfaced about the unborn babies she had aborted early on in her pregnancies, and persecuted by frequent dreams in which they were born, but shortly after they cried out in life, she strangled them. She had recurrent dreams of having two beautiful girl babies and falling in love with them, but then having to kill them under instruction of a military officer. In her nightmares she killed them with her bare hands, and had to bury them in an industrial compound, under harsh and glaring lights. The girls' features were hard to distinguish but their skin was dark, like hers. In the dream she was crying as she buried them but knew that she had to do so or they would be tortured and she would face prison straight away. The officer assured her she would be safe if she did what he said and went with him to a remote village where childless mothers gather. In her dream she doesn't understand why the babies need to be killed, but can see she has no choice. This dream appears to relate to her later fears about Isaiah's survival and her pervasive sense of guilt, fearing that she carried destructive forces inside her. The dreams suggest unconscious murderousness towards herself and her mother, as embodied in the girl babies.

During her early pregnancy, Tanya's (adoptive) maternal grandmother was diagnosed with pancreatic cancer, and died some three months later, when Tanya was seven months pregnant. She had been one of the only sources of consistent support to Tanya during her childhood, always treating her with special love and care, as opposed to her adoptive parents, whom she felt discriminated against her, preferring their own biological children, a boy and a girl who were several years older than Tanya. Her grandmother did not seem to share this bias, and showered Tanya with love and affection, seeing resemblances between them, although they were not blood relatives.

Her grandmother's death was deeply distressing for her, and she associated this profound loss with her own fecund state, feeling that she had swapped a life for a life. As her mental state deteriorated Tanya became more isolated, frightened to confide in friends or her partner about the many fears that plagued her. She found the movements of the baby inside her frightening and unpleasant. At times she did not know what was alive inside of her, imagining monstrous creatures, ill-formed half-humans and mutant babies. She felt afraid to let anyone know what she was imagining as she worried they would think she was 'mental'.

Tanya felt hollow, depressed and frightened, and her physical health also worsened as she developed gestational diabetes. Throughout this time, she had recurrent fantasies of her own birth and imagined herself as an unwanted, difficult baby in her 'real' mother's womb, with vivid thoughts of having carried something toxic inside that had led to her abandonment. She knew that she was not thinking rationally, but whenever she went for appointments she imagined she could see a look on the faces of the midwives that signified that something was terribly wrong with her baby. She found it hard to mourn her grandmother's death in an ordinary way, and did not want to visit her grave, or cry for her, but became deeply preoccupied with the idea of cancer and death, to the point where she was convinced that Isaiah would not live past the age of six months, as he too had something deathly inside him. The roots of her belief were difficult to disentangle, and impossible for her to put into words, but she had a profound conviction that he would die and, in the process, suffer terribly.

Tanya's actual delivery went smoothly and Isaiah was born at 38 weeks, a small but healthy baby boy with big brown eyes and his mother's dark skin tone. Throughout her labour Tanya had requested intense pain relief, saying she was too scared to be emotionally present during what she was sure would be a horrifying ordeal. She did not want to breast feed Isaiah, fearing that her milk would harm him and that she had nothing good inside her to offer him, but also indicating her wish to keep him at a distance, trying to protect herself from falling in love with a doomed creature. She left the hospital after one night, as there were no concerns about either her or the baby's health. When Isaiah was three days old Jesse went out for a few hours to his mother's house, leaving Tanya alone with the baby, hoping that she might get some rest, and pushing aside any concerns he had about her strange withdrawn state. Almost as soon as he had gone Tanya started to study the baby for signs of imminent disease, and soon identified what she believed were significant skin lesions on his upper thigh and some others in his mouth. She was distraught and held him close, feeling how fragile and tiny he was. She felt desperate, sad and alone, and had a sudden image of herself as this tiny creature, with a mother who didn't want her, in contrast to her own feelings of wanting to protect her baby in any way she could.

Tanya later described to me how she was frantic with the fear that Isaiah would suffer, as she had seen her grandmother do before she died, and believed he would follow her, and that neither deserved to endure such pain. She texted Jesse to say that everything was fine, and that she and the baby would both go to sleep for a few hours, but a plan formed in her mind. She remembered the dream and reinterpreted it as a prophecy, a sign of what she needed to do. She told herself that she would help his passage from this world and minimise his suffering, fearing that she and he would otherwise have to endure unbearable pain. She prepared his feed and decided to add strong pain medication that she had been given for emergency use after having a tooth extracted. She hoped that this would allow Isaiah to fall into a peaceful sleepy state, from which he would not awaken. At this point Tanya was shaking and crying, as she felt overcome with loving feelings, but equally terrifying thoughts about what awaited her son unless she 'saved' him.

Though she had not heard back from Jesse, and believed he would be some hours with his mother, in fact this did not occur. He had, he later said, 'a sixth sense' that Tanya was 'not right'. He had no sooner gone to his mother's house, some 20 minutes away, when he began to feel uneasy and said he needed to go back and check on Tanya and the baby, leaving his mother concerned and a bit hurt. As Jesse re-entered the flat he found Tanya crushing up codeine and ibuprofen tablets, next to a bottle of formula milk, in a near hysterical state. He took the baby away immediately and shook Tanya, asking her what was going on. Despite her terrible fear of what was happening in her mind, and about her son's future, Tanya had broken down and told him everything, including her plan to kill Isaiah to save him. She explained her conviction that he would die, and that everything she touched would perish, that nothing good could have grown inside her, and, though Isaiah was so good, he must have been contaminated by hidden poison. She had not been sure whether she would follow him to the grave or not, but had just 'known' that she must act. She thought that the dream images, in which the daughters were dark like her, related to Isaiah too, and that she had to bury him to preserve his immortal soul.

After quickly disposing of the crushed up medication, Jesse then called an ambulance for both the baby and his partner, as he was not sure he could trust that Tanya had not already poisoned Isaiah, and he was alarmed by what seemed her hysterical state of mind. She was subsequently admitted to a psychiatric ward, where she was allowed supervised access to Isaiah; Jesse spent every day over the next few weeks on the ward, in the grounds, bringing Isaiah to see Tanya and supporting both. The police were informed on his admission, and considered prosecuting Tanya, but as medical investigation revealed that Isaiah had not been harmed, and a thorough psychiatric evaluation and treatment for Tanya were in place, they took no further action.

Discussion of Tanya's persecutory ideas

Tanya was referred to me for psychological and psychotherapeutic treatment and we worked together for over two years, beginning while she was on an inpatient unit for six months. During this time, we were able to address underlying issues of loss and anger related to Tanya's abandonment by her biological mother, her sense of not 'belonging' anywhere and feeling that her adoptive mother hated her. This led to a profound sense of confusion about her identity. As Isaiah developed and became stronger Tanya was increasingly reassured that he would not become terminally ill and to address her grief about her grandmother's death, seeing how she had linked it inextricably with Isaiah's birth.

Both birth and death were mysterious and traumatic events in her own life, and there was a strong part of her that had considered it impossible that she could ever bear life and become a good mother. Pregnancy and childbirth had stirred up early and unconscious anxieties for her, alongside her grief about her grandmother and her fears for her baby. At times she was overcome with longings for an ideal mother who could hold and comfort her as she did Isaiah, and during those periods she would express anger at me for offering such limited contact – 50 minutes once a week – and at her adoptive mother for being 'fake' and 'useless'. In a sense she was envious of her own capacity to care for her infant son. While it was sometimes hard for me to remain calm in the midst of her emotional storm, her expression of need and anger as her own, not projected into Isaiah, nor converted into self-harm or self-reproach, was a healthy and requisite development.

Tanya's sense of guilt related to her own birth, and her belief that she had disappointed her mother(s) were crystallised during her pregnancy when her grandmother died and her own body had failed her. This had been converted into a quasi-psychotic conviction that her baby would die, leading, catastrophically, to her delusion that she would need to kill him to save him and her subsequent actions that could have actually killed him. At times her guilt and terror about what might have happened threatened to destabilise her, and I had to hold a clear and steady lifeline for her, allowing her to recognise that she had acted out of fear not rage, a misguided protectiveness, not hatred on that occasion. This work went alongside an exploration of aggressive feelings and fantasies about her own destructiveness and her sense of abject helplessness in the face of her newborn baby. She was able to confront her own hostility and rage at the grandmother who had died, the mother who had failed her and at me, her therapist who could not offer perfect care and reparation for earlier childhood trauma. I too had to bear this pain alongside her.

Fortunately, Tanya had chosen a loving partner, whose instincts were good and whose decision to return home may have saved the baby's life. He supported Tanya to seek urgent psychiatric and psychotherapeutic treatment so that her overwhelming fears could be addressed and she could begin to distinguish fear from fact, fantasy from reality.

This is a case that offers hope, but sadly, many other young mothers are not as fortunate, and choose to take what appears to them at the time to be a rational action, only then to live forever with regret or to take their own lives in compensation.

Central concerns in assessment

How can a clinician gain the trust of a mother who has tried to harm her child, and help her to connect to her own mind and the mind of her child? In order for her to see him as separate and in need of her care, she would first have to be helped to see herself as a subjective creature, not simply a recipient of abuse and object of neglect. In Tanya's case her difficulty in expressing her own vulnerability and sense of humiliation led to a greater fear that she would be punished and could contaminate her baby, feeding into a delusional belief that she would need to kill him to save him. Other women without such delusions see their babies as part of themselves (Welldon, 1988), narcissistic extensions whom they can mistreat as they mistreat themselves. These women require skill and sensitive work to help them see and accept their child's separateness.

A successful engagement at assessment can lay the foundations for therapeutic work, complex and tricky as it may be. An important issue in assessment is to consider the level of understanding the mother has of guilt, particularly in cases where psychosis is suspected. If she has been under the thrall of a false belief, approaching a delusional intensity, and this has led her to the decision to hurt her child, this conviction will protect her against feelings of guilt. However, as she begins to understand that the action that followed from her false belief was in fact unnecessary, the sense of guilt and loss can threaten to overwhelm her and become persecutory. While it is not always straightforward to distinguish between heightened levels of anxiety and false beliefs, like those Tanya entertained, and actual psychotic delusions, a skilled practitioner can begin to challenge these beliefs and untangle the complex strands of reasoning that have led to 'protective' action. It will be threatening and painful for a mother to acknowledge the harm to which she has put her child because of these fears and false beliefs. It is also indicative of mental ill health that many mothers who take action like Tanya did do so in secret, frightened of everyone around them and convinced that they must act alone, as no one is to be trusted. This can have catastrophic consequences for both mother and child.

When the history of a mother is already known to professionals, and includes attempts to harm or even kill her child, or herself, the therapist should bear this in the forefront of her mind during both assessment and treatment phases, and draw up a formulation of the significant factors that led to these attempts. This should be shared with the woman herself to establish a shared and collaborative working hypothesis related both to the risk of future harm and to reveal the meaning of the acts. The task of the therapist who works with someone who frequently enters into what can be considered to be psychopathic states of mind is to be able to tolerate these, without being either collusive (co-perpetrator, indifferent to suffering or excited by it) or victimised by it (hurt, angry, frantic with the wish to stop it) and allow the woman herself to be curious about what may lead to these states of mind, what function they serve and what would make it possible to relinquish them.

Zami: the impact of maternal and societal neglect on the developing self

Maternal neglect, the absence of care, is also a potent and destructive force, as the black feminist poet and author Audre Lorde describes. In her autobiography, or what she calls her 'biomythography', *Zami: A New Spelling of My Name* (Lorde, 1982), Audre Lorde reveals how the socio-economic context within which maternal care takes place cannot be ignored; the mother struggling to raise her children in situations of limited resources and a hostile environment may herself feel too depleted and persecuted to offer her children the emotional and physical care they needed. She explores the pain of both mother and child, and the mirroring between the society that overlooks the mother and the mother who neglects her child in turn. The excluded and exiled mother turns her own shame and rage onto her child, wreaking revenge in the private realm, in response to her humiliation within the public realm. Not only are mother and child often overlooked altogether, but when they are seen it is through a distorting lens. The colour of their skin shapes how they are viewed within white society, in ways that are not congruent with their own sense of themselves. The scared black woman can be viewed as the angry black woman, the timid child as unfriendly, or 'other'. This process is alienating, on both a social and psychic level. The self that is seen and responded to is not the self that is experienced from within, leading to a more or less constant state of distrust, disconnection and confusion. This self-alienation and misrepresentation is so disturbing and frightening that it can lead to violence; Ralph Ellison describes this starkly in his powerful portrait of the life of a young black man in 1950s Harlem, *Invisible Man*, discussed in the Introduction, and the tragic series of misconceptions and misrepresentations he endures.

Audre Lorde's mother is a woman of colour, away from her country of origin, the Caribbean island of Carriacou, raising a young family in a segregated and discriminatory New York City. She is left with intense and buried rage and a terror of letting her guard down. She is in a place where care is absent, where home and mother are no longer available to her, and is in turn brutal to her daughters, especially when they don't conform to expectations and threaten to bring shame on the family. In this way the daughters, especially the inquisitive and imaginative youngest child, Audre, are silenced, if not fully hidden. Lorde, in turn, spends much of her young life yearning for maternal care and understanding, to no avail. She recounts the neglect she endured, alongside beatings and verbal chastisement. Lorde recalls her painful, unmet needs for her mother's comfort, but remembers how, despite her brutality, her mother offers her lyrical words, snippets of songs and phrases from her birthplace that feed her imagination and offer a form of sanctuary.

Lorde's rage against this blindness speaks to an early environment in which her emotional states could not be named or reflected back to her, both because of her mother's refusal to allow her to express pain and because of the racism and censorship of wider society, that overlooked them both. Many imprisoned women could tell a similar story today; their lives of pain and trauma have to be borne and suffered in silence, communicated through encoded expressions of pain, sometimes written on their own flesh. Their rage and trauma remain largely invisible, disguised and hidden.

Anger, absence and hunger: the pain of neglect

Lorde describes how society cannot tolerate female anger and forbids its expression. Silencing the voices of women can be experienced as a repeated violation and act as incendiary to actual violence. She shows how for her, as for so many women with childhood trauma who face racial and cultural oppression, anger becomes a potent but hidden force, whose open expression is prohibited. She describes her own hunger to be seen and heard and the need for anger to be expressed.

It is considered unacceptable for women to express anger, particularly if these women are mothers, because of deeply held gender stereotypes and cultural norms relating to the sanctity of motherhood (Welldon, 1988); and if these women are black mothers, this censure is even greater. Women who have experienced early neglect and abuse, and who face current hardship, can feel overwhelmed by feelings of rage, frustration and desperation. It is not surprising, then, that when anger's expression is forbidden it goes temporarily underground, only to erupt explosively against those closest and most helpless to withstand assault – their children. At such times, these children become sources of persecution, as the mothers see them as witnesses to their inability to provide: as insatiable monsters who insistently demand to be offered that which cannot be given, such as food and comfort (Kruger & Lourens, 2016).

Hunger plays a central role, as both a psychic and a physical state, and can trigger violence in the mother–child relationship. Like the internal representation of a malevolent absent mother, the pain of hunger is savage and frightening. It is a toxic presence, a wild and ferocious force that can lead to violence.

Both anger and hunger can be felt in the guts as wrenching, churning pain; this physical state is felt to demand a physical release. This is an important feature of its primitive potency, in that it seems to bypass reason or thought. An important consequence of this is also that the child, consistently faced with an angry, withholding or traumatised mother in response to expressing her need, takes this in, incorporating it into herself (G. Byrne, personal communication, 2016). She associates it with the badness of her need – so what is taken in is not food but hatred, fear, helplessness. The baby introjects her mother's toxic feelings, and what is withheld becomes not an absence but a potent, malignant presence.

Women faced with this pervasive feeling of neglect are not only at increased risk of unleashing feelings of rage on their children and themselves, but can also find themselves searching all their lives for the sense of care and experience of being properly seen, understood and wanted. In her prose and poetry, Lorde describes the intensity of this unmet need for her mother's love and nurture in her poem 'From the House of Yemanjá'. In it, she describes her mother's longing for a lighter skinned daughter, who was not her. This left her starved of her mother's affection and desperate to be recognised by her, black as she is, in the image of the mother goddess Yemanjá. Lorde refers to her unfulfilled dreams for her mother's recognition and love, saying she is 'forever hungry for her eyes' (Lorde, 1973: 235).

The metaphor of hunger is clear here, as Lorde remains searching: hungry, angry and unseen.

Hunger of the body and hunger of the mind: clinical illustration

The absence of food leads to interacting psychological and physical deprivation, creating a toxic relationship between mother and child. A mother faced with her own hunger, whether because of poverty, limited food supplies, self-inflicted starvation or a religious fast, may not only be unable to meet the needs of a distressed and hungry infant but to find them intolerable, as the following clinical illustration shows.

Clinical illustration 2: Amira

Amira was a recent immigrant from a Middle Eastern country who found her husband's absence and the care of two small children increasingly unbearable. They were living in a small apartment and she was unemployed, though fully trained as an accountant in her country of origin. She was in her early 30s and felt increasingly alienated; her unhappiness eventually erupted into violence.

Desperate to please her neighbours and act as the 'perfect mother' she hid her post-natal depression and sense of profound alienation in her new country, and relatively new role. She had recently undergone the bereavement of a sibling and her aunt, both of whom died in her native country. These losses left her unstable and vulnerable, desperate for nurturance and care.

Amira started wearing a hijab following the deaths of her family members. Far from home and alone with only her children she felt guilty, isolated and desperate. Following a temporary separation from her husband she was tasked with the sole care of the children, aged two and five, both of whom were unsettled by the changes in their household. As they became increasingly disturbed so too did Amira, and she found herself unable to sleep and concentrate as she normally would. She found the hijab and reading the Qu'ran comforting but did not notice that she was increasingly neglecting her children's needs. She later described this as an attempt to bring her closer to God, but, in hindsight, saw that this was a futile gesture. She felt that what she portrayed of herself could only enhance her standing in the community, apparently unaware of the racist projections to which she was already subjected.

As her mood declined she started to hate her appearance, feeling she needed to diet to become a better shape, a more acceptable form of woman, partly to attract her husband back home. As her mood deteriorated she ate less and less; food preparation became increasingly burdensome. After a few weeks of dieting she felt weak, depleted and sick but triumphant in her defeat of her body's incessant demands for feeding. Her children continued to clamour for food, and on the night of the offence she found their cries unbearable. Additionally she had spoken to her grieving mother on the telephone and felt unable to soothe her and had attempted to speak to her estranged husband, but found him unreceptive to her. She was preparing soup for the children when they started to cry and wail, then argue with one another. Amira said she 'snapped' and took the stirring spoon she had been using when she entered their shared bedroom to sort out their difficulties. She then took each of their arms in her hands and placed the hot spoon on them, causing burns. She was subsequently arrested and charged with child cruelty and assault, to which she pleaded guilty.

Amira received a prison sentence, an outcome that horrified her. Once her crime was known within the prison she was bullied and intimidated, considered a monstrous inhumane mother, echoing something of how the local authority had viewed her, despite her admission of guilt. Her statements were devoid of emotion as she tried hard to keep control over her feelings and saw depression as a sign of weakness. To the professionals, and to the judge, Amira was the outsider and the alien whose anger could not be understood or thought about other than as the mark of her 'badness' and thus justification for further removal – to prison, where she could remain away, apart and Other. This view of her was maintained within the prison, although she was able to engage well in art therapy and felt accepted and understood in those sessions.

Amira's violent state of mind reflects the impossibility of caring for others when feeling so deprived herself; she enacted her sense of rage and injustice with the very tools of domesticity, subverting the expected role of carer and food provider. She inflicted injury on herself through starvation and hurt the children with this symbol of maternal care, the stirring spoon, usually associated with an idealised image of motherhood. Her hunger of the body and of the mind led to savage acting out and a cruel misuse of power; while she described this as an impulsive loss of control, the statements by the children indicated that she returned at least once to the pot to heat the weapon, suggesting a more calculated and sadistic form of punishment and expression of rage. Her act of injury using fire can be seen to express an elemental, primitive rage.

Amira subverted the very act of maternal care and nurturance, waging rebellion on the idealised notion of sacred motherhood. She burned the children who wanted her warm food and care; the marks on their skin were evidence of her own burning rage. This act of desperation and fury drew attention to her state of mind and led to protection for the children, but the underlying meaning of the burning, and its communication of distress, desperation and grief were not understood. She was configured solely as perpetrator, rather than perpetrator-victim, a woman who both inflicted harm and suffered in her own right; as a perpetrator she was condemned. Although our psychological service had recommended therapeutic assistance in place of custody, she was not afforded this 'luxury' and was instead imprisoned, albeit for a relatively short period of time.

Once Amira was released from prison she re-engaged with therapeutic services and we were able to reunite her with her children for contact, though she was not considered suitable as a carer for them. Her ex-partner was granted custody and she was allowed regular contact; this was closely supervised and conditional upon her full apology to them and assurance that she would never harm them again.

Her guilt and shame about her actions remained persecutory and therapy focussed on her attempts to understand the 'alien self' that had overtaken her on the night of the offence. During therapy her own early experiences of maternal neglect and inconsistent, fragmented care were gradually uncovered and her parenting strengths were supported. She was able to be warm, loving and attentive to her children, within the context of a holding therapeutic environment and to explore the meaning and harm of her violence against them, although she found this aspect of the work painful and disturbing.

Mothers who assault their children may have experienced emotional starvation throughout their lives but it is also crucial to acknowledge the impact of social and economic deprivation. Faced with needs that simply cannot be met, they may respond violently. The feeding situation, so clearly one of the most idealised and primitive expressions of maternal love, exemplifies the act of self-sacrificial giving and the abundance of resources. In reality, those mothers who simply cannot find the food to feed them can perceive their children's hunger as a shameful and persecutory reflection on their maternal capacity.

This is poignantly described by Kruger and Lourens (2016), who describe how poor women of colour in South Africa experience their children's hunger. They focus on the shame and rage of being met with children's hunger and the assumption that they can satisfy the demand – 'everyone asks me for a piece of bread'. The authors focus on how these mothers cope with the pain of not being able to provide for their children's needs and how intolerable this is. It can lead to violence to evacuate unbearable feelings of being fed from, demanded of and being unable to provide. Their violence then serves as evidence of their inabilities and imperfections, as though the social context does not exist. As the authors describe:

> A vicious cycle of hunger, sadness and anxiety, shame, anger and anomie, aggression and withdrawal, negative judgement, and more shame, are thus maintained. As such, the unbearable rebukes of hungry children can be thought of as evoking a kind of 'madness' in low-income mothers.

The widely held fantasy of infinite nurturance is that it comes from within, and that limited resources without are irrelevant. This is an idealisation of maternal capacity that can rapidly turn to vilification.

Mothers who articulate their wish to get rid of their children, whose needs are felt to be unbearable, shatter cherished taboos related to the sanctity of motherhood and the wish for mothers to have infinite capacities for care and nurturance. Yet there is a social context to this desperation. In some cases their resentment results in regretting having had children. Wright et al. (2014) describe how impoverished women in their study stated that they feel like rejecting their children and report that their participants described fantasies of infanticide, citing that focus group participants in Langa described how their extreme levels of poverty and inability to provide for their children led them to desperate thoughts of suicide and infanticide:

> And when you are poor you are always depressed, angry and facing problems. When your child asks for food you take out all your problems out on him by insulting or beating him up just because you yourself are defensive about your lack of provision as a parent. Most of the time you end up feeling suicidal and thinking about ways to kill yourself and your children, like bombing my house is a fantasy sometimes. Really because if you only kill yourself who is going to look after your children?
>
> (Wright et al., 2014: 38)

Conclusion

In this chapter I have identified powerful stereotypes about womanhood, and motherhood in particular, that contribute to the denial of female violence, despite the clear evidence that women, including mothers, do engage in murderous acts of their own free will, when in a particular state of mind.

It is essential to recognise that victim and perpetrator can co-exist in the same person, and to acknowledge that women, including mothers, can enter into psychopathic states of mind that are transient, but highly dangerous, within which they may inflict sadistic aggression on others. By meticulously tracing the roots of maternal violence we can understand its developmental history, meaning and current function, and identify therapeutic possibilities to overcome those states of mind that give rise to it. Simply addressing the intrapsychic difficulties will not, however, eradicate maternal neglect and violence. Women's harm takes place within a matrix of social and economic and intrapsychic forces to which they can react through violence, expressing pain, desperation and anger on their bodies and those of their children.

Note

1   Parts of this chapter revisit themes discussed in my earlier chapter 'Forever hungry for her eyes: The pain of maternal absence', first published in 2018 (Motz, pp. 67–81) in John Adlam, Tilman Kluttig and Bandy X. Lee (eds.), *Violent States and Creative States: From the Global to the Individual (Volume 2): Human Violence and Creative Humanity*, London: Jessica Kingsley. I am most grateful to the editors for their support and encouragement in this project.

References

Brookman F. & Nolan J. (2006) The Dark Figure of Infanticide in England and Wales: Complexities of Diagnosis. *Journal of Interpersonal Violence*, 21, 869–889. [PubMed].

Gauthier, D. K., Chaudoir N. K., & Forsyth, C. J. (2003) A Sociological Analysis of Maternal Infanticide in the United States 1984–1996. *Deviant Behavior*, 24, 393–405.

Jaffrey, N. (January 2012) Reconceiving Motherhood: Infanticide and Abortion in Late Colonial Mexico. *The Journal of Family History*, 37(1), 3–22.

Kruger, L. & Lourens M. (2016) Motherhood and the "Madness of Hunger": "... want Almal vra vir my vir 'n Stukkie Brood" ("... because everyone asks me for a little piece of bread"). *Journal of Culture, Medicine, and Psychiatry*, 40, 124–143.

Lloyd, A. (1995) *Doubly Deviant, Doubly Damned: Society's Treatment of Violent Women*. London: Penguin Books.

Lorde, A. (1973) From the house of Yemanjá. In *The Collected Poems of Audre Lorde*. New York: W.W. Norton and Company. (2002).

Lorde, A. (1982) *Zami: A New Spelling of My Name*. Berkeley: Crossing.

McDonnell C. G. & Valentino K. (2016). Intergenerational Effects of Childhood Trauma: Evaluating Pathways among Maternal ACEs, Perinatal Depressive Symptoms, and Infant Outcomes. *Journal of Child Maltreatment*, 21(4), 317–326. doi: 10.1177/1077559516659556.

Motz, A. (2001, 2008) *The Psychology of Female Violence: Crimes Against the Body* (second edition). Hove: Routledge.

Racine, N., Plamondon, A., Madigan, S., McDonald, S., & Tough, S. (2018) Maternal Adverse Childhood Experiences and Infant Development. *Pediatrics*, 141(4), pii: e20172495. doi: 10.1542/peds.2017-2495.

Spinelli, M. G. (Ed.) (2003) *Infanticide: Psychosocial and Legal Perspectives on Mothers Who Kill*. Washington DC: American Psychiatric Publishing.

Warner, M. (1998) *London Review of Books*. 1 January.

Welldon, E. (1988) *Mother, Madonna, Whore: The Idealization and Denigration of Motherhood*. London: Free Association Press.

Wright, G., Noble, N., & Ntshongwana, P. (2014) Lone Mothers in South Africa – The Role of Social Security in Respecting and Protecting Dignity Themed Working Paper 2 UK Department for International Development and the Economic and Social Research Council. https://assets.publishing.service.gov.uk/media/57a089eaed915d622c000469/60946_TWP2_Lone_Mothers.pdf

Chapter 3

The criminalisation of blackness

Maxine Dennis

At the Berlin Conference in 1885, when the German Chancellor, Otto Von Bismarck, and 16 European contemporaries set in motion the destructive act of looting Africa and arbitrarily dividing up and putting together communities that do not belong together, he established a chain of behaviour based on the principles of 'divide and rule', the aftermath of which we are still facing transgenerationally. In this chapter I discuss how this legacy impacts on black girls and women, and in particular the way they are treated within the criminal justice system and how they have come to see themselves. I believe that colonial object relations (Lowe, 2007) form the background of this interaction. I view the phenomenon of turning a blind eye, which refers to conscious and unconscious knowledge, as crucial to this process. In this mechanism we seem to have access to reality but choose to ignore it because it proves convenient to do so (Steiner, 1993). The aspect of reality which is known and turned away from is the impact of slavery, notably the slave–master–slave co-existence. I will explore how I consider that legacy of colonial object-relating to be implicit in the treatment of black women and girls in the criminal justice system.

We know when individuals are traumatised and unable to put their experience into words they are destined to repeat (Freud, 1920; Van der Kolk, 2015). The repetition compulsion of infighting, sabotaging attempts at self-determination, the replay of the helpless victim at the mercy of a perpetrator, who operates both without and within the individual, as an internal sabotage and a feature of psychic retreat (Steiner, 1993) is evidenced in Black, Asian Minority Ethnic (BAME) communities. Where one is born constrains the degree to which one has access to education, use of language, and this is further supported by gender bias, sexism, class or caste restrictions. These aspects of privilege and power intersect, as black feminist thinking has illuminated, and combine to create inequities that consign certain groups to states of powerlessness and degradation (Wekker, 2016). This reaction to the trauma of discrimination and intersectionality impacts on all people since both black and white are implicated in these dynamics.

I aim to explore intergenerational and transgenerational trauma in the criminal justice system. I will discuss how the negative internalisation of blackness leads to an individual feeling guilt, which can bind with a cycle of criminality and incarceration. I discuss how the internalised hatred and denigration of blackness can impact BAME communities and also how some of the fractures in certain aspects of the community can be replayed.

The experience of being marginalised

The environment which has to be negotiated when one is a minority is often a hostile one. This sets up a context where one constantly 'glances over the shoulder' (Philips, 2004, cited in Lousada, 2006), literally and symbolically, and in some cases this drives one to full paranoia. Even within the place where one is born, even in the United Kingdom (UK), one's home, the black person is constantly made to feel that they do not belong. One faces both the ongoing every day micro-aggressions alongside the constant refrain, 'Where are you from?' If one replies, 'From England, London,' the retort is, 'No, where are you *really* from?' Following on from this is the question, 'When are you going home?' The implicit message is clear: the black person is neither wanted nor 'really' at home here and belongs elsewhere. This message is internalised, with destructive consequences, or there is an ongoing battle against this position.

One's experience of even benign objects within this hostile context has an impact. If parents are subject to racism to the extent that it affects whether they can provide a 'good enough context' for their family then this is impactful. The primary carer needs to help with the acceptance of her child's own skin through their loving early relationship with the baby and young children, enabling a good internal object and the internalisation of a loving relationship. This facilitates an acceptance of the body self and the emotional self as both are intrinsically related.

Communities that are racially othered internalise adverse experiences in such a way that it supports, encourages and endorses criminality and violent acting-out. Internalising a sense of racial badness binds inside with ordinary developmental psychic procedures/processes around identifying good and bad, feelings of worthlessness and Oedipal conflicts. Here ordinary guilt and ordinary anxieties around what is good and bad are perverted through the internalisation of sanctions of the use of violence for everyday parenting so as to survive managing situations of racism (Coates, 2015; Fletchman-Smith, 2000). An example is found in Coates's descriptions of how physical punishment is more prevalent in black families in the United States as an attempt to ensure that offspring don't 'step out of line' and get in trouble; they need to be 'twice as good' as white children. The parents fear the consequences of what might happen if their children step out of line as a life and death issue.

Criminals from a sense of guilt

> In many criminals, especially youthful ones, it is possible to detect a very powerful sense of guilt which existed before the crime, and is therefore

not its result but its motive. It is as if it were a relief to be able to fasten
this unconscious sense of guilt on to something real and immediate.

(Freud, 1916: 332–333)

The above quotation highlights how individuals commit a crime because they
feel guilty. Their unconscious guilt precedes the crime, and subsequent punishment for the crime alleviates this guilt temporarily. To prevent further crimes
the underlying issue of a sense of badness needs addressing, otherwise there
will be ongoing attempts to obtain punishment through criminal enactment.
The non-facilitating environment is both the external, which may have been
further supported within their family structures, and a destructive internal
object-relating. If one's blackness is one's ruin, if one can be punished for
one's blackness, one can expedite the crime. The internal object-relating being
one of guilt for their badness; this is attributed to their blackness, which has to
be punished.

The mechanisms for achieving this punishment are repetition compulsion,
internalised masochistic guilt and sadomasochism.

The social or political system wants to encourage a definition of the black
self in approximation to 'the negro'[1] which is not a definition people gave
themselves but one that was imposed. Such a system 'blackened one set of
people' and 'lightened another set of people' and was supported by laws, religion, spurious eugenics and acts of emotional and physical violation. The fight
is for a category fallacy, as the idea of 'race' is itself spurious (Kolbert,
2018).[2]

In the UK and much of the western world we live in a perverse system
where the focus is on greed in the form of acquiring more and more wealth at
the same time as the systematic mis-education of our children. This mis-
education supports the physical, mental, socioeconomic, political, spiritual and
cultural disenfranchisement of people. This is a system which literally drives
some people mad. In this system white people don't need to think about themselves because they are seen as the norm and others are not seen (DiAngelo,
2018; Frankenberg, 1993; Ryder, 2019).

The historical context: impact on BAME communities today

I now turn to highlighting some central points in relation to the legacy of slavery and colonisation. I will make some reference to the United States and then
move to discussing the situation within the UK. The economic wealth generated by the trans-Atlantic slave trade fuelled the growth of the agricultural and
later the industrial age, and whilst it was abolished in the United States in
1865 its laws continued there until 1965 in the form of enforced segregation.
This did not allow black people to participate fully as equal citizens and
engage in the wheels of democracy. However, using the courts and the media

in the face of the mob violence, lynchings and the rise of the Ku Klux Klan, by 1919 an American racist ideology developed which was not restricted to the South. Whilst black people supposedly had freedom, they had to work for slave owners to pay the rent due to their profound economic, educational and social disadvantage. Although in England slavery had been abolished earlier than in the United States, in 1833, and there was no state sanctioned segregation, its impact was still evident via the class system. Areas like Liverpool, Cardiff and Bristol were key sites for slave traders and prospered from the black trade triangle exploiting African people whose forced labour generated Caribbean sugar, much of which was destined for Britain. This became the basis of the wealth and finery of many exclusive British homeowners. Wealth generated by slavery also formed the backbone of the banking and cotton industries. Estimates suggest that there were around 12 million Africans transported over 400 years of slavery, and many would perish before arriving in the Americas.

The trans-Atlantic slave trade was a lucrative system for the European countries that orchestrated the machinery of slavery and was maintained by the military and the church/religious authorities. The slave operated within a highly controlled relationship: the planter had his white family and kept a second family with his slave mistress. The children of the second family were afforded a privileged status and were perceived by some as having a right to be afforded freedom. It was these mixed parentage children who worked in the main house. The 'slave mistresses, would also have children by a black slave' (Lobb, 1876; Sterling, 1997). There were also restrictions around marriage. The master chose the names of the children and of course they could be sold. Slavery diminished the family structure and its effects would ensure families would not remain together. Ownership would be in the hands of the slave master rather than the parent, who was no longer in charge of their own destiny. There was a Hobson's choice: either endure a life of slavery or take the life of one's self or child (Carrol, 2019).[3]

In Queen Victoria's reign we initially saw slavery being replaced by racism and colonisation. The imperialism was based on the racist pseudo-science that 'some races were born to rule'. This notion that one's body (or mind) is the possession of another is a crucial aspect of colonial object relating and has direct relevance to the experience of black girls and women in the criminal justice system. How much one is in charge of one's self-definition is significant in this process of criminalisation. The extent to which one is relating according to the projections or role actualisation (Sandler, 1976) must be considered, and, unconsciously, individuals take on the distorted projections they receive.

The Victorians seemed to portray those of mixed parentage in a disparaging light. The portrayals of women with mixed parentage are contemptuous. We can see examples of this in Thackeray's novel, *Vanity Fair* (1848), where Rachel Swartz is portrayed as 'a mulatto' who is socially awkward and clumsy and often inappropriately dressed. In Charlotte Bronte's *Jane Eyre* (1847), Jane is trying to become the wife of Rochester but the reader discovers that he has a 'problem', a 'wife who has to die', who is of mixed parentage and described as a 'creole'.[4] One reading of this text is that the two female characters are both parts of Jane Eyre but it is significant how the evil self has to be the darker one.

Impact on the family

Through colonialism a dynamic is set up where pernicious in-fighting within black and Asian communities can manifest as an attack on the family and provide fertile ground for colourism (a hierarchy based on shade, envy, competition and rivalry) which leads to an attack on the self and one's own surroundings. We know that children who grow up in care can do badly in terms of mental health and educational attainment (O'Higgins, Sebba & Luke, 2015; McNiesh & Scott, 2014). The modern family is not what it was. It is easy to leave individuals in this family with an issue and label them as 'hard to reach' (Kassman, 2019) which speaks of us needing to move to them rather than imagining 'they are the problem'.

I have elsewhere spoken about the struggles with operating in the NHS, which is becoming an increasingly paranoid system where manic solutions are the order of the day. In such a system, which can generate mindless competition, it becomes hard to think (Dennis, 2012). The legacy of this relates to an earlier policy predicated on the idea that 'there is no such thing as society, only the individual. There are individual men and women and families' (Thatcher, 1987). This position is antithetical to people for whom the community is the central feature and who put into practice the idea that it takes 'a village to raise a child' (African proverb). But many of the structures important to creating support have broken down. It may not be surprising that the poor and disenfranchised and alienated will turn to apparently strong and caring 'leaders' who make themselves available, only to find that they are further exploited or neglected.

Windrush and its traumatic legacy

The aftermath for people in the colonies was the feeling that England was the mother land.

In the UK the ruling class needed a workforce and enticed people from the Caribbean to come to the 'motherland' to undertake work following the Second World War. Many young men and women served in British armed forces, as their countries were still under British rule, and responded to job advertisements to come to England. On 22 June 1948 the HMT *Empire Windrush* arrived at Tilbury Docks in Essex with about 500 migrants. However, neither the indigenous population nor the migrants were fully prepared for the montage of experience that played out: the violence in the form of a lack of access to housing, discrimination around work and racism: 'No blacks, no dogs, no Irish' was a sign regularly seen on boarding houses.

The grandparents of millennials were encouraged to come to the 'motherland' but they were not welcomed with open arms. Far from the warm embrace they were expecting, they found racism and discrimination, often finding it hard to get proper homes, make friends with British people or get jobs. They witnessed their children being discriminated against and abused at school for the colour of their skin. Under the Immigration Act of 1971 they were given the right to remain here permanently. Those who did not apply for a UK passport or did not have their official paper work were told they would have to leave and were denied access to free hospital treatment and the benefits of being a citizen of this country. This was in line with the rising anti-immigration sentiment in the West at that time. Quite incredibly, the government did not keep a full record of those who came (Gentleman, 2018) but we do have archives that carefully recorded the movement of slaves, along with livestock, during the slave trade. After a review of 11,800 cases, the National Audit Office decided in 2018 that 18 members of the Windrush generation who could have been wrongly removed would be helped to return. In addition, those removed or detained would get a formal apology from the Government. Prime Minister Theresa May said, 'No one from the Windrush generation would have to leave the UK. Windrush migrants were part of us and there was no question of forcing anyone who made their life in the UK and was here legally to leave' (BBC, 2018).

As a consequence of ongoing racism, discrimination and micro-aggressions many black people born in the UK or who have lived here for many years feel they are inhabiting this country with a 'double consciousness', looking at themselves through the eyes of the majority culture (Du Bois, 1897, 1994) or living here with a sense of a home being elsewhere, what Papadopoulos (2002, 2019) calls 'nostalgic yearning'. However, for those born here this is their 'home', but one where they feel unwanted. This is the brutal legacy of the UK's colonial past.

I suggest that we have turned a blind eye to what is in plain sight, there is a disavowal of the repudiated aspects of self or emotion into/onto the other, or at times a fetishisation of the other: the impact and consequences of slavery, including the idealisation of single black females as strong and invulnerable, the attack on a sense of community, social and economic structures supporting poverty and white superiority, and an (implicit) invitation to BAME people to attack one another and fight amongst themselves: the perpetuation of divide and rule. As described above, the principle of divide and rule, and not to educate, were the explicit policies of colonisation within Africa and the Caribbean, as well as within the apartheid regime in South Africa.

Marginalisation and its consequences: othering

The shame internalised from being brought up on the edge of society (being disenfranchised/poor) and the wish 'to live' and to acquire things (socially or materially) can be mitigated against by alternative systems to the mainstream. This can be seen in the dedication of what can be provided by gang membership and the love of the leader. Such 'leaders' usually notice the vulnerability of the young person – maybe giving them the trainers they want, or the money they need to help a parent out, or to pay bills because a parent cannot afford to, as the latest boyfriend is misusing the funds for alcohol or drugs. A gang leader presents himself as 'the saviour', or he is known in the community as 'the man', and much like the Pied Piper the young gravitate towards him and dependency begins. They act as a family, but a mafia family where the boundaries of a family are replaced by rules and a code of conduct where there is an awareness that breaking the code can lead to death. I think these life and death ways of functioning become a place where early feelings about experiences of pain, death, loss, separation, fracture, abuse can coalesce but not be dealt with.

The pressure of constantly being the one who is not the acceptable or desirable one is tremendous, as described earlier; when the BAME women/girl 'messes up' it is an indictment not only of them but 'their group' which produces an ongoing strain. In this scenario I propose that guilt is projected and 'the other' (BAME person) is created as the receptacle of this projection. This 'othering' has psychological sequelae, being framed and fixed by poverty and educational and societal systems. It is a system rather than just one event that creates this othering, a phenomenon which may feel hard to address for such communities. Thus no matter how hard the individual is attempting to affect the situation, any real change becomes problematic. I think there is just enough awareness and lack of awareness (a blind eye) to perpetuate this status quo.

There are of course the 'exceptional blacks', who are given a place at the metaphorical 'top table' and accepted as long as they do not 'step too far out of line'. We are reminded of what occurs when one does, such as Colin Kaepernick, an African American football player, who was chosen to lead an advertisement campaign for Nike after two years of not working. Part of the controversy around him is that he knelt instead of stood to the American flag, during the playing of the American National Anthem. He knelt in support of the Black Lives Matter campaign, in relation to ongoing killings of African Americans that have occurred in America. Whilst all lives matter, this goes without saying, what one is being alerted to is something at the heart of prejudice. Certain sectors of society are attacked, denigrated and hated with impunity. A black man can be killed in broad daylight. There are many examples of black people being killed.[5] However, as a wider collective there appear to be pains of discomfort at one end, or, at the other end, guilt, but mostly we get on with our lives. Certain sectors of society, the poor and disadvantaged, are left to carry the unwanted aspects.

At the time of writing, black people, including Sarah Reed in the UK[6] and Sandra Bland in the US,[7] are dying in police custody in suspicious circumstances, with no one being held accountable. They had already been imprisoned with little evidence, subjected to police brutality during and after arrest, and have not had proper legal representation. Data published by Inquest, the UK charity investigating deaths in custody, found the following in their ten-year study: 'BAME people die disproportionately as a result of use of force or restraint by the police, raising serious questions of institutional racism as a contributory factor in their deaths' (Inquest, 2018). The specific break-down is as follows:

- The proportion of BAME deaths in custody where restraint is a feature is over two times greater than it is in other deaths in custody;
- The proportion of BAME deaths in custody where use of force is a feature is over two times greater than it is in other deaths in custody;
- The proportion of BAME deaths in custody where mental-health-related issues are a feature is nearly two times greater than it is in other deaths in custody. (Inquest, 2018)

Colin Kaepernick is a person with the means to mitigate against the restrictions imposed from his protest; however those with less means are unable to protect themselves. This process occurs with black men and women. We need to keep in mind the limited power base which can be felt by those individuals who have been marginalised, grown up in care, are lone parent families and in households with low incomes.

The portrayal of black women as criminals

I want to focus on and describe the psychological criminalisation of women by starting with a particular example, Serena Williams. Here again another black person is seen as not conforming to the reassuring stereotypes which are meant to put her in place. We see in this particular example the mis-use of the black woman's body in order to exemplify part of the psychological process which is used to justify incarceration. During the US Open tennis final, Serena Williams received a code violation for coaching, a penalty point for breaking her racquet and a game penalty point for calling the umpire a 'thief', and was fined £13,000. The Women's Tennis Association have described the referee's actions as sexist and found that Williams's actions were no different to that of many top players during the heat of a championship game. Serena Williams was then portrayed as the 'angry black woman'.

It is relevant to examine how Serena Williams was portrayed and how black women have been portrayed at certain points in history. The 19th-century min-strel shows were popular in England and America and utilised gross caricatures of black people as the basis for their entertainment. In America, Blair Kelley (associate professor of history at North Carolina State University) explained that black women were often played by white men who painted their faces and donned fat suits 'to make them look less than human, unfeminine and ugly'.

Williams is then depicted in the media in a cartoon as a 'petulant, mannish figure' with the caption that the referee tells the opponent, 'Can you just let her win?' This supports the idea of the angry black woman who cannot be afforded any other role, class and position within society, especially if she does not assimilate and conform to certain stereotypes around looks and body shape. While those condemning her do not refer explicitly to her black skin, their distortions are based on implicit associations that she is lesser, other and wild, not fully human, connoting the body of a slave. I use this simple example to highlight how a heated exchange between a player and an umpire becomes contorted into the excessive and uncontrollable responses of 'an angry black woman', with the consequence of her needing to be firmly put in her place, like an animal in its cage.

The internalisation of racism

In the chapter 'The Fact of Blackness', Fanon (1952, 1991) talks of the black man having a divided self as a result of colonisation:

> I am a negro, it is a feeling of not existing – a toy in the hand of the white man. In the end he has to accept his colour as the amputee accepts his disability. He feels he has a part to expand to infinity and yet he feels paralysed. He is at a cross roads between nothingness and infinity and he weeps.

In 'I Am Not Your Negro', a 2017 documentary film based on James Baldwin's unfinished manuscript, *Remember This House*, he states that it is not easy to detect who possesses racist ways of being, because it is in all of us. Davids (2011) attempts to describe this analytically, calling this aspect the internal racist.

The internal racist is possessed by everyone and becomes more active under certain conditions. What we think we know is fuelled by our internal state. Psychic retreats are resistant to change precisely because they provide a refuge for both paranoid and depressive anxieties. This organised template governs relations with the object.

> No matter how hard *(s)he*[8] tries, the victim cannot be an ordinary human being. Like a mafia gang, this internal structure promises protection in return for loyalty.

> (p. 64)

Davids links the internal racist structure to the Oedipal situation, a position of insight within his psychoanalytic model. What is perhaps most helpful is that there is the hope of depressive position functioning; though at times of anxiety there is a return to paranoid schizoid functioning. It is not a static position and one can move to a more reflective place and out of it again. During the paranoid schizoid phase, the infant's mind defends against psychotic anxieties by splitting. It is exposure to a third, the father, or others outside the family, which help to ameliorate these anxieties, and, over time, these paranoid anxieties are worked through to more depressive position functioning (Klein, 1935, 1940). However, 'as the ego grows and develops, this experience shrinks, but is never totally obliterated' (Davids, 2011: 64). During periods of immense anxiety and uncertainty the experience resurfaces. Here, rather than hold onto any sense of complexity, one operates in a more one-dimensional way in relation to the other.

The toxic meanings ascribed to skin colour, and fear/hatred of darkness

An aspect of trans-Atlantic slavery is colourism, where those black people with a lighter skin are treated preferentially. These slaves were seen as more desirable and given less arduous work than their darker-skinned contemporaries. Black and white people are caught up in the aftermath of the internalisation of hatred, aimed at keeping black people divided. You would not get a white person asking if another was 'white enough', but they do speak of 'white trash', where trash refers to 'black' and its proximity to that trash.

As Baldwin describes in the 2017 documentary, 'I Am Not Your Negro', those who keep him and other black men in ghettos, or lynch them, become something monstrous themselves. Though they do not see him at all, as he really is, or the damage they inflict, he can see them all too clearly, acting out their hatred and evil (Baldwin, 2017) (see also Chapter 4 in this volume). This is an example of the traumatic invisibility of the victim of racism, and the destructive impact on the racist himself. The damage is compounded with Baldwin then staring at the monstrous face of the one who has ghettoised him. This is a powerful and violent image.

Everything that is faced can be changed but nothing can change until it is faced. We see this repeatedly with the way whiteness is preferred over blackness, seen as more desirable and acceptable (Baldwin, 2017). This also is seen in the way it's used in language. Some of the most powerful metaphors are taken from the Christian Bible and associate darkness with Satan and sin, while the light is symbolic of reason, goodness and Christ, the pathway to redemption. Heaviness and burden are likened to darkness while spiritual purity and heavenly states are the real: light in another sense. If light symbolises God, darkness connotes everything that is anti-God, the wicked. These dichotomies run deep in the psyche and manifest in the treatment of black minority ethnic people beyond conscious awareness. They take on concrete shape in the way that black and white is perceived. They continually shape and refine ideas about who is, and who is not, good, deserving and trustworthy. We speak of the 'black sheep of the family', 'the heart of darkness', the 'shadow side' and compare this to 'white as the driven snow', 'the lightness of joy', of being 'brought into the light'.

Annihilation of the other

Our reliance and use of these metaphors/unconscious phantasies unquestionably further entrench racism. They fuel our way of relating to the other, which can become fixed. They will influence the nature of relating in all sectors of the community. DiAngelo (2018) highlights how white people can enjoy segregation, universalism and individualism, entitlement of racial comfort, racial arrogance, racial belonging and psychic freedom, which are seen as more valuable – through representation in everything. Hence psychic freedom of the individual is seen as the dominating force in acts of racist violence, whereas what is actually going on is that this is not a mentally disturbed white man, but an ordinary one, who acts on the (unconscious and unstated) wishes of the dominant power structure. Thus an 'ordinary white man' can kill 49 people of colour[9] and his action be seen as unrelated to any other person from the white population; nor is it linked to explanations of white failings. It is understood as the expression of his individual failings or psychic disturbance, rather than a manifestation of the widely held feelings and unconscious wishes of the dominant power structure.

Trauma and attachment

We know from attachment theory and object relations that the early infant–caregiver relationship is important in terms of the sense of self and self-love. We know about the importance of parental and child relationships, attachments and mothering/primary caregiving. The importance of the early mother–infant relationship, and the breakdown of that early attunement, alongside mirroring and formulations of early experiences of containment (Bion, 1962), are crucial to later development. The reflective and containing functioning of caregivers enables mirroring, which is fundamental for the development of emotional experience, identifying and processing our mental states, and empathic engagement with others. The early experience of containment by another will enable later internalisation of containment and the capacity to manage and process intense feelings, including aggressive and sexual ones. For children whose mothers are in pain, whether mental or physical, this sense of containment may be impoverished, and they may develop heightened sensitivity to the mental state of others, and become less aware of their own sense of being seen. It is essential for the primary caregiver to take in anxiety and makes sense of it for the baby and infant. In so doing the infant is helped to develop an emotional language and a rich interior life to manage anxiety, relate to others (object relationships) and to make sense of the world. Trauma can have a devastating impact on the capacity to contain and on those exposed to it. As outlined in Chapter 1, the rates of trauma in women in the criminal justice system are high, and their incarceration can often retraumatise them.

Given the central importance of early attachments we need to be aware of how parenting practices and children's identifications with these practices impact on their development. The family scripts which impact on thinking and behaving are essential to the development of the individual's sense of self. This sense of self is shaped through our internalised beliefs and value systems and silence about the unresolved generational pain on the psyche/mental health faced by the challenges in daily life. Thus the impact on an infant of growing up with a mother/primary caregiver who has themselves faced racist projections and treatment is significant.

Intergenerational transmission of the trauma of racism

Sharpe (2016) states that living in the wake of slavery is living 'the afterlife of property, and living the afterlife ... in which the black child inherits the non/status, the non/being of the mother. That inheritance of a non/status is everywhere apparent now in the ongoing criminalisation of black women and children' (p. 15). How does one mourn the interminable event? Just as what she calls 'wake work' troubles mourning, so too does the wake and wake work trouble the ways most museums and memorials take up trauma and memory. *She refers to disrupting with pursuing un/imaginable lives.* It is hard to work through being invisible, lacking status if the sources of restriction continue to impinge on life and there is little opportunity to grieve and to realise aspirations or dreams.

We have to constantly keep in mind that for each person there is an intersectionality of their sexuality, gender, class and differing degrees of ability Crenshaw (1989). Any system seems to privilege just one aspect of BAME people, which is their blackness/skin colour, and becomes a receptor for unwanted projections from the other. History is not past, it is present, we are our history. But it may be something that can be faced with proper containment. Thus a racially abused/depressed mother in deprived social circumstances may not be able to contain herself without adequate support – and then the containment for the baby is impaired, continuing an intergenerational trauma.

I will now turn to two clinical examples which exemplify these points.

Clinical illustration 1: Ms S

Ms S is a 26–year-old woman of dual heritage; her father is of Jamaican origin and her mother white English. When she was six years old her father abused her sexually, which she remembered clearly when she was in a party dress on her way to a cousin's christening. Her parents had separated and she only saw him for special occasions. When she returned home she told her mother what had happened, what her father had done. Her mother, a woman who was herself alcohol-dependent, became highly distressed and put Ms S in a bath in which she had poured bleach. Ms S remembers her mother scrubbing her and trying to 'clean' her. While she knew that her mother was trying to protect her somehow, the feelings of being bad, unclean and damaged became associated with the darker colour of her skin (somewhat like her father's, unlike her mother's) rather than with the sexual abuse she had endured. She was not stopped from visiting her father and he both violent and sexually abusive to her on subsequent occasions. She eventually refused to go and see him when she was 11 years old and her younger sister was six, the age she had been when first abused. Although she found it difficult to protect herself from her father, she was able to take this on when contact with him would have exposed her sister to similar danger. Her sister would not go alone as she too was frightened of their volatile father. Although her white mother had been unstable, alcohol-dependent and not protective, Ms S retained a rather idealised image of her, viewing her as without choice and agency. In this way it was clear how she used splitting as an attempt to maintain some sense of world order, but with destructive consequences for her own psychic functioning.

She was a very well-groomed and attractive woman who had avoided close relationships, done well at school and acquired a well-paid and prestigious job in a bank. When she was caught and charged with fraud, related to presenting false cheques with funds taken from the bank, she was referred to the out-patient department of the forensic psychology and psychiatry service for evaluation, then received a probation order with the recommendation that she engage in forensic psychotherapy.

Although she was convicted when she was 26 she disclosed in therapy that she had a long history of shoplifting and fraud for which she had not been convicted. She presented herself as a white European woman, which she 'passed' for, as her olive skin and straightened, thick dark hair could be associated with Mediterranean colouring. She was able to acknowledge a deep sense of being fraudulent in her attempt to disown her father and his ethnicity, embodied in her. The unconscious reasons for her deception in relation to stealing, and the self-destructive aspect of her behaviour, as she stole from the organisation or 'body' that fed and housed her, in one sense, were the main themes of the therapeutic work. Although her outward presentation was of a composed, competent and elegant woman, underneath this exterior she was fragmented, enraged, humiliated and ashamed. The traumatic aspect of her experiences both of abuse and of the part of her that she identified with her father became expressed in her fraudulent activities and what appeared to be her unconscious desire to be caught and punished.

She engaged well in therapy for the first three months but then began to dis-engage, using as a reason her wish to pursue a retraining opportunity at college. Although she attended for approximately 36 sessions I felt that her decision to end the therapy somewhat prematurely reflected her terror of addressing her anger at her (white) mother and the fear that she had externalised her rage onto both her own dark skin through her disavowal of her link with her (black) father, rather than seeing it in its complexity and achieving a state of ambivalence. At some level she was aware of the self-and-other deception she was perpetuating in her self-presentation and her criminal activity could be seen as a form of truth-seeking – she was eventually found out to be in a state of deception and to be stealing from the organisation that symbolised the maternal body. In this sense her attack against the non-protective and neglectful mother was also externalised, but in a concealed way. She found it very difficult to express anger overtly and instead acted it out through her stealing, and through the self-harm that she eventually admitted to in therapy. She let me know that when she first saw me she would engage in delicate self-cutting on hidden parts of her body at least twice a week, hating her own body and the lies she felt it contained and concealed. By the time she left treatment she was no longer attacking herself with anything like this degree of regularity but was still keeping her 'weapons' of a razor and scissors in her drawer at home, 'as a last resort'.

Clinical illustration 2: Ms R

Ms R is a 25 year old well known to social services for violence directed towards her. Her mother was known to psychiatric services, having moved to England when Ms R was in her late teens. She had four children with her Eng-lish partner, who had grown up in care. When the youngest child was age three, her partner left the family. Ms R is the eldest child, and she was tasked with taking care of her three other siblings when her mother would leave to see her friends or go out. The mother felt out of place in the UK and had given birth to Ms R when she was herself only 17. She wanted to 'make up for lost time' and often went out to 'party' leaving Ms R in charge of her younger siblings. She formed relationships with several men in quick succes-sion, often introducing them to her children. At least one of these boyfriends was violent to her and towards the children, including Ms R, who tried to pro-tect her mother from the abuse and even called the police on one occasion. These partners were of different ethnicities. Ms R and her mother were black, subjected to abuse by the neighbours and one of these partners referred to Ms R's mother as a 'black bitch' and a 'ho', despite having pursued her.

When she was at school, Ms R was teased and bullied for being the daugh-ter of a woman known for her eccentric behaviour, dressing flamboyantly and having numerous boyfriends. She recalled being beaten up by a group of boys when she tried to defend her mother's name, and also believed that the teachers in charge of monitoring the playground at times simply looked on and watched, failing to protect her. She had felt singled out because of her mother's reputation and also because of the city, as the majority of the other children were white or Asian.

When she went to secondary school Ms R continued to be ostracised and became overweight, saying that she found comfort in overeating. She felt lonely and suffered more bullying by others in her year group, eventually making some friends with other young people who were 'outsiders' including a boy who believed he was gay, and two girls who adopted Goth personas. She had developed early and was much bigger than other girls in her year, for which she was also marked out, though some of the older boys were clearly attracted to her and made advances towards her. She spent much of her time outside of school taking care of her younger siblings and was often the target of her mother's aggressive outbursts. When she was 15 she became sexually active and eventually gave birth at 17, after a brief and unhappy relationship with a violent partner. He was white and the baby had very dark skin, appearing physically much more like her than her boyfriend. Her mother was furious that she had become pregnant and found it difficult to support her in her decision to keep the baby. She asked Ms R to leave and she was eventually housed in a bedsit where she and her baby lived. Although Ms R had the support of her maternal aunt she found it very difficult to manage the care of this young baby, and when he was five months old she reported to the health visitor that she was experiencing violent fantasies about him. She was living alone and her father was no longer maintaining contact with either Ms R or their son, saying that he didn't want the responsibility.

Isolated as she was, Ms R became increasingly depressed and frustrated by the restrictions on her life. She began to spend longer periods of time in bed and stopped attending the baby group she had joined. The health visitor became concerned about the apparent neglect of the baby. He seemed listless, failed to thrive and often cried for long periods of time. She alerted social services who then began a detailed assessment of Ms R and the baby, alongside assessing the other family members to act as carers. Ms R was deeply suspicious about the input of the local authority and hurt by her mother's abandonment of her and her son. Although she described feeling loving towards her baby, she also felt that he was just like her, a 'bastard' who had little chance of having a good future. He began to become more mobile and active, which seem to coincide with social services becoming alarmed when they noticed bruising on his legs and a burn mark on his hands.

Although Ms R denied that she had caused the bruising or being aware of his movements, saying that he had accidentally touched a hot iron she had left on the floor, the local authority became suspicious about the possibility that she may have deliberately burnt him. She adamantly denied this but reported one day to the health visitor that she had intrusive thoughts about hurting him, saw him as unwanted, and also believed that he was filled with anger and hatred towards her. She described feeling hurt that her ex-partner had abandoned them both and that this, in part, was to do with how dark their son was, explaining that she believed her partner had been racist and had not wanted to have a 'mixed race or black baby' in the family.

She narcissistically identified with the baby, finding it hard to see him as separate from her in any way, and was loathed to enrol him in a nursery, despite the local authority's strong recommendation that she do so. The concerns became more serious when she took a moderate overdose, while in sole charge of her son, although she contacted her aunt to notify her of this. Her aunt arrived at her home to find the paracetamol bottle in range of the baby, who was now crawling and appeared dirty and unhappy. He was subsequently placed under a care order, pending psychiatric assessment of Ms R.

Following the psychiatric evaluation, Ms R received a diagnosis of a personality disorder and was then referred to the complex needs service. She engaged well in the service, where she was seen by a therapist and used the sessions to acknowledge her guilt and shame and explore the underlying motivations/meanings for the offence. Eventually she admitted that she had lost her temper with the baby and put his hand on a hot kettle to punish him for what she perceived to be the intolerable demands that he placed upon her. She sought to understand her behaviour and to engage in the treatment offered in order to reduce the risk she posed. She explored her complex sense of identity, hatred of herself, her background, including a complicated set of feelings about her ethnicity and her fear that she was treated differently and more harshly as a young black woman than other white women. She saw a lot of herself in her son and had her fears that unless she understood herself better she would not be able to love him for who he was, separately from her, and offer him the stability and care he required, should he be rehabilitated into her care.

The therapy was of benefit in helping her to explore the complex feelings towards herself, of her self-hatred and towards abandoning parental figures, including her father, which were also projected onto her son. Her son was eventually returned with ongoing child care support. Her psychotherapy helped Ms R to begin to symbolise and mourn her losses, including her feelings of abandonment related to her mother, father and her whole experience of childhood. In becoming a mother she could now think about her need for mothering and develop a more coherent narrative about her experiences.

This case illustrates the internalisation of racist abuse, identification with her mother (identification with the aggressor) through lack of protection, the intergenerational transmission of abuse, and how Ms R was able to make good use of therapeutic input. Through the stark examples given above it is clear that conscious and unconscious manifestations of racism engender deeply traumatic experiences in victims of racist projection, inflicting actual as well as psychic violence, and re-awakening and deepening earlier experiences of trauma and pain.

It is important to explore carefully what we mean by trauma, which literally means 'wound'. Van der Kolk (2015) states that it is 'an inescapably stressful event that overwhelms people's existing coping mechanisms'; and Herman (1992) states that 'at the moment of trauma the victim is rendered helpless by overwhelming force'. We have to keep in mind that this is a combination of that event, that moment, that person's life, with that person's history, that makes it an individual experience. From neuroscience we are aware that child-hood trauma reduces one's capacity for language (Broca's area of the brain) and reduces one's capacity to put emotional experiences (the body experiences) into words (Van der Kolk, 2015). The smaller corpus callosum reduces com-munication between the left (logical, rational and language) and the right (emotional experience and processing, empathy and bonding) hemispheres. Van der Kolk (2015) states that because the traumatic event does not get pro-cessed in symbolic/linguistic forms, like most memories, but tends to be organ-ised on a sensori-motor level, as horrific images, visceral sensations or fight/flight reactions. Storage on a sensori-motor level and not in words is supposed to explain why this type of material does not undergo the usual transforming process. If a woman does not remember an experience in words, it becomes action; it is repeated without her knowing she is repeating it, and this becomes her way of remembering. Freud called this the repetition compulsion (1920) and I have provided examples of its expression in the case studies above.

Therefore the external event is experienced as confirming the worse internal fears and phantasies, in particular the imminence of death. Trauma impacts adversely on our capacity to symbolise and interferes with our capacity to mourn (Garland, 1998); furthermore the current trauma may be reactive to much earlier experiences, especially pockets of vulnerability (Segal, 1957). In working with trauma it is important to validate the experience, to enable some understanding of the internal meaning and help contain it (Levy & Lemma, 2000). I have shown how hard it is to do this in the face of racism, when the action and the permutations of this force are relentless and ongoing. It is diffi-cult to mourn a destructive 'gift that keeps on giving'.

Trauma and marginalisation: the violence of racism

> I am often conscious in groups, and in one-to-one situations, of my colour in relation to others. We don't have single identities but we are members of different groups who are better defined by class, gender, sexuality, the city, disability, religion, culture, language etc. Each of these categories expresses a power dynamic within the social order that defines the centre and the margins in relation to that category.
>
> (Dalal, 2002: 219)

Depending on which is at the foreground at any moment, we may find ourselves sometimes occupying the centre of a dynamic and sometimes the margins. What the marginalised groups are then forced to do, as a strategic necessity, is use the same weapon and assert a new essentialism at the margins. The point about being at the margins is that the centre finds it hard to hear, partly because what has been said is inconvenient. And so the marginalised are forced to shout and can end up sounding shrill. The power of the ideology is such that the 'whiteness' as organising principle is unconscious. In other words the white ensign as the centre is invisible, and it is only the black ensign at the margins that is able to be seen. Those at the centre feel themselves to be innocent, unfairly assaulted from without (Dalal, 1998: 206–207.

DiAngelo (2018) writes of:

> white fragility … where a minimum amount of racial stress becomes intolerable to a white person or system, triggering defensive moves, including anger, fear and guilt, and behaviours such as augmentation, silence, and leaving the stress-inducing situation … insulated environments of racial protection build white expectations for racial comfort while at the same time lowering the ability to tolerate racial stress. It is whiteness as a constellation of processes and practices rather than as a discrete entity (like skin colour) alone. Whiteness is dynamic, relational, and operating at all times on a myriad of levels.
>
> (pp. 1–2)

I hope to have highlighted the criminalisation of black women and psychic/actual violence committed through racist projections, behaviours, invisibility and the tremendous difficulty for the women themselves to separate out what is done to them and how they subsequently perceive themselves and their children. An irony is that whilst education is often seen as a route to enlightenment there is little awareness of miseducation in the sense of a black women not being presented with a history, at all, or with a mono-history that supports a lack of sense of self. That is, there is a gap or absence bolstering an alienation rather than giving a sense of access.

In any facility the therapy or therapeutic input the individual receives needs to be maintained and supported by the structures after they are discharged or run in parallel if they are outpatients. This therapeutic intervention should not be solely organised around traumatic incidents but an attempt should be made to understand the meaning of these to the individual/partnership/family, which requires understanding the broader context of the individual's life and functioning. The therapeutic aims include a connectedness with a sense of community, which means addressing the double consciousness[10] towards a more integrated sense of self.

In addition an intervention could include practical aspects, such as work and social skills training, which might be an important part of integration into society with a more coherent sense of self. The hope is that this coherent sense of self will be less vulnerable to the projections/fragmentation inflicted by white society on a black woman, enabling her to resist these projections, though at times these will be overwhelming. The connection to community can help to strengthen the individual against the weight of racialised attacks/projections.

> It dawned upon me with a certain suddenness that I was different from the others; or like, mayhap, in heart and life and longing, but shut out from their world by a vast veil.
>
> (Du Bois, 1897, p. 1)

This chapter has outlined the forces that combine to lead black women to perceive themselves as criminal, taking on the projections of a racist society. Despite the alienation and double consciousness this leads to, and the reinforcement of this distortion through the criminal justice system, I have outlined some interventions that can address this, enabling the women to face the meaning of their experiences, to feel a connection to community and to come to know themselves as they really are, released from the shackles of the presumption of white innocence and black guilt.

Notes

1 The word 'negro' is derived from the Latin, meaning black, as it does in Spain and Portuguese. Back in the 1700s and 1800s it was used by the slave master to summon his slave. It is currently regarded as an offensive term in the United Kingdom.
2 Throughout this book we will not refer to this notion of a construct of 'race' as if it refers to a meaningful construct, as we consider it empty and inaccurate.
3 Margaret Garner (1833–1858) had escaped from slavery with her husband and family. However, once caught she killed her daughter so that she would not have to face the prospect of a life incarcerated. She had tried to kill herself but was prevented from doing so.
4 Bertha Mason is the famous 'mad woman in the attic', whose 'insane, violent behaviour' is frightening to behold. Her laughter is described as 'demonic' (Bronte, 1848: 167), and she crawls on all fours, snarling and behaving in a bestial manner.
5 Cynthia Jarrett, died in 1985. Joy Gardner died aged 40 on 1 August 1993 after being arrested by specialist officers of the extradition unit of the Metropolitan Police. She was gagged with 13 feet of tape and the officers were later acquitted. Germaine Alexander was removed to a strip cell in prison. He was found dead with bruising all over his body. It was deemed to be due to natural causes aggravated by lack of care. Oliver Pryce aged 30 died on 24 July 1990 – verdict unlawful killing. Dereck Buchanan aged 19 died on 4 September 1988 from drowning whilst in police custody. Oluwashiji Lappite, aged 34, died on 16 December 1994 during a struggle with the Metropolitan Police; four years later the CPS reaffirmed their position that the officers would not be prosecuted. Winston Rose died aged 27 on 13 July 1981. He was restrained by police officers in a police van on his way to a psychiatric hospital.
6 www.theguardian.com/society/2016/feb/17/sarah-reeds-mother-deaths-in-custody-holloway-prison-mental-health
7 https://www.theguardian.com/us-news/2019/may/07/sandra-bland-video-footage-arrest-death-police-custody-latest-news
8 I have italicised and altered the gender in this quotation.
9 The Australian 28 year old, Brenton Tarrant, accused of killing 49 people at two New Zealand Mosques on 15 March 2019.
10 Du Bois referred to double consciousness as: 'It's a peculiar sensation, this double consciousness, this sense of always looking at one's self through the eyes of others … One ever feels his twoness, an American, a Negro; two souls, two thoughts, two unreconciled strivings; two warring ideals in one dark body, whose dogged strength alone keeps it from being torn asunder.' Other writers refer to proxy self, false self, black Atlantic self, black skin and white mask – i.e. colonialism becomes embodied; like Du Bois they are referring to a self that cannot embrace its full identity. This may involve where one is born and a historical/ancestral self. This will include individuals' mixed parentage negotiating many histories/multiple identities.

References

Baldwin, J. (2017) I Am Not Your Negro. Film Directed by R Peck.
BBC News (2018) What is the Windrush generation. https://www.bbc.co.uk/newsround/amp/43793769
Bion, W. R. (1962) *Learning from Experience.* London: Karnac Books.
Bronte, C. (1848) *Jane Eyre.* New York: Bantam Dell.
Carrol, R. (2019) Overlooked: Margaret Garner 1833–1858 Obituary. NewYorkTimes.com.
Coates, Ta-Nehisi (2015) *Between the World and Me.* Australia: The Text Publishing Company,
Crenshaw, K. (1989) Demarginalising the intersection of race and sex: A black feminist critique of antidiscrimination doctrine, feminist theory and antiracist politics, *University of Chicago Legal Forum* 140:139–167.
Dalal, F. (1998) *Taking the Group Seriously.* London: Jessica Kingsley.
Dalal, F. (2002) *Race, Colour and the Processes of Racialization: New Perspectives from Group Analysis, Psychoanalysis and Sociology.* Hove: Brunner Routledge.
Davids, F. (2011) *Internal Racism: A Psychoanalytic Approach to Race and Difference.* London: Palgrave Macmillan.
Dennis, M. (2012) Fighting for survival, *New Associations* 10:5. British Psychoanalytic Council.
DiAngelo, R. (2018) *White Fragility: Why It Is So Hard for White People to Talk about Racism.* Boston: Beacon Press.
Du Bois, W. E. B. (1897) 'The strivings of the Negro people.' *The Atlantic Magazine.* August.
Du Bois, W. E. B. (1994) *The Souls of Black Folk.* New York; Avenel, NJ: Gramercy Books.
Fanon, F. (1952, 1991) *Black Skin: White Masks.* London: Pluto Press.
Fletchman-Smith, B. (2000) *Mental Slavery: Psychoanalytic Studies of Caribbean People.* London: Rebus Press.
Frankenberg, R. (1993) *White Women, Race Matters: Social Construction of Whiteness.* Minneapolis: University of Minnesota Press.
Freud, S. (1916) *Some Character-Types Met in Psycho-Analytic Work.* Standard Edition, Vol 14. London: Hogarth Press.
Freud, S. (1920) *Beyond the Pleasure Principle.* Standard Edition, Vol 18. London: Hogarth Press.
Garland, C. (Ed.) (1998, 2007) *Understanding Trauma: A Psychoanalytical Approach.* London: Karnac. The Tavistock Clinic Series.
Gentleman, A. (2018) Home Office criticised for 'lack of urgency'. www.the guardian.com.
Herman, J. L. (1997, 1992) *Trauma and Recovery: The Aftermath of Violence—From Domestic Abuse to Political Terror.* New York: Basic Books.
Holmes, J. (2014) *John Bowlby and Attachment Theory (Makers of Modern Psychotherapy).* London: Routledge.
Inquest (2018) BAME deaths in police custody. www.inquest.org.uk/bame-deaths-in-police-custody.
Kassman, P. (2019) Conference presentation. *Youth Violence and Knife Crime in London Today: Going beyond the superficial approaches.* March. Tavistock Clinic Thinking Space.

Klein, M. (1935) A contribution to the psychogenesis of manic depressive states. In E. Spillius (Ed.), *Writings of Melanie Klein*. London: Hogarth Press, 262–289.

Klein, M. (1940) Mourning and its relation to manic-depressive states. In E. Spillius (Ed.), *Writings of Melanie Klein*. London: Hogarth Press, 344–369.

Kolbert, E. (2018) There is no scientific basis for race: It's a made-up label. https//www.nationalgeographic.com/magazine/2018/04/-race-genetics-science-Africa.

Lemma, A., & Levy, S. (Eds) (2000) *The Perversion of Loss*: *Psychoanalytic Perspectives on Trauma*. London and Philadelphia: Whurr Publishers.

Lobb, J. (Ed) (1876) *Uncle Tom's Story of his Life: An Autobiography of the Rev. Josiah Henson*. London: Christian Aid Office.

Lousada, J. (2006) Glancing over the shoulder: Racism, fear of the stranger and the Fascist state of mind, *Journal of Psychoanalytic Psychotherapy* 20(2):97–104.

Lowe, F. (2007) Colonial object relations: Going underground black-white relationships, *British Journal of Psychotherapy* 24(1):20–33.

McNiesh, D., & Scott, S. (2014) *Women and Girls at Risk: Evidence Across the life Course*. London: Lankelly Chase.

O'Higgins, A. J., Sebba, J., & Luke, N. (2015) *What is the Relationship between being in Care and the Educational Outcomes of Children?* An international systematic review Rees Centre for Research in Fostering and Education, University of Oxford September.

Papadopoulos, R. (Ed.) (2002, 2019) *Therapeutic Care for Refugees: No Place Like Home*. London: Routledge.

Ryder, J. (2019) *White Privilege Unmasked*. London: Jessica Kingsley.

Sandler, J. J. (1976) Countertransference and role responsiveness, *International Journal of Psychoanalysis* 3:43–47.

Segal, H. (1957) Notes on symbol formation, *International Journal of Psychoanalysis* 38:391–397.

Sharpe, C. (2016) *In the Wake on the Blackness of Being*. US: Duke University Press.

Steiner, J. (1993) *Psychic Retreats: Pathological Organisations in Psychotic, Neurotic and Borderline Patients*. London: Karnac.

Sterling, D. (Ed) (1997) *We Are Your Sisters: Black Women in the Nineteenth Century*, New York: W. W. Norton.

Thatcher, M. (1987) *Women's Own Magazine*, Thatcher Archive (THCr 5/12/262): COS Transcript.

Van der Kolk, B. (2015) *The Body Keeps the Score: Brain, Mind, and Body in the Healing of Trauma*. London: Penguin.

Wekker, G. (2016) *White Innocence: Paradoxes of Colonialism and Race*. North Carolina: Duke University Press.

Chapter 4

Caught in the racist gaze?

The vulnerability of black women to forensic mental health and criminal justice settings

Anne Aiyegbusi

Introduction

Black girls and women are likely to attract particular projections associated with low status, invulnerability, precocious or exaggerated sexuality, violence and other forms of criminality. A social unconscious loaded with their historical devaluation and disavowed brutalisation in Europe, and by the European diaspora over a number of centuries, brings to bear a particular type of racist imagery that is difficult not to internalise. This is especially so given the multi-faceted bombardment by which its messages are communicated. This perspective is rarely afforded relevance for making sense of the stressors affecting their lives, shaping their expressions of distress and influencing their over-representation in mental health and criminal justice settings.

This chapter will explore the social and interpersonal influences black girls and women are required to negotiate and how these factors impact on their psychological wellbeing and identity. I aim to outline the generational political and social contexts contributing to their over-representation in mental health and criminal justice settings. The way in which the most vulnerable become entangled in brutalising exchanges with authority, re-enacting historical racist atrocities, is elucidated. This includes the way they are typically framed through a lens of risk or dangerousness to a degree that overrides any vulnerability, suffering or distress.

The well-publicised story of Sarah Reed, a vulnerable black British woman who tragically ended her life while floridly ill in London's Holloway Prison, is presented to illustrate how black women's vulnerabilities and distress become framed and responded to in terms of risk and danger. This is followed by an exploration of the historical context of racism, how it intersects with gender and how its threads remain evident in society today. The particular burdens carried by black women within the racist frame are considered. It is suggested that re-enactments of historical racist trauma will most likely be evident in mental health and criminal justice systems.

The chapter will conclude with ideas about how professionals working throughout the network of forensic systems might employ knowledge and awareness of racist dynamics to avoid perpetuating racist trauma on black women who offend while experiencing psychological distress.

Black women and British prisons

The Lammy Review (2017) of the experience of Black, Asian and Minority Ethnic (BAME) people in the British criminal justice system identified an even greater disproportionality of black men and women in its prisons than in the USA, a country known for re-enacting the trauma of chattel slavery through its mass incarceration of black people. With regard to incarcerated women, the Corston Report (2007), a review of vulnerable women in British prisons, highlighted the doubly vulnerable status of black women. The recent joint publication by Women in Prison and Agenda (2017) about the experiences of BAME women in the criminal justice system, entitled 'Double Disadvantage', reported that 8.8% of female prisoners are black whilst only 3.3% of the general population are. Compared to white women, black women are about 25% more likely to be sentenced to custody at crown court. This disproportionality increases in the case of drug offences where black women are about 125% more likely to receive a custodial sentence than are their white counterparts. This chapter will argue that the root of what is baldly termed 'disproportionality' lies in centuries-old abuse of the black body and that the picture seen today reflects that history and its generational re-enactment.

Black women, mental health and prison: Sarah Reed

In order to illustrate the experiences of black women in the mental health and criminal justice systems, the tragic case of Sarah Reed is considered. Sarah Reed died in prison custody in 2016. Information sources within the public domain have informed this account, including: CCTV footage available online, referring to a prior incident involving Sarah as victim; the independent investigation into her death by the prison and probation ombudsman dated January 2017; the coroner's report dated July 2017; numerous articles published in *The Guardian* newspaper, including those which have reported interviews with her mother; and the website of Inquest, a British charity focusing its legal expertise on state related deaths.

Sarah Reed's tragic story has been well publicised in the British media. She was a young British-born black woman with a long history of traumatic experience and serious mental health problems who was found dead in the mental health assessment unit at London's Holloway Prison on 11 January 2016.

Sarah had been charged with assaulting a male nurse while sectioned in a mental health unit. She had admitted the charge. However, there were concerns about her fitness to plead. While living at home in the community she had failed to attend psychiatric appointments required for completing assessment reports to help the court determine her fitness to plead. So she was deemed unreliable. For that reason she was remanded by the court to prison in October 2015. The rationale being that, while detained in prison, she could not default on psychiatric appointments and so the assessment reports would be promptly completed.

While in prison she suffered cardiac symptoms, which led to her anti-psychotic medication being discontinued. Her mental health deterioration was observed and mainly conceptualised as difficult behaviour, such as the bullying and intimidation of others. She herself complained of being bullied, but this was never looked into. Subjectively, she appeared to have been frightened and lost. Despite her pleading for help to control the disturbing symptoms she was experiencing, the behavioural manifestation of her relapsing condition was responded to with disciplinary action rather than care and treatment. Mean-while, the length of time taken to complete the psychiatric assessments was not reduced by her detention in prison but prolonged, with Sarah not knowing what was happening to her. Uncertainty about the date of the court hearing to determine her future weighed on her mind. The fact she was a woman with long standing and serious mental health conditions and a history of trauma appears to have been lost sight of within a system not equipped to care for her. The fact that the sole purpose of her detention was for the completion of psychiatric reports was also lost sight of. In the time leading up to Sarah's death the prison had cancelled multiple visits including those from her family and solicitor, which of course compounded her isolation.

She had been transferred to the mental health assessment unit six days before she died because of her severely deteriorating condition, which wors-ened at a rapid pace once she arrived. Descriptions of her mental health are consistent with a floridly ill state. Sarah had been spending much time shout-ing and chanting in her cell. She also spat at people through the hatch in the door. For that reason, a screen was placed in front of it. It was in this sensory and relationally deprived environment that a seriously ill Sarah killed herself. She was found with ligatures made from her bed linen tied around her neck.

Sarah's personal story contains harrowing experiences. Ten years before she died she had experienced the death of her six-month-old daughter who had suf-fered from a degenerative medical condition. Compounding the traumatic experience of losing a child, Sarah and her partner were left to transport their daughter's body from the hospice where she'd died to the mortuary in their own car. This was a trauma from which Sarah was said to have never recovered. She'd suffered from formal mental health problems ever since. She had been given multiple psychiatric diagnoses over the years including emo-tionally unstable personality disorder, schizophrenia, bulimia nervosa and sub-stance misuse. Since diagnosis, Sarah had been detained in Holloway and other prisons and also been sectioned to mental health units.

Four years before her death, Sarah entered into the consciousness of the British public in a devastating way after being accused of shoplifting in a clothing store. CCTV footage of the aftermath emerged, showing her contact with the police. Sarah is shown being beaten by a male police officer. Even from the footage, her terror seems tangible as it registers in her mind that the police officer is going to assault her. As he does, her fragile body can be seen, like a rag doll, being hauled from a chair, pulled by her hair and physically dragged along the floor. The considerably larger male police officer then sits astride her, his knee in her back, while pressing on her throat, punching her around her head and face. Finally, she is seen face down on the floor, hands cuffed behind her back. She seems to struggle to breathe, to be contorting her neck in an effort to clear her airway. The police officer assailant was subsequently convicted of common assault, dismissed from London's Metropolitan Police force and sentenced to perform 150 hours of community service. This incident is said to have impacted on Sarah's already fragile mental health in a negative way. Another traumatic event from which it is said she never recovered. Deborah Coles, Director of Inquest, made the following statement about the circumstances surrounding Sarah's death:

> Sarah Reed was a woman in torment. Imprisoned for the sake of two medical assessments to confirm what was resoundingly clear, that she needed specialist care not prison. Her death was the result of multi-agency failures to protect a woman in crisis. Instead of treating her with adequate support, the prison treated her mental ill health as a discipline, control and containment issue. (www.inquest.org.uk/sarah-reed-inquest-conclusions)

This is a singularly horrifying account, but echoed throughout it are themes that are reminiscent of racist history and which are also known to characterise the experience of black women who come in contact with the mental health and criminal justice systems in the present day. This chapter will explore the historical, social and political contexts that underpin a system that so consistently and colossally underplays vulnerability while over-stating risk and dangerousness in black women.

'Race', racism and the systems upholding white supremacy and privilege

As Andrews (2018: xv) states, when it comes to the pain and brutality of racism 'connections of blackness … cannot be contained within national borders'. For that reason, an atrocity in one part of the world is felt and identified with by black people in all others such that geographical location, nationality and individual heritage are of little relevance in determining felt hurt and harm. It is with this in mind that the material of this chapter refers to racism and racist atrocities beyond the United Kingdom.

'Race' continues to impact on human relations in powerful ways, despite considerable evidence as to its biological irrelevance. Indeed the very physical characteristics relied upon to determine categories of 'race' have been found to be of no more than superficial import (Dalal, 1993, 2001; Kendi, 2016; Montagu, 1997; Richards, 1997). Despite being an empty and artificial construct in this regard, 'race' continues to bear a powerful social influence in day-to-day life, in a psychotic way, as though it has the capability to endow different so-called 'races' with qualities and characteristics that can be measured and categorised into hierarchies indicating varying levels of inferiority or superiority (Rustin, 1991; Frosh, 2013b). This process is called racism, which thus intertwines with 'race' which is its inevitable corollary (Dalal, 2002).

In terms of the roots of racism, Kovel (1988) explains how the history and appearance associated with black people has so 'bedevilled' (p. 62) Europeans. The devil existed as a black entity within European fantasy and thought long before Africans came to be sighted by them in the sixteenth century. Once they were seen, their dark skins and cultural differences were such that they slotted neatly into the European imaginary as an embodiment of the devil and, as such, became convenient receptacles for all that was considered bad, bestial, evil or dirty. The perceived devilishness of the African also offered the European an opportunity to construct and later internalise a contrast for themselves, that of the superior, saintly, pure, clean, white. This dynamic is at the core of white supremacy. Without blackness to project disavowed negative characteristics and experience onto and into, there is no whiteness.

When justification was needed to make good on an opportunity to considerably enrich the life experience of Europeans and produce white utopia on foreign soil (Penna, 2016), 'race', as a construct, with its attendant hierarchies, was consolidated. The Americas and the Caribbean islands with their fertile lands were discovered by Europeans who recognised that there were phenomenal economic gains to be had if only the mineral rich lands could be worked and the potential fruits of their fecundity reaped. A solution was found in enslaving Africans, utilising physical and cultural difference to degrade them to the status of animals or, at least, not full humans, and forcing them to work on this land. Doing so required profound criminality (De Gruy, 2017), including a psychotic level of self-deception (Rustin, 1991) to justify and implement the scale of dehumanisation required for enforcing such a brutal regime. This was maintained for centuries, therefore producing generations of victims and perpetrators of this specific traumatic abuse. The traumatic trans-generational impact of slavery is further described in Chapter 3.

As De Gruy (2017) has stated, the institution of chattel slavery cannot be disentangled from its violence as it was:

> through violence, aggression and dehumanisation that the institution of slavery was enacted, legislated and perpetuated by Europeans.
>
> (De Gruy, 2017: 35)

Fletchman Smith (2000) also notes that the whole social structure upholding slavery, including the sites of its bodily enactment, the plantation societies, were actually criminal enterprises, created solely for the abuse of human beings. Furthermore, as this regime took hold, powerful legal, political, religious and medical institutions colluded in the deception required to so designate Africans as inhuman or subhuman in such a venal way. Race and racism are embedded in psychological and social domains with regard to the history of relations between Africans and Europeans. Indeed, racial categories were used to underpin other social, political and economic systems of power for centuries, and in the most extreme circumstances of which segregation, apartheid and colonisation come to mind – they have served as a rationale for 'superior races' to dehumanise within brutal regimes and perpetrate atrocities on those deemed inferior (Anderson, 2016; Clarke, 2003; Dalal, 2001; Kendi, 2016). Importantly, the flimsy construct of race is in and of itself a convenient while tragically convincing lie used to justify brutal dehumanisation for material gain and emotional self-delusion. The notion of white supremacy appears to be particularly intoxicating and difficult to relinquish. This may go some way to explaining why it is so difficult for so many white people to consider the artificial nature of race and its global impact on humanity, past and present. Toni Morrison (1992: 52) explores how race is used by whites:

> Africanism is the vehicle by which the American [white] self knows itself as not enslaved, but free, not repulsive, but desirable … not history-less but historical … not a blind accident of evolution, but a fulfilment of destiny.

Generational trauma and the social unconscious

Frosh (2016) describes the apparent intangibility of generational transmissions of trauma which nevertheless unconsciously link networks of people to a shared experience. If not brought to consciousness and worked through, this historical trauma risks being re-enacted. So, if not processed by one generation, it is handed down to the next and so on. The social unconscious may mediate the way racist experience, whether as victim or perpetrator, becomes transmitted through generations of a society to influence present day relations (Einhorn, 2007; Frosh, 2013b, Frosh, 2016; Wilke, 2007, 2016). It has been argued that the trauma of institutionalised racist abuse and terror such as was evident in slavery, segregation, colonisation and apartheid has been generationally transmitted through the social unconscious. The result is that relations between the descendants of both victims and perpetrators carry internalisations of the original racist conditions (Volkan 2001).

The racist gaze

A number of authors have elaborated upon the racist gaze, which is regarded as central to understanding how racism is both communicated and perpetrated at the level of the visual register. Though referred to in the literature by a variety of terms including the 'white mirror,' 'mirror as camera' and 'the white gaze', it is widely recognised by black people, who are required to contend with it on an hour-by-hour, day-by-day basis but not by whites (Yancy 2017).

Fanon (1952) brought into sharp focus a particular type of alienating, racist gaze that he observed to characterise interpersonal exchanges between coloniser and colonised. He builds on the concept of double consciousness, which was first described by W. E. B. Du Bois (1903), explaining that when the racist white person looks at a black person they convert the person they see into something debased and dehumanised. This distorted picture is then mirrored back into the mind of the black person, who then comes to experience their own self in the same degraded way, objectified into what Fanon (1952, p. 2) calls 'a zone of non-being'. Double consciousness captures the way black people are required to grapple with this powerful, 'thrown back', degraded image while trying to maintain congruence with their true selves.

Frosh (2013a: 148) captures what has been written about the racist gaze:

The gaze is both destructive and admiring; or rather it is full both of hate and of desire, and as such is marked by envy and by a search for a mirror that will reflect difference. The white subject needs the black to define itself; and it desires the black as the repository of those necessary things – above all sexuality – which it has repudiated out of anxiety and self-loathing.

Frosh (2013a) describes this phenomenon within the context of colonialism and observes that the black person is denied the kind of reflection that would enable the status of subject. Instead, it is argued, they are met with the kind of psychotic gaze that would be in keeping with the status of object. Khanna 2003)) describes this gaze in terms of 'mirror as camera' (p. 187). The author notes the impact of 'mirror as camera' and describes it as undermining any sense of creativity, integration or autonomy the black person might otherwise have. Yancy (2017) describes it as 'the white gaze' through which the black body is both weaponised and criminalised yet simultaneously experienced as both monstrous and desired.

On the receiving end of the racist gaze, 'what she or he sees is not a look of recognition coming from the other, but a look of distain, fear or blank incomprehension' (Frosh 2013a: 147). Indeed, Frosh goes further in stating that the power of colonisation lay in its ability to extract the source of subjectivity from the colonised, and that this power became institutionalised and was repeatedly reflected in the gaze, which rests on the skin through a process that Fanon (1952) described as epidermalisation, referring not only to the visibility of 'race' but the effects of the racist gaze which overemphasises the visible and bodily in a way that is aggressively disorganising and narcissistically traumatic. It breaks down the humanity inherent in self-representation and forcefully replaces it with a form of objectivity which, as we have seen, when en masse, becomes internalised.

Hook (2012) describes the racist gaze as the primal scene of racism. He describes how the degree of othering involved in the racist gaze can be experienced as violently denying the black person access to the fantasised and subjective goodness of whiteness and therefore to humanity (Hook 2012). At the same time, the only aspects of the black person that are valued are those that mirror or comply with the wishes of the white person. Thus an internalised split emerges within the psyche of the black person, one that is represented by the title of Fanon's book: *Black Skin, White Masks*. Hook (2012) explains that the racist gaze activates this split which he describes in terms of (a) a real but bad black self who is embodied but is silenced and devoid of subjecthood, and (b) a good but false white self who is disembodied, has subjecthood and can speak as long as it is only in the master's voice (i.e. wears the white mask).

Yancy (2017) links the racist gaze to centuries of black pain and suffering through violence and sadism to the black body, which has been dehumanised through its lens. Yancy describes its power in present day America where it is ever present, requiring black people to pre-empt the white response to their every move, avoiding any sudden movements, especially within closed or confined spaces like lifts where such movements could be misinterpreted as threatening. In a state of hyper-vigilance and attempting to over-control bodily comportment in a non-threatening way, Yancy describes a form of genuflecting which is an approximation to bowing and scraping, in order to assure that they will not be perceived as physically threatening. As such the experience is more typically akin to experiencing bodily confiscation. After all, black bodies have been subject to more than mere symbolic white violence historically and continuing into the present day. Yancy refers to how this violent history is replicated and repeated throughout American society, having been generationally transmitted. Butler (1993) also describes how the racist gaze distorts what is seen, misattributing impending violence and the threat to blacks in a way that ultimately underpins in America the frequent beating and killing of unarmed black people by white law enforcement agents who even in the face of clear video evidence contradicting their accounts are able to avoid conviction by claiming self-defence due to being in fear of their lives. Once these cases are examined before predominately white courts, the scenarios are further distorted under the racist gaze. Butler (1993) explains this in terms of the murderous violence that is projected onto these black people in the context of full force racist imaginary and gaze. Psychotically the black person is murdered as the carrier of a threat that was projected onto them by their killer. Once examined further in what Butler (1993) describes as the saturated visual field of a courtroom the violence is symbolically repeated and then validated. Such is the interplay between the racist gaze and structural violence. Under prevailing law, such murderous actions are justifiable.

The white gaze is propelled by racist fantasies. As such, the black person becomes the embodiment of disavowed white projections, especially with regard to sexuality. Yancy (2017) elaborates how the black body is both regarded as bestial and threatening while also being sought out for white sexual contact and fantasies. Therefore the black person is experienced 'as sexual, aggressive and physical' (Frosh 2013a: 147) and envied, desired and hated at the same time. This is particularly toxic to black people. Due to the nature of the projections, the racist white needs the denigrated black in order for self-definition, as a receptacle for all that they have discharged from the self through anxiety and self-loathing, especially sexuality (Fanon 1952; Frosh 2013a). Whiteness is imbued with delusions of pureness within which a disavowal of sexuality is entrenched. Therefore, the black person is forced to contain these disavowed sexual aspects and so is fantasised as a sexualised beast, becoming the focus of white envy and desire while simultaneously experienced as a threat to both their potency and their purity. Further intensifying the lethality of the racist gaze is the fact of its internalisation by black people who come to experience themselves and each other through its hateful lens.

Black women's burden?

In the context of powerful racist dynamics evolving from abusive historical contexts, what is the position of the black woman and does she carry a particular burden? Is there a particular way she is impacted on by the racist gaze? Hook (2012) points to the conflation of three key Fanonian concepts that constitute the racist gaze: epidermalisation; the violence of desubjectivisation which is a necessary part of racist objectivisation; and the role of desire and sexual anxiety which is seen as being at the root of racism. With regard to desire, Hook (2012), who takes the context of apartheid-era South Africa as an example, explores this a little further. He explains the immense defensive energy that is involved in repressing racist desire so that the racist never has to be aware of it even as it drives their behaviour in relation to blacks. As a result, racist desire is expressed in the form of repudiating violence. Hook (2012) refers to the work of Cronje, a fierce advocate of apartheid in South Africa and consequently a critic of any notion of whites and blacks having sexual relations and producing 'mixed race' children. He saw racial segregation as the way to resolve this threat. On the surface, segregation was promoted in order to keep whites safe from the desirous blacks' gaze. Hook (2012) notes that a denied function of segregation was actually to remove the black woman from the desiring eyes of white men. He points to the way the worst racist regimes have prohibited inter-racial marriage ostensibly to avoid racial mixing, while black women have nevertheless consistently given birth to 'mixed race' children throughout these regimes. In terms of American history, Oluo (2018) points to the routine rape of African women by white men. Yancy

2017) discusses this phenomenon in terms of another lie, one that involves the racist imaginary positioning the monstrous black male rapist as a threat against the pure and fragile white female body. Yet the rape of black women by white men is deeply rooted in the history of politically sanctioned racist societies and a factor that remains visible in these communities today, the irony of which is apparently not recognised by either the racist imaginary or gaze. This serves as evidence of a key psychological and moral manoeuvre at the core of racism, which culminates in a particular burden carried by black women. It arises from the legacy of a legitimised social system rendering them captive, voiceless and dehumanised and thus prey to institutionalised sexual violence by whites. At the very same time, they were being framed through the racist gaze as unwanted, un-human and undesirable. Yet at the same time, they were regarded through the racist gaze as sexually dominant vamps capable of corrupting decent white men.

In exploring the generational legacy of this impossible position, bell hooks (1992) notes that in popular culture black women's bodies gain attention only when being offered up and sexually deviant; in other words, she says, '"hot" and highly sexed' (p. 66). This position, according to hooks (1992), parallels the lies inculcated during slavery where the institutionalised rape of African women by white male slave masters and workers was represented in terms of the wild black seductress overpowering virtuous slavers. De Gruy (2017) describes how the 'bitches' and 'hos' (p. 131) depicted in music videos are the modern day internalised and commodified manifestation of how the black female body has been represented as '"hot" and highly sexed' in order to mask its historical and ongoing degradation and exploitation.

The '"hot" and highly sexed' (hooks 1992: 66) black woman trope exists alongside others, such as 'Mammy' (hooks 1992: 74). Through the racist gaze, black women have been considered bad, inferior and even incapable mothers (Washington 2008). Yet in another example of psychological contortion, their service in the raising of white children and the caretaking of white homes appears to have been de rigueur throughout socially sanctioned systems of racism and beyond. Parks (2010) explores the archetype of the strong black woman, noting the way the lives of black women have been taken control of and directed in the service of everybody else. She notes that central to this particular stereotype is the convenient delusion of the black woman as invulnerable, able to cope with unending stress and demands while requiring nothing for herself. Parks (2010) links this to the black woman trope of Mammy which was constructed by slave owners as a form of propaganda to support the lie of the contented slave. According to bell hooks (1992), racist incidents are seen differently by blacks and whites. She says blacks see with the pain of historical context while whites typically ignore it. As such, she says, some people of European heritage have an unconscious longing to restore the continent's racist past, including with regard to black women's bodies, when they were a commodity, starting from the slave block, available to any white person with money to buy them for domestic service and the full range of child rearing duties including breast feeding. In particular, hooks (1992) draws attention to the way black women's bodies have been used psychologically in relation to that of the white, with their body parts attributed to heightened sexuality while saturated with projections of ugliness, inferiority and badness.

An elaboration of the racist gaze concerns perceptions of beauty. Whiteness has long been the international standard for female beauty. De Gruy (2017) describes how the process of enslavement led to anything identified with Africa, particularly physical features, as being loathed by blacks as well as whites. The impact of the racist gaze on black girls is brilliantly and devastatingly depicted in Toni Morrison's (1970/1999) *The Bluest Eye* whereby the fictional protagonist, Pecola Breedlove, is unloved, unprotected and repeatedly treated with brutality and contempt as someone mirrored through the racist gaze as an ugly, worthless, black girl. Having internalised a self-representation that has been confiscated and then 'thrown back' to her through the racist gaze, Pecola fantasies about having the exemplar of whiteness: blue eyes. Blue eyes would, to her mind, change her wretched life and lead to her being loved and cared for. As racialised trauma and pain accelerates in her life, Pecola retreats further into psychosis believing that she does indeed have blue eyes. As Yancy (2017) reminds us, there are many non-fiction versions of this process as can be seen in the popularity of skin bleaching amongst black women, despite its known toxicity, scarring and poisoning of its users. In other words, internalising the racist contempt for black women's bodies is widespread and capable of inducing illness both physically and mentally.

Gendered permutations of the generationally transmitted racist gaze keep black women and girls in their place in the context of enduring dynamics that maintain white supremacy. That is often as ugly, unwanted and defective mules nevertheless fantasised to provide endless sexual and domestic service. Describing the generational trauma carried by descendants of slaves which she has theoretically conceptualised as post-traumatic slave syndrome, De Gruy (2017) explains how those who for one reason or another have not acquired the tools to defend themselves against the ongoing projections they face, come to enact the degrading and self-defeating roles ascribed to them by the dominant culture. It may be added that those who deviate from these expectations are likely to be met with hostility and quickly viewed through the gaze as aggressive and dangerous, justifying their criminalisation.

Black women and racist atrocity re-enacted

Given the power of historical racist trauma and resultant tropes for black girls and women that are felt to be a burden to carry in the modern day, what does this mean for those who find themselves in forensic mental health and criminal justice settings? To what extent can these systems enable the trauma and racism of slavery and other racist atrocities to be re-enacted in the present day? If we return to the tragedy of Sarah Reed we may find an answer. To begin with, she and the product of her body, her baby, were treated as if they were inhuman. In the face of her baby daughter's death, she was expected to personally transport the corpse to the mortuary, an experience that is not surprisingly judged to have precipitated severe mental health problems. While experiencing these problems, her overstepping the bounds of what was socially acceptable were responded to with disproportionately severe sanctions. Her allegedly transgressing the law in a case of shoplifting was experienced by a white male police officer as justification for him to brutalise her fragile looking body, treating it as though not human. It is a scene saturated with insinuated sexual rage and violence by a white man in power against a disempowered and vulnerable black woman. When she assaulted a male nurse while legally detained in a mental health unit she was treated as a criminal and not as mentally ill. Ironically, her mental health was nevertheless of such concern it warranted psychiatric assessments as to her fitness to plead to the charges she had already admitted to. In her mentally ill state she missed appointments and was again criminalised and incarcerated in prison. When her mental health further deteriorated because her medication had to be discontinued, she was found not to have been treated with care, but with discipline and punishment within an environment completely unsuited to her level of distress and vulnerability. At no point in this tragedy does it appear she was primarily perceived as a person with complex needs within forensic services but consistently as a criminal who needed control and seemingly the severest punishment possible. So this case demonstrates that, yes, when rendered defenceless in the face of it, the forensic system is capable of enabling the trauma and racism of slavery and other racist atrocities to be re-enacted in the present day.

Future practice developments

It may be argued that one of the ways in which the historical burden on black women is played out in the modern day is in the dearth of influential black women's voices in the narrative of forensic services. This seems particularly so in relation to the experience of black women caught up within the system. This absence of voice is particularly problematic when thinking about practice developments aiming to increase staff sensitivity including awareness of how their racialised perspectives inform attitudes and behaviours around black women. Self-awareness appears to offer a key to understanding and working productively with the dynamics of racism. After all, it seems preposterous to imagine internalised racial perspectives wouldn't emerge in settings where multi-ethnic clientele and colleagues are the norm (Knight 2013). So it seems obviously important to understand how unconscious processes within individuals, teams and organisations can operate to bring about re-enactments of historical racist traumas. In other words, how the racist atrocity of yesterday becomes replicated, emerging as today's tragedy.

In a context that is replete with education for clinicians and other professional staff, barely anything exists that addresses racism beyond a very surface, corporate level. It may also be expected that structured staff groups, such as those offering space for reflective practice, addressing unconscious processes operating in the workplace and their impact on emotional experience and therapeutic relationships, might offer support for staff working in these complex and forensic settings. It might be expected that psychoanalysts, group analysts and other psychotherapists would be able to support forensic professionals to work with what Knight (2013) refers to as the racialised unconscious. Unfortunately, psychoanalytic, group analytic and other psychotherapeutic trainings barely skim matters of racism. This means it is questionable how much expertise exists on a day-to-day basis to utilise reflective spaces for supporting and developing staff caught up in racist dynamics with the people they care for. Yet, in practice the relevance and trauma of racism in impacting on the lives of patients and prisoners seems crucial to understand if it is not to be enacted and re-enacted. In the case of black women, awareness of the historical context through which the racist gaze has constructed them, their bodies and their lives might help to engender compassion in professionals who may then be more able to question their perceptions and characterisations, recognising tropes such as 'strong black woman' and notions of 'hot and highly sexed', including the possibility of this imaginary being internalised. In doing so underlying vulnerability and distress may become more visible and obvious. At worst, it may avoid the type of racialised re-enactment that seemed evident in the case of Sarah Reed, a particularly vulnerable black woman.

So, it seems that what is required is the voice of black women with lived experience working in partnership with professionally trained practitioners to support and train staff working in all aspects of the forensic system. A model exists for partnership working between those who represent the voice of lived experience and those who represent the voice of the professionally trained. This model is typically termed 'co-production' (Lewis et al., 2017) and offers a way to improve the experiences of marginalised and stigmatised groups whose needs are not readily understood or represented in most mainstream professional trainings and practices. To achieve a position where the voice of black women who have experienced forensic systems is celebrated for the richness and validity of its narrative, the defensive structures that uphold racism in practice need to be addressed. As it is, defensiveness due to discomfort involved in considering the role of ancestral perpetrators, their generational transmissions and indeed the pain of internalised racism where relevant, appear to maintain the status quo with traumatic content and its repetition typically remaining unseen by professional staff. Meanwhile, in an epidermalised way, vulnerable black women remain highly visible, and therefore vulnerable to becoming caught firmly in the racist gaze.

References

Anderson, C. (2016) *White Rage: The Unspoken Truth of Our Racial Divide*. Bloomsbury. London.

Andrews, K. (2018) *Back to Black: Retelling Black Radicalism for the 21st Century*. Zed Books. London.

Butler, J. (1993) Endangered/Endangering: Schematic Racism & White Paranoia. In: *Reading Rodney King. Reading Urban Uprising*. Ed: R. Gooding-Williams. Ch 1, 15–24. Routledge. New York.

Clarke, S. (2003) *Social Theory, Psychoanalysis and Racism*. Palgrave MacMillan. Basingstoke.

Corston, J. (2007) *The Corston Report*: *A Review of Women with Particular Vulnerabilities in the Criminal Justice System*. London: Home Office.

Cox, J. & Sacks-Jones, K. (2017) Double Disadvantage: The Experiences of Black, Asian, and Minority Ethnic Women in the Criminal Justice System. https://wearea genda.org/wp-content/uploads/2017/03/Double-disadvantage-FINAL.pdf.

Dalal, F. (1993) 'Race' and Racism: An Attempt to Organise Difference. *Group Analysis*. Vol 26, 277–293.

Dalal, F. (2001) The Social Unconscious: A Post-Foulkesian Perspective. *Group Analysis*. Vol 34, No 4, 539–555.

Dalal, F. (2002) *Race, Colour and the Process of Racialization. New Perspectives from Group Analysis, Psychoanalysis and Sociology*. Brunner-Routledge. Hove.

De Gruy, J. (2017) *Post Traumatic Slave Syndrome*. JDGP. USA.

Du Bois, W. E. B. (1903) *The Souls of Black Folks*. Amazon Classics. Seattle.

Einhorn, S. (2007) Response to Lecture by Gerhard Wilke. *Group Analysis*. Vol 40, No 4, 448–456.

Fanon, F. (1952) *Black Skin: White Masks*. Pluto. London.

Fletchman Smith, B. (2000) *Mental Slavery: Psychoanalytic Studies of Caribbean People*. Rebus Press. London.

Frosh, S. (2013a) Psychoanalysis, Colonialism, Racism. *Journal of Theoretical and Philosophical Psychology*. Vol 33, No 3, 141–154.

Frosh, S. (2013b) *Hauntings: Psychoanalysis and Ghostly Transmissions*. Palgrave MacMillan. Basingstoke.

Frosh, S. (2016) Born with a Knife in Their Hearts: Transmission, Trauma, Identity and the Social Unconscious. In: *The Social Unconscious in Persons, Groups and Societies. Vol. 2: Mainly Foundations Matrices*. Eds: E. Hopper and H. Weinberg Ch 1, 3–20. Karnack, London.

Hook, D. (2012) *A Critical Psychology of the Postcolonial: The Mind of Apartheid*. Routledge. London.

hooks, b. (1992) *Black Looks, Race and Representation*. Southend Press. Boston.

Kendi, I. X. (2016) *Stamped from the Beginning: The Definitive History of Racist Ideas in America*. Nation Books. New York.

Khanna, R. (2003) *Dark Continents: Psychoanalysis and Colonisation*. Duke University Press. North Carolina.

Knight, Z. G. (2013) Black Client, White Therapist: Working with Race in Psychoanalytic Psychotherapy in South Africa. *The International Journal of Psychoanalysis*. Vol 94, 17–31.

Kovel, J. (1988) *White Racism: A Psychohistory*. Free Association Books. London.

Lammy, D. (2017) *The Lammy Review: An Independent Review into the Treatment of, and Outcomes for, Black, Asian and Minority Ethnic Individuals in the Criminal Justice System*. HM Government. London.

Lewis, A., King, T., Herbert, L. and Repper, J. (2017) Co-production: Sharing our Experience, Reflecting on Our Learning. ImROC Briefing Paper. ImROC. Nottinghamshire.

Montagu, A. (1997) *Man's Most Dangerous Myth: The Fallacy of Race*. Altamira Press. California.

Morrison, T. (1970/1999) *The Bluest Eye*. Vintage. London.

Morrison, T. (1992) *Playing in the Dark: Whiteness and the Literary Imagination*. Harvard University Press. Cambridge, MA.

Oluo, I. (2018) *So You Want to Talk about Race?* Seal Press. New York.

Parks, S. (2010) *Fierce Angels: The Strong Black Woman in American Life and Culture*. One World Books. New York.

Penna, C. (2016) Reflections on Brazilian Social Unconscious. In: *The Social Unconscious in Persons, Groups, and Societies*. Vol. 2: Mainly Foundation Matrices. Eds: E. Hopper and H. Weinberg. Ch 8, 139–158. Karnac. London.

Richards, G. (1997) *'Race,' Racism and Psychology. Towards a Reflexive History*. Routledge. London.

Rustin, M. (1991) *The Good Society and the Inner World: Psychoanalysis, Politics and Culture*. Verso. London.

Volkan, V. D. (2001) Transgenerational Transmissions and Chosen Traumas: An Aspect of Large Group Identity. *Group Analysis*. Vol 34, No 1, 79–97.

Washington, H. A. (2008) *Medical Apartheid: The Dark History of Medical Experimentation on Black Americans from Colonial Times to the Present*. Anchor Books. New York.

Wilke, G. (2007) Second Generation Perpetrator Symptoms in Groups. *Group Analysis*. Vol 40, No 4, 429–447.

Wilke, G. (2016) The German Social Unconscious: Second Generation Perpetrator Symptoms in Organisations and Groups. In: *The Social Unconscious in Persons, Groups and Societies. Vol. 2: Mainly Foundations Matrices*. Eds: E. Hopper & H. Weinberg. Ch 4, 61–80. Karnac. London.

Yancy, G. (2017) *Black Bodies, White Gazes. The Continuing Significance of Race in America*. Second Edition. Rowman and Littlefield. London.

Chapter 5

Prostitution

Visible bodies, hidden lives

Anna Motz

As Farley says, 'the harm of prostitution is socially invisible, and it is also invisible in the law, in public health, and in psychology' (2003: 247). The subject of prostitution is an emotive one, inspiring passionate ethical, philosophical and legal debates between those who view prostitution as a choice that women make to enter the 'sex trade' and those who see it as a form of social, psychological and sexual oppression in which men predominantly exploit women. It is underpinned by a clear economic structure and is a lucrative business, particularly for the pimps who prostitute them. Similarly, the various trajectories into the sex trade are complex and traumatic, as are the psychological consequences of engaging in this work.

Many women in the criminal justice system have been involved in prostitution: 21% of women in one prison said they had been involved in prostitution, most linking it to drug addiction (74%) and over a quarter (26%) to having been abused (NOMS, 2012). In this chapter I focus on the experiences of women within the criminal justice system, including those who have not been charged for offences related to prostitution but who have histories of prostitution and other forms of sexual exploitation. Women involved in street-based prostitution who misuse drugs and/or alcohol are amongst the most vulnerable, marginalised and stigmatised groups in our society.

I outline the traumatic experiences and violent and coercive forces that entrench vulnerable young women into prostitution, as well as the intra-psychic factors that can contribute to their enmeshment in this work. I use anonymised case material to illustrate how women's experiences related to prostitution have profound psychological and social consequences for their lives.

I argue that prostitution is not a manifestation of an individual woman's disturbance of mind, but rather reflects structural violence and a social and economic system that uses women's bodies to create profit, and to maintain particular power dynamics in which women, and particularly poor women, and those who are on the fringes of mainstream society, are exploited. I explore the association between substance misuse, prostitution and homelessness and address the notion of the un-housed mind and its connection with a body that is treated as public property.

The language of prostitution

Working girls, prostitutes, whores, hookers, hustlers, tarts, hos, sluts, slappers, slags, fallen women, white slaves, streetwalkers, ladies of the night, call girls: these are often terms of denigration, abuse and contempt referring to women who exchange sexual activity for payment of some form or other. The women are also described as being 'on the game' or working 'in the oldest profession' both of which are more oblique references to selling sex, implying that prostitutes are participating in a game with rules, or entering into a profession; the terms denigrate the women, highlighting them not as subjects, but as sexual commodities, debased and 'fallen'. Indeed, the term 'prostitute' can be traced to the 16th century, when it was a verb, in which someone is offered up for sale from the Latin *prostitut-* **'exposed publicly, offered for sale'**, from the verb *prostituere*, from *pro-* **'before'** + *statuere* **'set up, place'** (*Oxford English Dictionary*). This conveys the crucial sense in which the subject of commodification has been configured as an object, rather than as a subject.

I suggest that these denigrated terms reveal the disavowed shame of (men's) sexual impulses, projected onto women whose sexuality is 'for sale'. Women who sell sex can be treated as the 'poison containers' into which unacceptable urges, the wish for sexual satisfaction or control, are located. This is a form of projection, in which unacceptable feelings are placed into another, only then to be attacked. The bodies and minds of prostitutes are denigrated both by those who have exploited them and by other members of the public. 'Innocent' women walk free, while prostitutes are criminalised, or viewed as deserving of harm. As Richard McCann, son of Peter Sutcliffe's first victim, Wilma McCann, poignantly notes in Carole Hayman's film *No One Escapes*: 'they talked about "prostitutes" being killed, as opposed to "innocent women"'.

The question of terminology is a vexed one and the terms chosen will convey particular societal attitudes.

'Sex worker' is a term used to describe any individual who has been involved in prostitution, pornography or any other aspect of the sex industry. The term 'sex worker' can appear more respectful than the terms for prostitute outlined above, but it can be misleading and euphemistic as the work referred to is the sexual commodification of the woman's own body. The Sex Workers Collective of Great Britain accepts the use of the term 'sex worker' as a legitimate description of a role and argues that sex work is a trade like any other that can be entered into without coercion. Furthermore, an overly protectionist attitude in relation to sex work serves to deny women their agency and to denigrate them. Given that there are generally men involved in selling the woman's body for sex this term may, however, falsely imply that this is work freely chosen. I suggest that the notion of agency is misplaced here, particularly for girls abused early in life, with highly limited opportunities to escape a relentless trajectory of further brutality and exploitation. Black, Asian and Minority Ethnic (BAME) women and migrants are often particular targets of such exploitation.

This view of the agency and choice of the 'sex worker' is contrary to the findings of a research study that explored the strong links between poverty, drug dependency and prostitution:

> The term 'sex worker' is aligned with a view that selling sex should be recognised as a job like any other; however, this is not a view that reflects the narratives of the women interviewed for this research. All but one of the women interviewed for this research described experiences of violence in the course of their 'work', alongside experiences of drug dependency, poverty and homelessness. The term 'sex worker' implies a level of agency and choice that was not described by the majority of women we spoke to. At the same time, the term 'prostitute' is historically laden with institutional and cultural discriminations against women who sell sex, and defines and labels them by that act. In research interviews, we asked women for their preferred terminology and used that terminology through-out interviews. For the purpose of this briefing, we have used 'women involved in prostitution' as a term that does not define women by the act of selling sex, but also recognises that selling sex is not a job like any other. (Drugscope and AVA, 2013)

Rachel Moran, Founder of Space International and author of a powerful autobiography describing her experiences in prostitution, *Paid For: My Journey Through Prostitution* (2015), considers it as a system of compensated sexual abuse. She argues further that the term 'sex worker' is an attempt to normalise a fundamental abuse of human rights. She described her mixed emotions most recently as The Sexual Offences Act was passed in Ireland in April 2017 and the counter-argument was made by Senator McDowell that prostitutes choose their 'profession' out of free will, further implying that they were predatory creatures, preying on innocent men. She describes her memories of the women with whom she worked, which haunted her during the Senator's evidence: 'The first time Annie (some names have been changed to protect identities) got out of a john's car, lost, used and broken. The first time I saw Louise shove a needle in her arm. The last time I saw Maebh, except I didn't really see her, because her coffin was closed' (Moran, 5 April 2017)

Moran's description reveals how many women involved in prostitution have unseen pain, or become invisible through death, like her friend Maebh. Moran argues against the 'happy hooker' myth, claiming that the reason the women and girls in red light districts and brothels have ended up there is because of adverse life experiences outside of their control, including poverty, limited educational opportunities and childhood sexual abuse.

Women working in street prostitution, residential prostitution (brothels) or as escorts have been found to have similar difficulties both while working and when attempting to exit the trade (Bindel et al., 2012).

Poverty and survival sex

Changing Lives is a charity with regional centres in the Northeast, Merseyside, Humberside and Doncaster, devoted to working with the most vulnerable people in society, including women who have been sexually exploited and experienced 'survival sex'. Their Executive Director Laura Seebohm visited Parliament in May 2019 to provide evidence to the Work and Pensions Committee. The evidence session was part of an inquiry into the relationship between the introduction of Universal Credit and the number of people engaging in survival sex.

The findings obtained by Changing Lives showed that when women find themselves in economic hardship they are forced to sell sex, and that Universal Credit exacerbated this level of poverty.

> Laura quoted a woman we support who stated the stark reality. 'I hate sleeping on the street. I try to find a punter who will let me sleep for free sex. I hate it, but I hate sleeping on the streets more.'
>
> The Committee Chair, Frank Field MP, said 'Our heads have been knocked off by your evidence' after hearing the stories of women forced in desperation to exchange sex for the means to feed, house and warm themselves and their children. (Changing Lives, 2019)

Language, agency and meaning

The words 'entered into' and 'exited from' are often used in relation to prostitution, alluding, I believe, to the metaphor of prostitution as a world or cavern that has narrow and treacherous passageways into and away from its centre.

Other connotations of this metaphor of entry and exit clearly relate to the nature of sexual activity itself, bringing to mind the sense in which the body of the prostitute is entered into and exited, in various ways, depending on the negotiation that has taken place. This is a significant metaphor, conceptualising prostitution as a place one finds oneself, rather than a form of becoming, and similarly the prostitute herself as an object, a piece of land (or 'ass') to be invaded and then departed from, as dictated by those who purchase or rent her. She is the object, while the purchaser is the subject. At its heart, prostitution is the objectification of another, for the sexual satisfaction of the subject. In Chapter 6 I discuss the ways in which prostitution can also take the form of self-harm by proxy.

The Swedish philosopher and feminist, Ekis Ekman (2013), writes in the preface to her book, *Being and Being Bought: Prostitution, Surrogacy and the*

Split Self: 'Prostitution is, in reality, very simple. It is sex between two people – between one who wants it and one who doesn't. Since desire is absent, payment takes its place.' She argues that what makes prostitution possible for the woman who sells sex is the implicit assumption that 'I am not my body', which requires her to split off part of herself. This splitting requires distancing herself from part of her being, and this has significant psychological, social and economic consequences. She compares this with the position of a surrogate mother, whose body is required, and similarly bought, in order to produce a baby for others. The parallels are powerful and disturbing, bringing into sharp relief the reality that women's bodies are bought and sold without regard for their minds.

Many women who work as prostitutes want to leave, finding it frightening and degrading. Exiting prostitution poses grave difficulties, particularly as those profiting from it can become threatening; this will be discussed later in this chapter. The vast majority of prostitutes have been victims of violence, sexual, physical and emotional abuse in childhood and adolescence and have histories of being in local authority care; recent studies demonstrate the high proportion of women and children who have been trafficked into prostitution. Trafficking refers to the exploitation of a person, or groups of people, for the economic benefit of another person, or group of people, and has been likened to a form of modern slavery. While not confined to prostitution, it also applies to this sexual exploitation of people, who may be brought to work in cities and towns in the United Kingdom crossing international borders, or within the same towns and cities. Despite its connotation of traversing geographical areas, the term refers to the use of an individual, without their consent, or involving coercion, for the economic benefit of another person or group of people; and while there are some ambiguities in its usage, its meaning is quite clear in relation to the control, coercion and exploitation of vulnerable girls and women.

The glamorised conception of the 'high class escort' or 'happy hooker' starkly contrasts with the brutal reality of life on or off the street. The experience of many women who have engaged in prostitution and other forms of sexual exploitation is that it further increases the real risk of incurring bodily and psychological harm, including substance and alcohol misuse, PTSD and even death, as there are very high rates of mortality amongst prostitutes. Foremost among the health risks of prostitution is premature death. In a 2004 US study of almost 2000 prostitutes followed over a 30-year period, by far the most common causes of death were homicide, suicide, drug and alcohol-related problems, HIV infection and accidents – in that order. The homicide rate among active female prostitutes was 17 times higher than that of the age-matched general female population (Potterat et al., 2004). This reveals the actual risk faced by prostituted women and the often unconscious perception of these women as bodies, experienced so as to be brutalised and battered into oblivion, literally or metaphorically.

The invisible harm of prostitution extends to children whose mothers are injured or incur criminal convictions as a result, as well as those children who are at direct risk of harm by clients. Attempts to conceptualise sex work as a freely chosen 'trade' gloss over the direct and indirect dangers of prostitution, whether on the street or in a brothel, ascribing choice where there is no choice.

Traumatic trajectories

The question of whether women have a real choice to enter into prostitution and other aspects of the sex trade is far from straightforward, as the following clinical cases illustrate. Women with histories of trauma, exploitation and disrupted early attachments may become prostitutes out of economic necessity and limited options, encouraged by other young people whom they have met in the care system, or coerced into it by older men and women. Some have been trafficked from other countries specifically for the purpose of sexual exploitation. Rates of exploitation of trafficked girls and women are detailed in the recent report 'Disrupt Demand' (2019).

Some women describe prostitution as a choice they have made, raising questions about the power of unconscious forces; I suggest this choice is not one that is made with full awareness of the opportunities for sado-masochistic re-enactments, nor is it one whose risks were anticipated by the young girl who, though coerced into it, may imagine (or have been led to believe, falsely) that she was free to choose to do otherwise. For girls who have been sexually exploited, neglected and abused during their early lives, sex work may appear to offer a means of power, revenge or 'mastery of trauma', and some describe the sense of thrill that being chosen and desired can give them. But for many, if not most, the sense of being wanted is transient, and the reality of sex work is that it requires both dissociation from feelings – emotional and physical – and pretence. In order to meet the wishes of the customer the prostitute not only needs to offer sex, but to pretend to enjoy it. This element of deception is further alienating for the woman, contributing to the destructive dynamics implicit in 'the game' of prostitution. The dissociation required to perform this role compounds the sense of the split self that Ekis Ekman describes.

Colonised exploitation

The issue of prostitution is especially relevant to the lives of black and minority ethnic women and girls in the criminal justice system. Racial and sexual abuse of young girls and women are linked, suggesting the existence of an underclass, whose bodies can be bought and sold by those in positions of power and privilege.

The campaigner and feminist author Bindel (2018) outlines the links between slavery and prostitution and the particular discrimination that black women suffer when they are prostitutes:

Many women of colour have spoken about being raised under a cloud of sexual expectation that leads to them being vulnerable to prostitution. Meanwhile, many white men appear to expect girls and women from particular ethnic backgrounds to be particularly 'suited' to the sex trade.

Taina Bien-Aimé, a Haitian-American woman, is executive director of the Coalition Against Trafficking in Women. She says, 'I learned as a young girl, listening to my mother and aunties around the kitchen table, that men coveted our bodies,' she says. 'Our full lips and breasts, the way we swayed our hips, the brown hues of our skin had always been targets for the male gaze, sexual harassment and rape.' She explains: 'The Spaniards first, followed by the French and later the Americans, desecrated indigenous and enslaved African women in Haiti as misogynistic rituals; a pattern found across the "New World". Prostitution is a legacy of that systemic oppression.'

During prostitution, says Bien-Aimé, the same pattern emerges as did during the slave trade: 'The only difference with the enslavers is that these men, just a few generations later, pay for that access to black female bodies. Prostitution is not a concept found in indigenous languages – it's colonised exploitation.'

The hidden homeless

Women constitute a considerable percentage of the 'hidden homeless', since they are less likely to sleep in public spaces due to their vulnerability and their heightened risk of sexual and physical assault (Watson, 2016). Homeless women are 'hidden from view and hidden from services' (Reeve, Casey and Goudie, 2006: 2). The patterns of female homelessness are distinctive and often less evident than those of men. For instance, unhoused women frequently experience sexual assault, periods, pregnancies, motherhood and having to negotiate male-dominated services, all the while living in unstable circumstances with marginalised resources (Warburton, 2017). Their reproductive capacities, the relative vulnerability of their bodies and their common experience of sexual abuse by men all contribute to the increased and unique risks that women face.

Homeless women are significantly more likely than homeless men to be involved in prostitution. For instance, approximately one-quarter of St Mungo's female clients have been involved in prostitution, compared to 2% of male clients. Over a third of their female clients who ever slept rough were involved in prostitution (St Mungos, 2014).

The link with homelessness as an entry point into prostitution further testifies to its danger, a forced choice to escape other risks and survive on the streets. As Jasinski et al. (2005: 56) describe in their study of the lives of homeless girls and women in the United States:

Another way the women strategized to avoid violent sexual activity was to engage in sexual behaviour in exchange for money, food or safety. It is important to note that this exchange was exploitive and abusive of the women; however, on the streets it was one of the only options available to them.

Nearly half (45%) had spent some time in prison or jail as adults. In addition to involvement in criminal activities, survival strategies employed by homeless women often include prostitution to trade sex for money, shelter or drugs. These types of activities put women in risky situations and increase their risk of victimisation. In this study only a small proportion of the women indicated that they had worked as a prostitute or as a stripper at some point in their lives. What is perhaps more disconcerting, however, is that about a fifth of the women who had worked as a prostitute at some point in their lives had been forced to do so. Compared to women and men in large national samples, the homeless women and men in Jasinski's study experienced much higher victimisation rates, across different types of victimisation. Similar to prior work on homeless populations, the women in their sample were also perpetrators of crime.

The abusive and violent partnerships that women on the street are much more likely to form than 'housed' women are products of unconscious and conscious societal beliefs that these women are no more than objects, possessions to be treated without respect or dignity – they are denigrated, hurt and violated. I have described the links between homelessness, exploitation and violence extensively elsewhere, focussing on the impact of violent relationships (Motz, 2014). Homeless women who become involved in prostitution may be attempting to control their own exposure to sexual use and abuse, but find themselves, once again, being treated as the possession of another, and forced to open themselves to the needs, desires, cruelty or abuse of another, a customer who pays for this use of them. Furthermore, he will require them to act as though the sex was freely chosen, and enjoyable, leading them to develop the split way of relating (Ekman, 2013).

Neglected girls: the care system and prostitution

The homeless and young girls in care, or 'looked after children', are essentially cast out of the mainstream, and become far more vulnerable to abuse and assault because of their 'invisibility' and outsider status. Young people in care are particularly exposed, having fallen outside the family systems designed to protect and nurture them, seeking affection and attention elsewhere. Although the ultimate aim of the care system is to offer surrogate protection, nurturing and monitoring to the most vulnerable, the reality is often starkly different, and those young people are further placed at risk. The recent, highly publicised, cases of young girls in care being sexually exploited by gangs of men in

Oxford, Rochdale and Derby for financial, psychological and sexual gratification are stark proof of this. In Oxford seven men were convicted of charges including rape, arranging prostitution and trafficking vulnerable young people: most of these were girls living in local-authority care. These girls were groomed by gangs of men who would seduce them with apparent affection, drink and drugs, offering them what appeared to be an escape from their constrained lives within the care system. Issues of ethnicity emerge in these cases in that both in Rotherham and Oxford the gangs of men were Muslim Asians and the victims were primarily white British girls from the care system. It is possible to wonder about the unconscious forum for revenge that males facing discrimination in the United Kingdom sought on the bodies and minds of powerless young predominantly white women through sexual denigration and commodification. The girls often saw these men as trusted father figures or boyfriends, revealing the intensity of their own unmet needs for care.

Shockingly the systems designed to care for these girls turned a blind eye to their whereabouts, as if colluding in the mistaken belief that these young people were unworthy of protection, despite their status as vulnerable children in need of care. These 'looked after children' were anything but. They were neglected within the care system, much as they had been neglected at home. From this vantage point, it is clear to see the attraction of the attention offered by the men who groomed them – the world of sex and drugs would appear, on the surface, a welcome release. It is clear that entering into the dangerous and harmful world of prostitution and the associated activities of pornography and stripping is far from a choice in the usual sense of the word. Indeed, the most vulnerable girls in society are targeted for sexual exploitation and deceived into believing that their abusers are friends and lovers concerned for their welfare. As one of the girls who had been sexually exploited described to me, she had never been loved, and the experience of being groomed, 'possessed' and marked as someone's property, even branded with the man's initial, felt like being loved.

Clinical illustration: Maja, 24, from local authority care to street prostitution

Maja had received a suspended sentence for stealing, on numerous occasions. When I met with her for assessment for psychotherapy at the forensic outpatient clinic I was first struck by her direct manner and the way that she wore clothing too light for the harsh winter. This immediately drew me into a protective relationship with her as she seemed to convey her sense of neglect and vulnerability, alongside her evident sexuality, as she was athletic and her clothing revealed this. I found myself worried about the unwanted attention she might get from some male patients, also offenders, seated in the waiting area.

Maja described to me how she had been one of five children who were born to drug addicted parents in a northern city. She had grown up without any sense of parental care and been left to fend largely for herself, describing herself as 'feral'; she had spent time in children's homes sporadically. In one of those homes she had been physically and sexually abused repeatedly by a residential worker and ended up running away, only to find herself placed in a 'secure children's home' where she was accommodated with girls who were criminal as well as others who ran away from home or care.

When she was discharged from the children's home she ran away to London and began living on the streets, was befriended by an older man and young woman, her own age, and ended up 'turning tricks' for money and a place to stay. Tragically her own parents had become infected with HIV, possibly as a result of their intravenous drug use, and her mother died when she was only 19. Maja had recently discovered that she too was HIV positive and this shocking news had brought her to a state of despair, but also motivated her to attend to the crisis in her life and finally make urgent changes. She had no history of using violence though she had often been on the receiving end of it. She came to our first appointment session with a sense of desperation to engage with psychotherapy and free herself from addictions.

Despite this wish for life Maja described how she had been using prostitution to fund her drug habit which itself had developed during her experiences of homelessness and abuse, and how she had experienced this sense of relentless pull towards instability and the risk of death. For this girl, who had been born into a household filled with death, her own life was worth little. She had felt savagely wounded from the start, without any real expectation of a different life.

It is possible to understand Maja's involvement in prostitution as a complex interaction between her vulnerability, which had been repeatedly exploited by others, and an unconscious compulsion to repeat and re-enact the sexual abuse that had been inflicted on her, believing herself to this time be in control of it. That is, her economic, social and psychological vulnerability led to her being targeted for sexually exploitative work. This resonated with her own unconscious sense of guilt and wish to master her earlier trauma through engaging in something that replicated it, with the hope that this time she would not be left humiliated, hurt and betrayed. On a conscious level she wanted to leave this work and lead a life free from the risks and brutality she frequently experienced.

There were important aspects of splitting in her prostitution. Maja used one part of her body to secure gratification for another part, namely her addiction; these were separate aspects of the divided self – the body that could be given up for sexual use and the body whose pain could be eased through a narcotic. This also soothed and anaesthetised her mind. There appears to be a common link in the experiences of prostitution and drug addiction, in that in both cases her body was the container, the recipient of substances taken in, sometimes in a toxic form, a violent intrusion. Drugs can be used defensively against the sense of shame. At times Maja felt that she was a body only, rather than a subjective creature, a mind in an inviolate body whose ownership was not under dispute. Ironically, Maja's substance addiction did not protect her from pain, but increased her vulnerability to further abuse and exploitation as she was increasingly dependent not only on drugs to anaesthetise her against pain, but also on those who supplied them.

Maja felt that she was 'contaminated' and should have a 'Do not enter' sign on her as she felt her HIV status made her a toxic entity, the embodiment of 'damaged goods'. She was tormented by the idea that her former clients might have contracted the disease when they had insisted they would have unprotected sex with her, before her diagnosis. She felt guilty and frantic when she thought that her 'negligence' could have brought about a punishment to these men, whose contact details she would not have, and held herself responsible, even though it was they who had insisted that she dispense with protection. She felt dirty and disgusting; her unconscious fantasy was that it was also this inner poison within her that had somehow infiltrated her parents' bodies and made them ill. This kind of magical and destructive thinking tormented her and she felt that she could only find release from her own self-loathing when she cut her skin, using her sharp razors to slice through her pale, delicate flesh.

Maja's scars were alarming to see, some were fresh and looked raw; significantly she did not wear clothes that concealed them. It was as though she was cutting out unwanted parts of herself, and her past, through her savage attacks on her own skin, and she made no apology for this through attempting to cover the wounds. I was able to witness them and to bear the anger and despair I felt they clearly expressed. During the course of our work together Maja was able to uncover other aspects of herself that she considered shameful, including her grief for her parents and deep fears for her own health. I reflected that her revealing clothes showed me the vulnerability of her body, and pointed to a history of neglect, where she was literally and emotionally exposed to the elements; her self-harm wounds also felt like emblems conveying violence – and this too was an important communication.

The outcome of our work was that she began to take care of her health, attending her appointments with me and other health professionals reliably. This self-care marked a significant change in her psychological state in that she was able to treat her body as part of herself, not an unwanted and alien object. She began to talk more freely about her feelings and her dreams, nightmares and hopes for the future, and she formed a relationship with a friend, who later became her lover. This friend was female, and knew about her HIV and her history of prostitution, but still accepted and loved her. Although she had sexual relationships with women before, none had been significant, as this one was. She felt that, for the first time, she could have an intimate sexual relationship from which she did not need to dissociate.

Maja felt she was finally able to form and feel some kind of connection between her mind and her body, and allow touch to be gentle and wanted.

Although she did not articulate this, I felt that this possibility had partially come about because of the strength of our connection too, where my mind had been allowed to make contact with hers, and I was allowed to bear the pain of her past and present experiences. To the extent that her use of her own body had reflected both her savage impulses, and a wish to be punished (and punish others) – she had been caught up in a form of violence and self-harm – her capacity to reflect on herself and to relate to others – both to me and her partner – seemed to have increased, and the destructive pattern to have broken, at least for the time being.

Discussion

Maja's alienation from herself was partly a product of societal violence and inequity; the system around her had propelled her towards the streets as a false form of sanctuary, and her prostitution had been largely ignored by the services designed to protect her, as if her only worth lay in her sexual value to strangers. She had internalised this message and also relied on selling her body for sex as a form of economic and social survival, though doing so also put her at risk and consolidated her sense of primarily being a body for others to use and abuse. She had good experience of therapeutic contact, which had then led the way to making connections with others around her who could offer her support and, significantly, to establishing an intimate relationship with another person. In order to survive prostitution, she had learned to split off her feelings from her experiences, to dissociate, but now she was learning to integrate her mind and her body, to allow another to touch her emotionally.

As a psychotherapist, psychologist and forensic practitioner in women's prisons and secure and community mental health settings, I have worked with many women with histories of prostitution that they find painful to relate. My experience is that none of the women I have encountered described prostitution as empowering, or a viable choice amongst others, but have felt strongly that it was something that was done to them, or their only choice. While I would have much preferred to hear the women describe tales of emancipation, freedom and choice, instead I have heard histories of desperation, coercion and violence. When I interviewed her in 2017, Sister Enda of Anawim Charity Birmingham, said of her 30 years in Street Outreach, 'I have never met a woman who said she had *chosen* prostitution' (personal interview, 2017). In a sense, prostitution had chosen them, as these women were propelled on a traumatic pathway from being abused children to prostituted women.

References

Bindel, J. (26th June 2018) What the Sex Trade Has in Common with the Slave Trade. *Aeon Essays*. https://aeon.co/essays/what-the-sex-trade-has-in-common-with-the-slave-trade.

Bindel, J., Brown, L., Easton, H., Matthews, R. and Reynolds, L. (2012) *Breaking Down the Barriers: A Study of How Women Exit Prostitution*. London: London South Bank University.

Changing Lives (2019) Universal Credit and Survival Sex, 24 May. www.changing-lives. org.uk/news-stories/universal-credit-and-survival-sex-changing-lives-give-evidence-in-parliament/.

Drugscope, AVA (Against Violence and Abuse) (2013) *The Challenge of Change: Improving Services for Women Involved in Prostitution and Substance Use*. London: The Pilgrim Trust.

Ekman, E.K. (2013) *Being and Being Bought: Prostitution, Surrogacy and the Split Self*. North Melbourne: Spinifex Press.

Farley, M. (2003) Prostitution and the invisibility of harm. *Women & Therapy* 26(3/4), 247–280.

Immigrant Council of Ireland (2019) Disrupt Demand: A Comparative Report.

Jasinski, J.L., Wesely, J. K., Mustaine, E. and Wright, J. D. (2005) The Experience of Violence in the Lives of Homeless Women: A Research Report. Unpublished Report commissioned by the US Department of Justice and available at www.ncjrs.gov/pdffiles1/nij/grants/211976.pdf.

Moran, R. (2015) *Paid For: My Journey Through Prostitution*. London: W.W. Norton & Company.

Motz, A. (2014) *Toxic Couples: The Psychology of Domestic Violence*. Hove: Routledge.

NOMS Women and Equalities Group (2012) *A Distinct Approach: Guide to Working with Women Offenders*. London: Ministry of Justice.

O'Connell, M. (2019) *Disrupt Demand: Executive Summary*. Immigrant Council of Ireland.

Potterat, J.J., Brewer, D.D., Muth, S.Q., Rothenberg, R.B., Woodhouse, D.E., Muth, J.B. et al. (2004) Mortality in a Long-term Open Cohort of Prostitute Women. *American Journal of Epidemiology* 159, 778–785.

Reeve, K., Casey, R. and Goudie, R. (2006) *Homeless Women: Still being Failed yet Striving to Survive*. London: Crisis.

St Mungos (2014) Rebuilding Shattered Lives: The Final Report. www.mungos.org/publication/rebuilding-shattered-lives-final-report/

Warburton, H. (2017) An Exploration into the Lives of Homeless Women. Unpublished thesis, University of Sheffield.

Watson, J. (2016) Gender-based violence and young homeless women: Femininity, embodiment and vicarious physical capital. *The Sociological Review* 64(2), 256–273. doi: 10.1111/1467-954X.12365.

Chapter 6

Self-harm, inscriptions and survival

Anna Motz

Introduction

In this chapter I describe how women in the criminal justice system, including those in secure mental health settings, use self-harm to contain and communicate violent feelings, experiences and thoughts. I argue that self-harm has a hopeful function for many women, and is not simply a pathological expression of despair, nor necessarily a suicidal act. The addictive, intoxicating aspect of self-harm (see Chapter 8) creates intense feelings in staff, and this is part of its communicative power. I will explore how practitioners respond to self-harm, and how some responses are enactments, with destructive consequences. I consider self-harm separately from suicide, though the two can be linked.

Suicides in custody

Death in custody is a tragic issue, and suicide a central concern; the suicides of seven women in one year catalysed Baroness Corston's 2007 report calling for an urgent review of women's sentencing. Figures show that 93 women have died in prison in the 11-year period between 2007 and 2018, with almost a quarter of these occurring in 2016, making it the deadliest year on record. Of the total, 37 were self-inflicted, 48 were non-self-inflicted and 8 were not yet classified by 2018 (Bulman, 2018). The high rate of suicides and non-self-inflicted deaths that may have been preventable suggest that anticipated reform of women's prisons has not taken place (Inquest, 2018).

It is argued in this chapter that self-harm is a communication that, when understood, can reduce the risk of suicide. I describe how women's self-harm can be thought about, understood and sensitively responded to, reducing the emotional toll on workers and the risk to the women themselves. My model of self-harm (Motz, 2009) conceptualises it as a communicative act, as well as an attack on the woman's own body, and the body of the mother it represents.

Eating disorders are a graphic manifestation of this violence. The woman's hope is that her body will sustain this attack, and that others will be able to recognise her unconscious wishes and the meanings of these acts.

The impact of self-harm can be visceral and bodily. The responses of others, whether punitive or rescuing, can contribute to its potency and the secrecy that often accompanies it. To understand the potency of self-harm, its shame and its thrill, it is essential to consider how responses to it can perpetuate it, creating destructive re-enactments between the woman who self-harms and the worker who attempts to 'treat' or stop her from doing so. The purpose of this chapter is to help practitioners to stay still in the eye of the self-harming storm, offering thoughts about how to understand its roots and functions, as well as to identify the feelings it evokes. I will outline recent therapeutic interventions and their evidence base, both in high security hospitals (Jones, 2017) and in prisons (Walker and Towl, 2016).

Trauma and its inscriptions: self-harm and tattoos

There are important literal and symbolic uses of self-harm as a form of inscription, making links with the practice and function of tattooing as marking, possessing and articulating the body. Like tattooing, marking on the skin through cutting or scarification is felt to be a form of self-expression and to have enduring personal significance. This is revealed in the following passage by the Haitian–American author, Roxanne Gay:

> My first tattoos were small, tentative. With each successive one, the ink has gotten bigger, spread wider across my skin. I love the act of getting a tattoo. It's not so much about the design as it is the experience of being marked. I love watching the artist set up the workspace, ink, needles, razor. With my tattoos, I get to say, these are choices I make for my body, with full-throated consent. This is how I mark myself. This is how I get my body back.
>
> (Gay, 2017: 168)

Self harm and its meanings for women in the criminal justice system (CJS)

Women in the CJS have unusually high rates of sexual, emotional and physical abuse in their background, including bodily trauma, even when compared to men in the prison population. Too often their bodies have been violated, harmed, prostituted and scarred, and their minds similarly intruded upon. Women may react against this misuse of their bodies by asserting control over them in various ways, as Gay (2017) describes above. Self-harm through cutting, burning, substance misuse or disordered eating can express the wish to assert control over the bodies that were once, or continue to be, abused by others.

Self-harm serves many purposes, some of which a woman may be unable to articulate fully as they are not consciously known. On a conscious level, self-harm offers her a powerful form of release, self-expression, a sense of power and perverse mastery of helplessness. It can be both a source of shame and pride. Once self-harm begins it is difficult to give up, as it has an addictive quality that contributes to its power. It can be both a secret and a shared language, one with meaning and symbolism for the woman who employs it, and a communicative power that impacts on those who encounter it.

Self-harm has a powerful visceral impact on others, and creates a pull to action, rather than thought, in witnesses to self-harm, as well as those who engage in it. This countertransference response must be resisted and understood to develop reflective, rather than reactive, responses on an individual and organisational level. In her chapter entitled 'What Happened?' Aiyegbusi (2019) further describes the impact of working with women with these presentations.

Suicide and self-harm are acts with unconscious meanings, communications that convey, in action, repressed thoughts, feelings and fantasies that cannot be allowed into consciousness or be put into words. While women may have conscious motivations and reasons for self-harming, or suicidal acts, there are also unconscious forces of which they are unaware, and yet driven by. The compulsive force of the wish to self-harm is intense, and it can be seen as an attempt to reverse earlier trauma or injury, to mark it, or to wreak revenge for it, by punishing the parents in the cruellest way possible – depriving them of their child, as Stekel (1910) describes. This chapter explores some of these underlying conflicts and needs that are expressed and revealed through self-harming acts.

Inscribing trauma

Freud (1914) described how acting out was the substitute for remembering traumatic childhood experiences and was unconsciously aimed at reversing that early trauma. The person is spared the painful early memory of the trauma and, through action, transforms the early experience, which was originally suffered passively, into one where they are active, and in this sense the action serves to master the trauma. However, if these early memories and feelings cannot be symbolised or represented in the mind, they remain unconscious and unprocessed and will continue to be expressed in action. This is the essence of what Freud (1920) described as the repetition compulsion that indicates an unresolved conflict or unarticulated need.

Elimination fantasy

This term was used by Campbell and Hale (1991) in relation to the fantasy in which harming the self is used to expel toxins, to eliminate bad or impure thoughts and feelings. The person who cuts their wrists and releases blood is attempting to evacuate the badness from their body and mind, and freeing themselves, in fantasy, from impurity. This is a form of purging, with religious overtones, and in some ways follows a similar model, dependent as it is on the notions of: 'good' and 'bad', purification and punishment, the spirit guiding the body.

Women who have had early experiences of sexual violation, in which their body was abused by others, may locate their feelings of guilt, shame and anger in their bodies and seek to use these as the site where these feelings remain, as a kind of depository. When frightening, sexual or angry feelings and thoughts arise in the mind they need to be evacuated; cutting, hurting or harming the body can be a way to transfer these unwanted impulses and memories to a familiar wasteland.

In earlier experiences of abuse this type of splitting enabled the victim to keep her mind 'pure', as she dissociated from her body in order to survive painful, humiliating and frightening feelings; this relief from splitting her mind and body enabled her to ignore the violation and pain she was subjected to through sexual abuse. One consequence of this splitting is that it can continue even when sexual experience is no longer abusive, having served once as a powerful survival strategy, victims of sexual abuse may find that they still cut off or dissociate from sexual activity later in life even when it is wanted and consensual. The primitive mechanism of splitting creates a false sense of safety and a division between good and bad places in the self. Although splitting involves a disconnection between mind and body, it is fundamentally preservative, allowing the woman to feel that at least a part of herself is good. Self-harm also uses splitting, as the body is attacked in an attempt to preserve the mind as a safe place. Once the act of self-harm is complete the woman feels she has 'taken care' of her bad feelings, and discharged them onto the desecrated body that deserves this brutal treatment. She may feel ashamed and guilty about harming herself, in whatever form she has chosen, but this is still preferable to the feeling of being contaminated from within, in her mind and very being. Campbell and Hale (1991) refer to this as the fantasy of the 'surviving self' that is opposed to the expendable body, and argue that this fantasy underlies actual suicides as well as non-suicidal self-harm.

Splitting and identification with the aggressor

A woman may attack her own body in order to test its strength, and to decant the toxins of her mind onto this 'other' part of her, which she may see as the site of original damage. She hurts her own body because she sees it as a bad or alien part of herself, and wants to split off from it. The 'her' that she identifies on and in her body is unwanted, and must be 'cut out' or punished, while the 'her' that she locates in her mind is her 'real' self, that must be protected.

At times she feels totally cut off from her body, and has a tremendous urge to assault it, to make it feel pain and bear the marks of injury. This separation of mind and body, of thought from sensation, is a common feature of dissociation in traumatic situations. A person who is tortured can dissociate, or cut out, from the excruciating pain and humiliation they are forced to bear, in order to survive this traumatic experience. The mind becomes symbolically disconnected from the body and from the present experience, and becomes a separate place of safety, at least temporarily. This dissociation can happen automatically, rather than being consciously chosen, though at times the suffering body is longing 'not to be there' and wants to float free, with a mind that can disconnect and escape. It can feel quite separate and apart from the body that is hurt, serving a protective function at the time of the trauma, as the 'real' self, the thinking, watching ego, is experienced as other to the frightened part of the mind still attached to the powerless and violated body. The wish to numb and dissociate can also be met through the use of substances, that offer temporary escape.

During self-harm a woman's body represents the victim part of herself that she can attack and harm, while her mind is preserved as a pure place, protected from damage. Her mind is now in identification with the aggressor, and though this may be against her conscious wishes, it serves a crucial unconscious purpose. In this way she is employing a primitive defence of splitting which reflects an early wish to separate the world neatly into good and bad, and to project bad feelings from inside onto the outside (Klein, 1946). By damaging her body she asserts that her mind is the good, pure place, freed from destructive feelings and thoughts. The destructive impulses are all placed on the body, which is used as the bad object, the canvas upon which she paints her dark imaginings.

This form of splitting has a tremendous appeal, creating a false certainty in which good and bad can clearly be demarcated. It allows painful thoughts and feelings to be translated into actions, which also serves an important function, as the manic defence of activity can feel a relief compared to the weight of memory, replete as it is with depression, despair and shame. In a graphic example of splitting, a young woman seen in therapy only ever harmed one side of herself, her right side, as she felt that one part of her was bad, damaged, deathly, and the other part contained goodness, hope and the possibility of redemption. I use the term 'redemption' deliberately, as the split self, and the notions of good and bad, punishment, sin and purification, have strong parallels with religious beliefs and primitive rituals of poison elimination. The ultimate aim of these acts of separation, attack and violation is not, however, to destroy the object (the body) but to keep it alive, to test its capacities and to have it contain and withstand destructive impulses, as well as to serve as a living memorial to them, and to the violations they signify.

Interestingly, this denigration of the body and its use as a 'poison container' can also be found in sexual risk-taking and through violent relationships, in which self-harm can be administered by proxy, as described below.

Self-harm by proxy: violent relationships

The need to harm oneself can be met through a relationship where another takes the role of aggressor and the woman's violent impulses are disavowed and located in the arms of her partner. The partner, in turn, disavows his or her own vulnerability and helplessness, feeling relieved of a sense of power-lessness as it is located in their victim-partner. Through this unconscious sado-masochistic contract, the beauty and the beast can maintain a psychic equilibrium and create a false dichotomy in which one is helpless and the other omnipotent; one strong and the other weak.

Closer exploration of the underlying dynamics can reveal that, in fact, the apparent victim wants their partner to identify with her unwanted aggressive impulses and to enact them for her, longing for a sense of pain, violation and injury. Paradoxically the apparent victim can control the apparent perpetrator and, through projective identification, free themselves from the guilt and pain of aggressive impulses and locate them all in their partner. They will not 'need' to harm themselves as their partner will take care of this, abusing them both physically and mentally. The force of the underlying, often unconscious, contract between the two is powerful and maintains relationships that are clearly destructive to both.

The entrenched nature of these dynamics, and the unconscious wish to repeat the trauma, is evident. This can be seen when women who were in destructive and masochistic heterosexual relationships outside prison repeat the dynamics of the abusive relationship within custody, this time with a female partner. The deep need for this repetition reveals itself through this relationship and can be seen in the following clinical illustration.

Clinical illustration: self-harm by proxy in a toxic relationship

Friends, Amber and Mia, both single women in their late twenties, were drinking together in their shared flat one night when Dwayne, someone they considered more of an acquaintance than a friend, came over to join them. He was someone whom they would see in the pub, a friend of mutual friends, but neither woman was intimate with him. He had previously attempted to have a relationship with Mia but she had rejected him, as she was, at that time, in a relationship with another woman. When Dwayne arrived he had been smoking crack cocaine and was in a disinhibited state, making lewd jokes about the women being 'gay' and asking if he could 'join in', or just watch them have sex. Amber and Mia were not in a sexual relationship with one another, but both had shared their stories of being sexually abused in their childhood: Amber by family members and Mia by a residential social worker in her children's home. Enraged by his propostition, they held Dwayne hostage and tortured him, burning him with scalding liquid, poured over his arms, and beat him with a belt.

They were united in their hatred of the victim, whom they saw as predatory and he became the embodiment of the various men who had abused them, sexually, physically and mentally throughout their early lives. It seemed that in an attempt to avenge the sadistic treatment they had previously suffered separately, together they enacted humiliating scenes of sexual violation with someone who represented their abusers during this four-hour period in which they barricaded him in their flat. Eventually, after they released him, both pleaded guilty to false imprisonment and grievous bodily harm (GBH). The women each received prison sentences but were sent to separate prisons, and the judge commented on the toxic nature of their friendship, speculating that, alone, neither would have subjected Dwayne to this torture. Welldon (2011) describes this as a form of 'malignant bonding' in which a couple form a poisonous bond, turning against a third in order to further their own destructive excitement.

Once in custody Mia formed a relationship with a woman with a history of abuse; she perpetrated violence on this woman, who herself had fled from an abusive male partner and ended up living on the streets where she got involved in robberies. Amber, who also became sexually involved with another woman in prison, was, in turn, the victim of physical and emotional abuse by her. Amber's choice of partner could be seen as a form of self-harm by proxy. The violent assault on their victim was re-enacted in their intimate relationships in custody, in one case as perpetrator, in the other as victim.

Despite her dominant stance in relation to her prison partner, where she was the perpetrator of abuse, Mia self-harmed prolifically, using any weapons she could find and frequently fashioning ligatures. Prison staff described their sense of helplessness as they would continually take away items with which she could harm herself, only to find she had simply created other objects to use as weapons against herself. On one occasion she was ligaturing under a blanket while having an apparently calm and reasonable discussion with her personal officer (a prison officer assigned to her care, with whom she could have one-to-one sessions) who was horrified when she discovered this when Mia passed out. Losing consciousness was like a dress rehearsal of death, and left officers needing to cut Mia's ligatures.

This episode reveals the complexity of the self-harm, in that not only was Mia hurting herself, but also tricking the officer, with whom she had a good and trusting relationship, and, in one way, testing her capacity to watch her closely enough, and then to bear the hostility and fear that the self-strangulation generated in her. Mia later used sessions with her personal officer to describe feeling desperate to hurt herself as she was filled with guilt and self-loathing about her violence towards her girlfriend. She hated the fact that she was in prison, wasting her life, saying she found it hard to put that into words. She denied any sense of triumph in managing to tie a ligature while talking to someone whom she trusted, and who trusted her, maintaining that she had been determined to tie this piece of material around her neck before the officer came by to check on her, and that she felt she could not stop or resist this impulse. Helping her to put these feelings into words rather than actions was the aim of the therapy that she was then offered – a group run along mentalisation-based therapy lines. This therapy was effective in helping her, after some time, to reduce her impulses to self-harm.

Victims and perpetrators in self-harm

Rather than viewing self-harm as a straightforward attack on oneself, it is important to recognise it as an act of violence and aggression that has multiple victims, and that is inflicted, at least in fantasy, by multiple perpetrators. In other words, the woman who attacks her body may, in that moment, be identifying with her own abuser, as represented in her violent assault, with her body being identified as the victim. At the same time, other people are also hurt through the self-harm, including those who are tasked with keeping her safe, in this case the prison officer, in other cases parents or lovers. In fantasy, the mother, whose body is symbolically encoded on the woman's own, is also attacked.

At its most extreme, in suicide, the woman murders herself and kills off the mother she embodies. Tragically, pregnant women who kill themselves are murdering not only themselves, but their unborn child, and leaving behind mothers, fathers and sometimes children who mourn. This form of death is not unusual in pregnancy and often takes a particularly violent form that is considered unusual in women. (Khalifeh, Hunt, Appleby and Howard 2016).

Self-made fantasy

In her work on self-harm and body modification, Alessandra Lemma (2010) refers to the 'self-made body' which is the narcissistic fantasy that underlies manic attempts to change and transform the body. She argues that self-harm, like body modification, is an attempt to create a new self, to cut away the old, unwanted body in favour of a new, desired one. There is a fantasy of rebirth through one's own actions, as if carving out a new shape.

The way the self-harmer relates to herself is as if she can create herself through acts of self-mutilation and chosen cosmetic procedures designed to remodel the self so as to attack and sculpt it into an object of one's own creation. This links to the ideas expressed in Malan's (1997) work on anorexia nervosa, murder and suicide. Malan views these as attempts to deny need, want or dependence. In the fantasy of self-creation, the woman's attacks on her body are part of a reshaping and reconfiguration of it, over which she believes she has omnipotent control. This also echoes the idea of reclaiming the body that Gay describes in relation to tattoos.

Creating clear boundaries: carving the self

Self-harm can be a way of creating a boundary, a dividing line between self and other, good and evil, feeling and non-feeling. At times of inchoate feeling it is possible to carve out a sense of selfhood through cutting, burning or transforming the body in some way. Skin is the boundary, the protective shield that separates self and other, but also the point of contact with another, and the line between inside and outside, the surface on to which sensation is felt – it is boundary, site of perception and point of impact. Separation can be seen as the loss of the shared skin, and contact with another can be experienced as a form of penetration, threatening the skin's barrier. Anzieu's (1989) notion of 'the psychic envelope' is relevant here, as he describes how skin functions to contain and create a sense of oneself, carrying with it the bodily memories of the earliest relationship with the mother. He cites the functions as including that of inscription, containment and protection.

In her work on unconscious uses of the female body, Pines (1993) describes the impact of trauma on the skin and on other facets of the body. Bick (1968), too, provides rich illustrations of how the path of early experience can be traced on the skin, as well as its disorders. The link with early infancy and its embodied memories is central. When someone penetrates their skin, defaces it, marks or bruises it, there is a violent intrusion from the external world onto the point of contact with the internal world, and the harmed person is left damaged, momentarily disfigured and filled with impinging sensations. To do this to one's own body is essentially to become other to oneself, to enact a split and an attack that could come from an alien outsider. Cutting the skin expresses a divided self and is, in a sense, a reflection of the earliest relationship between the self and another. It also creates a boundary, a demarcation point between amorphous states of grey emotion and the colour of a wound; the sensation of pain interrupts this dreary state of nothingness as it punctures and punctuates it.

In *Skin Game*, Caroline Kettlewell describes her overwhelming urges to cut herself, and the comfort and peace it afforded her. Much as I describe above, she uses the razor to kill off the awful feelings inside her and to create a sense of self-identity. She writes:

> So when I discovered the razor blade, cutting, if you'll believe me, was my gesture of hope. All the chaos, all the sound and fury, the confusion and uncertainty and despair – all of it evaporated in an instant I was for the minute, grounded, coherent, whole. Here is the irreducible self. I drew the line in the sand, marked my body as mine, its flesh and its blood under my command. (Kettlewell, 2000: 37)

Her body is used as the object onto which these aspects of a divided self can be expressed, both as aggressor and nurse, in the service of the final aim of reintegration and creation of a coherent sense of self. The skin as boundary acts as a kind of psychic container, but for those who do not have an interior sense of integration, the disintegration is played out on the body and its surfaces.

The anthropologist and psychiatrist, Armando Favazza, has described self-injury as a means of returning to one's body after a period of disassociation: '[One] of the sure ways to end these episodes of depersonalization is to cut yourself,' he described in an interview on National Public Radio, 'Those who engage in self-harm see the blood, and they say, "OK, that's where my body is because the blood is coming out of my skin, and I know where the boundaries of my body are."'

Untouchable: self-harm as a defence against intimacy

Self-harm serves as a powerful defence against intimacy in two primary ways: firstly, it immerses the woman in a sadomasochistic relationship with herself and so protects her against intimate contact with another; secondly, in a concrete form, the marks and injuries of self-harm disfigure her, both preventing her from revealing herself to others, and offering a rationale for this retreat.

The woman makes herself untouchable, confirming her inner sense of unworthiness and otherness. The scars and mottled skin offer her a reason to hide, and they also confirm her sense of damage, now externalised. She creates a barrier between others and herself. She sees herself as outside of society, as an Untouchable, a pariah who contaminates others and is herself already poisoned, corrupted and damaged. Like the Untouchables in India, now called the Dalits, considered to be 'beneath' even the lowest of the lowest four castes, many women who self-harm view themselves as beneath contempt, as they have internalised the hatred and dismissal with which others have treated them. The only touch that can be controlled and borne is one that is self-inflicted and painful. To make oneself untouchable by others, through self-mutilation, can feel like a powerful defence against intimacy, similar to the compulsive use of food for comfort and control that Gay (2017) describes in *Hunger*, after a devastating experience of gang rape. Eating both comforts and protects her, shielding her from the possibility of further violation and abuse, but it also leads her into a destructive cycle of self-loathing. The link between self-protection and self-harm is clear: what appears to others to be destructive is felt by the woman herself to be a fundamental act of self-preservation. She renders herself untouchable for protection, because she has an inner sense that this is the truth, that she is unworthy and broken.

Self-harm and inscriptions: signing with a scar

Self-harm can be used to carve experiences onto the body, making public private pain: 'deliberate self-harm is a symptom of internal distress, which has both a private and a public message' (Adshead, 1997: 111). The notion of signing with a scar, as described by Gillian Straker (2006) suggests that self-harm acts as a form of autobiographical narrative, in the form of flesh wounds. It expresses the feelings of the woman who self-harms and inscribes her narrative. The self-harm acts as a signature, a form of 'writing oneself' even if the only person who can decode the text, with all its meanings and signifiers, is the woman herself. Others, who may not be aware of the significance of the marks, will still receive the communication they convey – the responses to self-harm are often visceral, highly disturbing and powerful.

Straker describes how the affective message that self-injury conveys can be a more primitive and urgent form of communication than language. It is clear that articulate women, who can express themselves in words as well as images, at times feel that this is not enough to communicate the intensity and urgency of their emotions effectively. Self-harm has a primitive immediacy and power that words do not, or do not yet. She points out that the language of self-harm can eventually be replaced with the language of words, once the person has felt she is understood and that the message inscribed on their bodies has been received. Straker terms this self-creation through self-harm 'signing with a scar' and views it as a form of affective communication. It is an affective mode of expression that is not just an inadequate form of language for the inarticulate. Through this language of the body, feeling states are preserved, not lost and distanced through language.

Suicide and its prevention

Although self-harm is often not an attempt to kill oneself, it is a fact that a history of self-harm increases the risk of suicides. The Corston Report was commissioned in 2005 as a response to an unprecedented number of suicides in women's prisons: in 2003 there were 14 and 13 in 2004, of which six occurred within a one-year period in HMP Styal. The report compiled by Baroness Corston at the request of the then Home Secretary, Charles Clarke, is an independent review that stresses the urgent need for reform of women's prisons and a reappraisal of how female offenders are treated within them. In her passionate and well-substantiated report, she further notes that:

- Outside prison, men are more likely to commit suicide than women but the position is reversed inside prison;
- Self-harm in prison is a huge problem and more prevalent in the women's estate. (Corston, 2007: 3)

However, in 2015 the 100th woman to kill herself in custody was a landmark that went unreported, causing little stir in the public imagination but throwing into sharp relief the sense in which women in custody are disregarded, both in their lives and deaths.

Simply being in prison is a traumatic situation for women who may have to leave children and other family members suddenly, losing homes and a sense of identity. Further experiences within custody may re-enact their earlier experiences of hopelessness, despair and fear, leading to desperate attempts to escape. The 2018 report on suicides in prison by the charity Inquest made the following recommendations to reduce the numbers of women dying in custody and upon release:

- Redirect resources from criminal justice to welfare, health, housing and social care;
- Divert women away from the criminal justice system;
- Halt prison building and commit to an immediate reduction in the prison population;
- Review sentencing decisions and policy;
- An urgent review of the deaths of women following release from prison;
- Ensure access to justice and learning for bereaved families;
- Build a national oversight mechanism for implementing official recommendations. (Inquest, 2018: 20)

Treatment approaches

Psychodynamic psychotherapy and suicide prevention

Walker and Towl (2016) describe evidence-based programmes for preventing suicide and self-harm in this population and offer a powerful argument for the need to use this research to inform staff training within the criminal justice system. They also describe the profound impact that suicide has on the prison officers who work with and care for the women. The results of their empirical research were that the presence of prison officers checking in with the women reduced the rate of self-harm significantly, as much as the use of a particular treatment protocol, indicating that relational security has the greatest impact on reducing the likelihood of self-harm or suicide.

The Women Offenders Self Harm Intervention Pilot II (WORSHIP II) study was conducted in three female prisons in England and piloted a treatment intervention for self-harm (Walker and Towl, 2016). WORSHIP II specifically aimed to reduce thoughts and actions of self-harm and suicide risk through an evidence-based intervention, psychodynamic interpersonal therapy (PIT), which is also known as this conversational model. Walker and Towl (2016) found efficacy in the method for reducing the rates of self-harm and attempted suicide. Significantly, the increased levels of contact with a personal officer were also effective in reducing the rates of self-harm, suggesting that simply being kept in mind was tremendously important for women in custody, and that the sense of loneliness and neglect was overwhelming, leading them to injure themselves. The principal finding was that the relational function of self-harm was evident: simply having more contact with a personal officer reduced the frequency of self-harm. This important treatment trial is now being replicated in seven women's prisons, in the project entitled WORSHIP III, beginning in 2018.

Psychoanalytic psychotherapy

Working in a psychoanalytically informed way in individual therapy allows the practitioner to gain a rich understanding of the woman's inner world, and to have a sense of the complexity of her earliest attachments. Through the transference, the woman will project feelings from early in life onto the therapist and may view her as alternately withholding, cruel and punitive or as an idealised mother figure, a benevolent and all powerful nurturing presence. In either case, the transference will tend to be intense, and any breaks or gaps in treatment will have a significant impact.

The work will be slow and gradual, as the therapist sensitively explores the meaning of the self-harming acts for the woman, the underlying feelings and fantasies that drive them, and how this serves as part of an overall constellation of difficulties for her. In this model the symptom of self-harm is not focussed on to the exclusion of other aspects of the woman, and the therapist is careful not to become too interested in the acts themselves, focussing instead on their underlying meaning and how they can be thought of as the external manifestation of inner conflicts. The therapist holds the notion of the unconscious at the forefront of the work, bearing in mind that the woman herself is not necessarily conscious of her motivations for self-harm. Her dreams, associations, fragments of memory and feelings about the therapist are all vital clues in piecing together the puzzle of how and why this particular woman self-harms.

Individual psychotherapy can take place within custodial settings, and within secure mental health units, although the culture of the unit will determine whether this approach is viewed as suitable. The need for attachment based treatments is widely recognised across the Women's Offender Personality Disorder Pathway.

Working psychoanalytically or in psychodynamic psychotherapy with self-harm leads to strong countertransference responses, as the depth of anger and despair is often projected onto the therapist, who then identifies with those feelings. Sometimes the anger can be turned against the patient, at other times against the therapist herself. Monitoring and reflecting on these powerful communications, sometimes felt viscerally, is essential in enabling the therapist to resist either retaliating or surrendering under their impact. Through close supervision of one's own response, and reflection on the nature and impact of the communication, the internal world of the woman who self-harms becomes clearer, and eventually one can use this insight to help the woman put her feelings into words.

I have discussed the pull to action and to strong feelings that self-harm can generate, as it intoxicates as well as deadens those who encounter it (see Chapter 9). In her classic paper, 'Addiction to Near Death', Betty Joseph (1982, p. 451) describes the pressures felt by an analyst working with patients masochistically intent on enacting destructive impulses, even attacking the therapeutic relationship itself:

> It is familiar to us and has been well described in the literature (Meltzer, 1973; Rosenfeld, 1971; Steiner, 1982) that such patients feel in thrall to a part of the self that dominates and imprisons them and will not let them escape, even though they see life beckoning outside.

The task of the analyst here is not to get caught up in these projections, but to help the person see that the addictive use of self-destructive activity, including ongoing, deathly ruminations, is defensive, covering up underlying fears and anxieties that should instead be brought into the therapeutic work. She becomes the repository of hope for the patient.

Trauma-informed therapy: the sense of self starts from the outside in

The body ego, as Freud (1923) termed it, is the first ego, and disruptions in its care have a profound impact on the development on the psychic structures, the ego or the sense of self in mediation with the external world. For many women with disturbed histories of attachment their bodies remain the site of emotion, and act as containers of their pain. Words have less impact than wounds.

Jones (2017) conducted research with and by females in a high security hospital, where they were placed instead of prison for their own protection and to reduce the risk of violence towards others. She analysed their understanding of their self-harm alongside the views of nurses who worked with them, and then compared the two sets of responses. In the trauma-informed service for women, established in Rampton Hospital, the notion that the first ego is the body ego finds confirmation, as sensory modalities of treatment appear more effective than 'talking cures' when women are in a heightened state of arousal.

The context for her study is the National High Secure Healthcare Service for Women (NHSHSW) which opened in 2007 following the closure of all other high security healthcare services for women. The NHSHSW provides assessment and treatment for women detained under the Mental Health Act and who are classified as posing a grave and immediate danger to others. Care delivered within the NHSHSW is grounded within the guiding principles of trauma informed environments. This philosophy of care is predicated on the notion that women patients in high security facilities experience heightened and usually chronic levels of distress which can be communicated through violent and dangerous behaviour (Jones, 2017; McMillan and Aiyegbusi, 2009).

In her phenomenological analysis of how women in high security services understood their self-harm, Jones found the following themes: observable behaviours and responses; blocks to getting help; change over time; an entity to be endured; an emotional experience; a physical experience; being alone. She compared this to the nurses' understanding of the patients' self-harm.

Jones's research revealed that there were marked differences in the two groups in terms of their understanding of the patients' experience of distress; she found that the women patients placed emphasis on the physiological/sensory aspect of their distress, whereas nurses placed emphasis on the emotional aspect of the patients' distress. The implication of this finding was that at times of heightened distress the patients did not feel they were understood by the nurses. The findings also highlighted areas of unmet need, including family involvement in care and a perceived lack of support to enhance family contact. Loneliness was identified as a significant stressor for the women, and was identified as an ongoing risk of harm.

Jones's research concluded that for the women who self-harm, the body and its responses were primary and that they craved recognition of this, and treatment addressed at this level is needed. She developed techniques including grounding, aromatherapy, guided relaxation and other sensory methods to enable women to develop the capacity for self-soothing at times of intense distress, and when tempted to self-harm in extreme ways. The women created their own individual documents mapping out their particular expressions of self-harm and how best to modify these where possible. These were shared with their nurses and therapists and helped the women to feel that they had a better understanding both of the triggers for their self-harm and, the most helpful, compassionate responses to the acts themselves. Jones worked alongside women in the wards to ensure that staff were aware of the roots of the distress and how best to respond to its expression. As Chapters 9, 10 and 11 explore in depth, the impact on staff of working with women who deploy self-harm and other violent communications is intense and can be overwhelming, creating the risk of retaliation and other enactments. How these are understood and resisted is central to the task of rehabilitation and recovery.

Conclusion: self-harm as a sign of hope

I have described self-harm as a communication and expression of hope (Motz, 2010), in that it can be a means of self-expression and an attempt to reach out to another human being who will be able to decode the message and respond with understanding rather than condemnation or pity. It is important to keep this in mind when faced with women who self-harm rather than to view it as a nihilistic or death-seeking act.

Self-harm is not necessarily a suicide attempt nor attention-seeking behaviour: it is a communication that contains within it the hope that there will be a response. While self-harm is a complex set of behaviours, with different meanings in different contexts, it should be considered to be akin to the hopeful aspect in the antisocial tendency, as described by Winnicott (1967). Like other behaviour considered to be antisocial, self-harm is actually hopeful, revealing an attempt to find a helpful response to distress: 'In the hopeful moment ... the environment must be tested and re-tested in its capacity to stand the aggression, to prevent or repair the destruction, to tolerate the nuisance, to recognise the positive element in the antisocial tendency' (Winnicott, 1967: 312).

Although self-harm is viewed with horror and incomprehension by many, its origins and communicative purpose should not be ignored. In self-harm the body is the environment that is called upon to survive the destructive act and 'house' the toxic feelings that drive it. The sense of release once self-harm has been enacted is not just felt viscerally, but also emotionally, in the relief that there is a 'survivor' self, symbolically located in the body. To extend this idea of hope contained in the concept of self-harm as a communication, the external body that can tolerate the assault is not just the woman's own body, but the bodies and minds of those who come into contact with her. The hope is that they will respond to the woman who self-harms with interest, care, curiosity and compassion, and enable her to make sense of her distress and rage. Unfortunately, all too often, this unconscious hope is not met, and self-harm is treated with contempt, derision and disgust. Although unwanted, this response may also confirm the woman's sense of herself as she 'really' is, and meet a need in her for punishment and rejection. A different response, one of a real attempt to understand and relate to the woman who self-harms, can eventually stop the cycle of repetitive and intensifying self-destructive action, and I suggest that it is this unconscious hope that underlies much of self-harm.

Self-harm has a multitude of meanings and purposes. It serves significant functions for women and is associated with trauma that cannot yet be spoken about. Women in the criminal justice and secure mental health systems have high rates of trauma, and, consequently, high rates of self-harm. Settings must be trauma-informed with staff trained and supported to manage their counter-transference, contain the women's distress and reduce the rates of self-harm and suicide.

Self-harm is most helpfully thought about in relational terms, as expressing unmet needs from earlier disturbed attachment relationships that are now played out on the self. It serves the function of mirroring in those for whom the early caretaker has not provided this. The skin, rather than the eyes or arms of the mother, becomes the reflective surface. This is a hopeful conception of self-harm that links it to the creation of an embodied identity, rather than consigning it simply to the realm of pathology. Its purpose and meaning for a particular woman, at a particular time, requires sensitive and patient enquiry before it can be understood and decoded.

For many women, including those in custody, self-harm is not about suicide but about survival:

> That's when I wanted to cut. I cut to quiet the cacophony. I cut to end this abstracted agony, to reel my selves back to one present and physical whole, whose blood was the proof of her tangibility … The chaos in my head spun itself into a silk of silence. I had distilled myself to the immediacy of hand, blade, blood, flesh.
>
> (Kettlewell, 2000, p. 27)

This chapter has conceptualised self-harm ultimately as an attempt at relating to others, and an expression of the hope that this wish will be fulfilled. Self-harm can arise out of loneliness but, paradoxically, can also serve to keep others at bay, reflecting both desire for intimacy alongside the fear of closeness to another. It marks the body for the woman and has a narrative purpose, as the woman can use the language of the body to 'write herself' in the hope that another will ultimately be able to read her story.

References

Adshead, G. (1997) Written on the body: Deliberate self-harm and violence. In E. V. Welldon & C. van Velson (eds) *A Practical Guide to Forensic Psychotherapy*. London: Jessica Kingsley Press.

Anzieu, D. (1989) *The Skin Ego*. New Haven, CT: Yale University Press.

Corston, B. (2007) *A Report by Baroness Jean Corston of a Review of Women with Particular Vulnerabilities in the Criminal Justice System*. London: The Home Office.

Bick, E. (1968) The experience of the skin in early object relations. *International Journal of Psychoanalysis*, 49: 558–566.

Bulman, M. (2018) Nearly 100 women die in prison over 11-year period due to 'glaring failures' by government, says report. *The Independent*. https://www.independent.co.uk/news/uk/home-news/women-inmates-deaths-prison-uk-government-failure-protection-police-figures-a8330576.html

Campbell, D. and Hale, R. (1991) Suicidal Acts. In J. Holmes (ed.) *Textbook of Psychotherapy in Psychiatric Practice* (pp. 287–306). London: Churchill Livingstone.

Freud, S. (1914) Remembering, repeating and working through. In J. Strachey (ed. and trans). *The Standard Edition of the Complete Psychological Works of Sigmund Freud*. London: Hogarth Press.

Freud, S. (1920) *Beyond the Pleasure Principle (The Standard Edition)* (trans. James Strachey). New York: Liveright Publishing Corporation.

Freud, S. (1923) *The Ego and the Id in Beyond the Pleasure Principle and Other Writings*, reprinted 2003. London: Penguin Classics.

Gay, R. (2017) *Hunger: A Memoir of my Body*. London: Corsair.

Inquest (2018) *Still Dying on the Inside: Examining Deaths in Women's Prisons*. London: Barrow Cadbury Trust.

Jones, J. (2017) How distress is understood and communicated by women patients detained in high secure forensic healthcare, and how nurses interpret that distress: An exploration using a multi-perspective interpretative phenomenological analysis. University of Derby, DProf thesis.

Joseph, B. (1982) Addiction to near death. *International Journal of Psychoanalysis*, 63:449–456.

Kettlewell, K. (2000) *Skin Game: A Memoir*. St Martins Press: London.

Khalifeh, H., Hunt, I. M., Appleby, L. and Howard, L. M. (2016) Suicide in perinatal and non-perinatal women in contact with psychiatric services: 15 year findings from a UK national inquiry. *The Lancet Psychiatry*, 3(3): 233–242. https://doi.org/10.1016/S2215-0366(16)00003-1.

Klein, M. (1946) Notes on some schizoid mechanisms. *International Journal of Psychoanalysis*, 27: 99–110.

Lemma, A. (2010) *Under the Skin: A Psychoanalytic Study of Body Modification*. London: Routledge.

Malan, D. (1997) *Anorexia, Murder and Suicide*. London: Butterworth Heineman.

McMillan, S. and Aiyegbusi, A. (2009) Crying out for care. In A. Aiyegbusi & J. Clarke-Moore (eds) *Therapeutic Relationships with Offenders: An Introduction to the Psychodynamics of Forensic Mental Health Nursing*. (pp. 171–186). London: JKP.

Meltzer, D. (1973). *Sexual States of Mind*. Perthshire: Clunie Press.

Motz, A. (2010) Self-harm as a sign of hope. *Psychoanalytic Psychotherapy*, 24(2): 81–92, DOI: 10.1080/02668731003707527.

Pines, D. (1993) *A Woman's Unconscious Use of Her Body*. London: Virago.

Rosenfeld, H. (1971) A clinical approach to the psychoanalytic theory of the life and death instincts: An investigation into the aggressive aspects of narcissism. *International Journal of Psychoanalysis*, 52: 169–178.

Straker, G. (2006) Signing with a scar: Understanding self-harm. *Psychoanalytic Dialogues*, 16: 93–112.

Steiner, J. (1982) Perverse relationships parts of the self: A clinical illustration. *International Journal of Psychoanalysis*, 63: 241–252.

Stekel, W. (1910) Symposium on Suicide. In P. Friedman (ed.) *On Suicide* (pp. 33–141). New York: International Universities Press.

Walker, T. and Towl, G. (2016) *Preventing Self Injury and Suicide in Women's Prisons*. Hampshire: Waterside Press.

Welldon, E.V. (2011) Perverse transference and the malignant bonding. In B. Kahr (ed.) *Playing with Dynamite: A Personal Approach to the Psychoanalytic Understanding of Perversions, Violence and Criminality* (pp. 50–59). The Forensic Psychotherapy Monograph Series. London: Karnac.

Winnicott, D.W. (1967) Delinquency as a sign of hope. A talk given to the Borstal Assistant Governors' Conference, held at King Alfred's College, Wincheste, April 1967.

Chapter 7

Taboo
Female psychopathy and sexual offending against children

Anna Motz

> Here's the smell of the blood still. All the perfumes of Arabia will not
> sweeten this little hand.
>
> (Macbeth, Act 5, Scene 1, 50–52)

In this chapter I discuss two phenomena that have traditionally been the
domain of male offenders, psychopathy and sexual offending. I explore their
manifestation in women, and the vilification of these women. Firstly,
I describe the notion of 'female psychopathy' and its depiction in popular culture. I challenge the utility of the concept of psychopathy and suggest that it
should instead be replaced with the notion of 'psychopathic states of mind',
arguing that cruelty and reckless disregard for others can occur when women
are under tremendous psychic pressure, rather than as a result of pervasive
characterological disturbance.

I then discuss female child sexual abuse and its treatment. We know that the
actual prevalence rates are hard to detect, and that the conviction rates of
women who sexually offend against children is far lower than the number of
offences reported by victims: 'The sexual abuse of a child always takes place
in secret: therefore, the true prevalence of any form of sexual abuse of children
will always be secret' (Saradjian, 2010).

Psychopathy

What are the features that render an individual psychopathic, and is this
a concept relevant to women? A fundamental feature of psychopathy, as
defined in relation to men, is their capacity to inflict cruelty and harm to
others without remorse, empathy or inhibition, to enjoy aspects of their sadism
and wrongdoing. It is often used as a moral term as well as a psychological
one, and connotes an individual who has essentially stepped outside of humanity altogether. The concept derived from Hervey Cleckley, in his seminal book
The Mask of Sanity, originally published in 1941 (reprinted 1976) and later
developed by Robert Hare (1980).

Hare created the 'gold standard' measure, the Psychopathy Checklist, subsequently revised and often used in the Screening Version (PCL: SV) to enable the distinction of psychopathy from antisocial personality disorder through specific traits, such as emotional detachment, grandiose sense of self-worth, manipulativeness, lack of empathy, superficial charm, shallow affect, parasitic lifestyle, irresponsibility, impulsivity and social deviance (Cooke & Michie, 2001). The classification and its measurement has mainly been applied to men, whose 'natural' aggression and ruthlessness appears in toxic form in psychopathy.

As Logan (2011) argues, the psychopathic woman has often been overlooked, and her agency and violence viewed as deeply unnatural. She describes the depiction of the alluring, highly dangerous 'femme fatale' who appears in fiction and drama as the prototype of this, and emphasises that such a woman acts against deeply entrenched gender stereotypes. The personality features that have been identified in the literature as characterising female psychopathy tend to fit stereotyped conceptions of the 'femme fatale', including 'seductiveness', deceit and the capacity to manipulate others. Recent literature has identified a strong link between borderline personality disorder and the diagnosis of psychopathy in women (McKeown, 2010; Sprague et al., 2012).

In popular culture the female psychopath is almost always someone who uses her sexuality as a powerful means of manipulation and weaponry. Aileen Wournos, the American serial killer, is depicted as a seductress who lures her victims into her web, only then to kill them, rather than a prostituted woman who took revenge through murder on a client who raped her; Wournos then repeatedly re-enacted this revenge killing. That is, the trauma underlying the violence was ignored. In his role as consultant to the popular television show *Killing Eve*, featuring a female psychopath in the starring role as Villenelle, Consultant Forensic Psychiatrist Mark Freestone acknowledges that as there are so few female psychopaths he based her character on a male. Nonetheless he has attempted to give this character a more realistic complexity in her functioning and underlying motivations, though she too is portrayed as a very beautiful and alluring woman with seductiveness, youth and sexual freedom. In a recent interview Dr Freestone describes the development of her character, an entertaining one, in a show that has attracted great success, including BAFTA awards.

In this interview, Consultant Forensic Psychiatrist Mark Freestone describes how he uses the notion of 'the mask of sanity' as a basis for Villanelle's character. This mask hides her true self, including the aggression and sexual desire that defines her. The seductive mask allows her to interact with others but underneath there is murderous rage, manipulation and sadism. When she is wounded she adopts a further mask of vulnerability and becomes the predator, not the victim, as we can see happen within an episode. Her history of adversity has enabled her to develop adaptive, if cruel, survival mechanisms. Having lived through a childhood characterised by abuse and neglect with a criminal father and no mother, she has had 'training' as an assassin, with skills learned from her abusive history. He notes that the character is even more psychopathic when she is vulnerable and that female psychopaths per se have rarely been identified in the psychological literature on psychopathy. He deliberately chose a male profile in order to highlight Villanelle's unusual levels of brutality and savagery.

'The psychopathic woman, in many respects, remains elusive ... case studies must form part of the investigation of female psychopathy if this construct is to be better understood in women' (Kreis et al., 2012: 267)

In her study of psychopathic personality disorder in women, Mette Feibert Kreis further addresses the neglected issue of female psychopathy using a dimensional model, Comprehensive Assessment of Psychopathic Personality (CAPP) (Cooke et al., 2012), alongside the Psychopathy Checklist Screening Version (PCL:SV) (Hare, 2003) to investigate the construct in women, and to gather a picture of how it manifests in them.

Psychopathy is a severe personality disorder with a complex and extensive theoretical and clinical history. It is intrinsically linked with the concepts of personality and personality disorder generally. The conceptualisation of psychopathy is still passionately debated, especially the relevance of antisocial and criminal behaviour to the construct. Another debate centres on the structure of the Psychopathy Checklist-Revised Edition, which has become synonymous with the psychopathy construct, bringing with it even more conceptual confusion. This is the complex and indistinct foundation from which a conceptualisation of the construct in women is to grow. Not many references have been made to women in the historical psychopathy literature; what is known about female psychopathy to date is based on the male template. Kreis (2009), Kreis and Cooke (2011) aim to identify the characteristic features and typical expression of the construct in women, and consider how this compares to its expression in men.

According to this model, both males and females are considered to differ significantly from others who are not psychopathic, and to show individual differences in dysfunctional personality traits and presentation. The CAPP has been shown to be more gender sensitive than the PCL:SV, which was designed using men. The authors suggest that some CAPP symptoms may be particularly relevant to psychopathy in women, including 'lacks emotional stability', 'manipulative' and 'unstable self-concept'. This model for assessment uses a dimensional approach including emotional expressiveness, attachment and behavioural domains that lead to a far more nuanced and gender sensitive picture of women with psychopathic characteristics than other measures. It is a conceptual map that can be used with individual women and lends itself to case study, offering a rich measure of a particular woman's style of interpersonal relating, typical behaviour and self-concept.

The notion of psychopathy assumes a qualitative difference between 'psychopathic' women and others – in terms of fixed, characterological structures, rather than emphasising the role of early trauma – and the development of defences and modes of survival that enable women to survive in an unsafe world.

Clinical illustration 1: Phoenix, a female psychopath?

Background

Phoenix was referred to me for forensic psychological evaluation in a criminal case relating to charges of cruelty and neglect of her two daughters. She was a 45-year-old mother of two, with a long history of mental health problems, resulting in admission to psychiatric hospital on three occasions. Additionally, she had been convicted for acts of cruelty against animals (dogs and cats) within the past ten years. She had also been charged with two counts of violence against her partner and was found to have been the perpetrator of serious non-accidental injury to her two daughters, Jade and Rosie, aged three and five at the time. Her sister had reported her after hearing from Jade about how her mother punished her, and then seeing cigarette burns on her arm. Rosie also had bruising on her body and appeared frightened in her mother's presence, frequently wetting and soiling herself. She had told the police that sometimes 'Mummy beats us' and described being locked in cupboards for long periods of time. Although Phoenix had separated from the girls' father shortly after Rosie's birth, she had a stable partner with no history of violence or criminal convictions; he was often away for long periods of time, as he worked as a long-distance lorry driver. It was evident to Social Services that this mother was incapable of looking after her daughters with any degree of warmth, consistency or care, and it was proposed that if the father did not assume the main responsibility for the children, they would be removed and taken into local authority care. She and her partner were both facing criminal charges for cruelty, neglect and aggravated bodily harm in relation to Jade and Rosie.

Discussion of the assessment

I met with Phoenix on three occasions to explore with her the offences for which she was charged, her background history and her current therapeutic needs. She was guarded initially but willing to engage in the assessment, despite the obvious sense of apprehension she showed, and her reluctance to relate details of her unhappy past. At moments I could see glimpses of a softer, more vulnerable woman, beneath her hard and mask-like exterior.

Although she denied the offences, Phoenix acknowledged that she frequently had thoughts of harming these girls, especially Jade, in whom she said 'I saw a lot of myself.' When asked to elaborate on this she described herself as having been wilful, naughty, bad, angry, destructive and out of control. She had moments when she felt like murdering her daughters. Her elaborate violent fantasies about what she could do to them, and the pain she wanted to inflict on them, were alarming for me to hear, and also frightened her. Phoenix frequently had vivid fantasies of punishing her children severely, gagging them with cloths, punching them or making them scrub the kitchen floor clean with a toothbrush, using bleach and scalding hot water. Exploration revealed that she had herself been punished in these ways, by both mother and stepfather, who felt she was 'a bad apple'. She had hated her sister, who was disabled and treated with far more tenderness and care. Phoenix associated her disability with weakness, softness and shame. At school she had been teased for having a 'spastic' sister.

Phoenix insisted that she had never acted out these fantasies of re-enacting her own harsh treatment with her daughters, but acknowledged that she found their behaviour difficult to bear and felt that 'they got away with murder'. It seemed that she identified with them and wanted to attack them as she herself had been attacked, as if this would free her from the humiliating position of being helpless and small as she would then become the powerful aggressor. Significantly, she would feel provoked by their tears as well, as a part of her couldn't bear signs of vulnerability and sadness, in herself or in others.

At times in the interview it was as if she were not fully present and had detached herself emotionally, creating a stark incongruity between the disturbing material she was presenting and her manner. The chilling sense I was left with came from her emotional distance from the destructive wishes she disclosed and a sense of profound contempt for vulnerability, in herself or others. She described her sister in contemptuous terms with little sense of compassion, empathy or care, clearly viewing her as both unworthy of care and as having triumphed over her by securing her mother's attention. She only showed softness when describing how sometimes she would be asked to help give her a bath and then she and her mother would work together and her mother would be kinder to her; this was one of her only positive memories of contact with either mother or sister.

It was painful for Phoenix to reflect on how her own mother had treated her in childhood, as she had suffered long periods of time with other family members when her mother had sought periods of respite from caring for her sister, and her. Her mother had several boyfriends before meeting her second husband, a man with alcohol dependence and violent tendencies. Phoenix had never known her biological father. She had truanted from school, had a history of harming family pets and antisocial behaviour including fighting at school and shoplifting, multiple sexual relationships and poor relationships with others. Her relationships with women and girls were particularly problematic and she largely directed her aggression towards females. In adolescence she had become sexually active and was befriended by a gang of older men who appear to have exploited her sexually and introduced her to prostitution.

Although abusive, she viewed these men as her friends and protectors, maintaining ties to some of them currently.

Phoenix felt outside of society, on the edge of sanity and on the outside of her own mind, as she experienced her thoughts and feelings as 'other', not really part of her, but forces that overtook her. Her presentation fitted the description of 'the alien self' as described by Bateman and Fonagy (2004) in which an infant with an impoverished experience of reflective parenting develops a sense of fragmentation and perceives 'unacceptable' impulses within the self to be alien and unintegrated. She acted out angry feelings towards herself and others, cutting her legs and arms from an early age and sometimes burning them.

Countertransference

Phoenix presented as guarded, chaotic and unpredictable, engaged and interested at moments, but 'vacant' and distant at others. My countertransference was one of interest, curiosity but also a strange sense of fear, rejection and failure, as my steady attempt to engage her was not enough to keep her fully in the room. I saw flashes of vulnerability that seemed quickly to be covered up with a sense of flight and a guarded, hard exterior. Phoenix was quite beautiful, and wore her colourful clothes with grace, bringing a wild exotic bird or flower to mind, and this was at odds with the shabby, grey premises of the council building where the interview took place. Her status as dual heritage was difficult for her to speak about, as her father had been a malignant absence in her life, and any contact with him had been problematic. She referred to herself as black, and chose partners who were Afro-Caribbean, but did not consider ethnicity an important issue for her although she disclosed that she had also suffered racial abuse at school in a predominantly white area, and would be asked why she didn't look like her mother and if she were adopted. At this moment I felt in touch with a sadder, more vulnerable part of her and she powerfully communicated to me a sense of being an outsider, not belonging.

Phoenix knew that her father had a history of mental illness and could be violent at times, but his presence in her early life was so shadowy that it was almost impossible to gain a real, nuanced picture of him. At times I felt that she longed to meet him, but had to cover up her sense of missing him and her complicated fears about being like him, as if to acknowledge that worries or a feeling of pining would be unacceptable or shameful. She recalled that in childhood she had often wished he would come and take her to live with him and his extended family, rescuing her from her brutal home-life, but he never did. Her sense of herself as dual heritage was conflicted and troubling as her father represented dark, dangerous forces, like mental illness and violence. In contrast, her white mother, whom she did not physically resemble, looked calm on the outside and 'fitted in' to the local community, though she experienced her as violent and unpredictable. Her mother's dangerousness was invisible to all but Phoenix herself.

Although her childhood recollections evoked my sympathy, her presentation of current events awakened anger, particularly when faced with descriptions of her cruelty to animals, which she acknowledged, and about which she seemed only minimally concerned, stating that she didn't treat her dogs like that now. I found her brutal descriptions of her daughters most difficult to listen to, and also confusing as she spoke about very young children as though they were much bigger and more powerful than she was. I found myself challenging her about factual issues related to her daughters and saying that they couldn't possibly be responsible for the levels of damage she described, including deliberately drinking bleach and wilfully hurting one another – her own treatment of these girls had an impact. This was a fruitless discussion and I had to rein myself in as we were simply getting entrenched in an argument, in which her rigid position was reinforced and my own sense of injustice and despair stopped me from engaging her effectively.

In order to counteract this sense of being at war, I needed to take a break and reflect on my own anger, fear and confusion. When we resumed the interview I was able to adopt a more neutral stance as I had understood that for Phoenix she was the helpless victim of her daughters' incomprehensible actions and that she felt hated by them, much as she had by her own mother and stepfather. Her distorted perceptions of them reflected her narcissistic relating to them, where she saw them as reflections of herself, to be treated with the same contempt and cruelty as she had been treated. I had to understand her position and help her to view herself in a different way before she would have a chance of seeing her children differently. This insight was important in enabling me to anchor my countertransference rage, and my own identification with her maltreated daughters. I had to step back from what felt like a visceral experience of being gagged and wanting to rip off the constricting material, and had to enter Phoenix's world, seeing things through her eyes, unbearable as this was.

Assessment considerations

I was asked to consider whether Phoenix suffered from psychopathic disorder, and additionally whether she would address her parenting difficulties in therapy. The court heard that her sister considered her to be a 'psycho' and to manipulate and control the responses she created in social services professionals. I was requested to determine if she met the criteria for antisocial or psychopathic personality disorder. In addition to the worries about her capacity to bear her children's needs in mind and attend reliably to their welfare, the Social Services were also concerned by reports of her involvement in prostitution, engaging in sadomasochistic sex in which she was the dominating partner and reports of animal cruelty in her childhood. There was a description in her medical records of her as 'displaying cruelty to animals and towards younger children' at primary school, and describing her tendency to isolate herself from others for extended periods of time, but then flipping into being an outgoing and charming personality with a great appetite for parties and nights out. Social workers involved with Jade and Rosie had described her as 'manipulative' and 'ruthless', with a capacity for 'superficial charm', inadvertently evoking terms that are often used in descriptions of psychopathy.

It was, in my view, essential to consider in more detail the nature of Phoenix's internal world, to look carefully at her history of violence and cruelty to animals and younger children and to attempt to draw a picture of the meaning and function of these acts. The familiar scenario of brutality, humiliation and helplessness she had experienced was being re-enacted with her own children. Had she been too maltreated and disconnected from her own mental states to be able to relate to her own mind and the mind of another with empathy and concern? Or was all evidence of need or vulnerability in herself and others to be attacked and obliterated, as too painful a reminder of her own earlier helpless state? She clearly had a strong need to take back power and control and to inflict pain on others, finding some relief in the sadistic sexual practices she had engaged in during prostitution, and also in hurting animals, vulnerable creatures helpless to defend themselves, much like her own daughters, with whom she identified and treated as narcissistic extensions of herself.

Understanding cruelty and danger: psychopathic states of mind

I saw Phoenix as someone who frequently found herself in a 'psychopathic state of mind' and felt that the question of her potential classification as a psychopath was unhelpful and distracting. It implied that the 'answer' would offer certainty about her prognosis and the likely trajectory of her life, addressing the central question of future risk once and for all.

When I explored her early life with her, Phoenix seemed to come alive, though she found it hard to tell a clear narrative, and it was striking how she moved back and forth in time. At some moments I felt she was telling me about a current situation, rather than a historical one; at others, I believed she was giving me a description of her early life with her mother and younger sister, only to learn she was talking about herself and her daughters in the present. Although this was confusing at the time and served to 'wrong-foot me' so that I would need to check, rewind and clarify, interrupting the flow of the story, when I reflected on it later I realised that this confusion of the past and the present is characteristic of trauma – reliving the past as if it were the present, experiencing current events as if they were happening to a younger self in a frightening past state of being. Far from an irrelevant and distracting detail that needed correction, this confusion between past and present was a crucial piece of data, a countertransference experience that offered insight into how Phoenix functioned and how confusing, unstable and chaotic her states of mind were. It was clear that she was devoid of any sense of an under-lying, coherent and intact adult self and that at times of heightened emotions she would see her children not as they actually were, but in identification with them, as the child she had been, in relation to the mother she had faced. She would not, at those moments, see herself as an adult in charge of them, but would, and had, become destabilised by their neediness, their vulnerability and their fear. It was in this state of mind that she wanted to harm them, to silence and subdue them, as representatives of her unmet needs, unheard cries and savage feelings that had found no home in her own mother.

Phoenix's childhood had been characterised by disruption, maternal absence and cruelty. She was left with an underlying sense of being nothing and no-one, marked by her visible difference and invisible trauma. I considered her aggression to be defending her against underlying feelings of shame and humiliation. She guarded herself against revealing any 'softer' feelings and considered these unacceptable, expressing pain through violent actions, taken both against others and herself, some-times through savage acts of self-harm. Her daughters did not provide the solution she had hoped for to her unhappiness, and the comfort she still longed for. Like many other deeply disturbed young women with impoverished experiences of being mothered themselves, their children function as narcissistic extensions of themselves (Welldon, 1988). The baby can be seen as the good object which the 'bad' woman desperately needs as a receptacle for her projections. In her mother's fantasy the unborn infant is the embodiment of a loving creature who confirms the mother's regenerative power and the existence of some good in her. This idealisation can lead to disappointment and depression when the infant is actually born, awakening rage in the mother.

I outlined this formulation in my assessment and described how a course of forensic psychotherapeutic treatment could enable her to address both victim and perpetrator aspects of herself, without denying her accountability or relinquishing her agency. Such work requires the dedication and consistency of a practitioner trained in psychotherapeutic approaches to working with violent and perverse individuals, informed by a full understanding of the consequences of trauma, and the dynamics that may dominate a therapeutic relationship, such as the invitation to become the harsh judge of the woman's actions, or, alternatively, to become either a passive bystander or injured victim of her aggression. Close supervision and proper training enables forensic psychotherapists to resist these (unconscious) traps and enactments, and to offer a neutral space in which women who enter psychopathic states of mind can begin to explore and understand what leads to these lapses in their ordinary functioning.

Psychopathic states of mind

This model – of a violent psychic intrusion of a past experience into the present, such that the former victim of trauma now becomes a perpetrator, while feeling her-self to be the child victim – is well described by Anna Freud's (1936) notion of identification with the aggressor. It is like a force, a vortex of feelings, that threatens to overwhelm the person, who may, like Phoenix, resort to violence, or imagine a violent scene, in order to try and restore a kind of peace, and free themselves of overwhelming and unbearable emotions. Someone in this state of mind cannot conceive of the mind of the other in empathic terms. I would consider it a 'psychopathic state of mind' that comes and goes, rather than a psychopathic personality disorder. This transient state of mind is associated with not caring, not knowing, not wanting to think or being able to connect thoughts and feelings, actions and consequences, self and other. In this state it is impossible to make the kinds of links essential for symbolic functioning and to distinguish between fantasy and reality. This state of mind can enable acts of sadism, violence, sexual abuse or even murder.

Female child sexual abuse

Sexual abuse of children was, historically, considered to be a crime perpetrated solely by men. Although the majority of convicted sex offenders against children are male, there is growing recognition that female sex offenders exist and that the true prevalence rates are difficult to estimate given the reluctance of victims to report them.

The impact of female sexual abuse on children is destructive and significant, as shown in the following poem, written by a survivor of female sexual abuse at age 14.

Untitled poem (written 1974)

It was a dying night
I lay in my bed
And waited
Silently waited

Not a step I heard
No voices
When silence entered my room

Did I hear?
Did I tremble?

Still I lay
I lay
All alone

A blue cloak she had
The silence
To hide me in
And carry away
Like one carries a child

Did anyone hear?
Do our hearts remember?

No storm was there that night
Just a moon
Far in a distance
So red

But blue
Was the bosom of the silence
Where I lay

Carried away
To the night
So stormy
To the mountains
And a house
Windows facing the North

There she laid me
Facing the North

Her cloak all over
Her blue cloak
All over me

I sang a song
A song of the unspoken years
Lost in the unknown

Who was crying?
Was it me?
Or the trees?

With the longing known

So great
Only by the ocean
Far out in the North

That moment
The sky
So dark
The clouds
Like the souls of the birds
Gone long ago

(Lea Getu, 2018)

The greater shame of abuse by a female, and the fear of being disbelieved, often inhibits reporting. Despite this, we can estimate that the male-to-female ratio of sexual offenders is 1:20. However, while only 4–5% of all reported sexual offenders (Cortoni & Hanson 2005; Cortoni et al., 2009) are female, self-reports by victims indicate far higher rates. The 2017 Crime Survey for England and Wales indicates that 83% of victims of sexual offences do not report their crimes. The actual extent of the problem is even more difficult to determine than it is for male offenders.

Pathways to sexual offending

Recent research identified that female sexual offenders followed three main 'pathways', or trajectories, to offending. While one of these pathways was found to be similar to that previously reported in male sexual offenders, the others were unique to women (Gannon, Rose & Ward, 2008). This outlines how certain factors causing women to start, and then to continue, offending against children differ from those that underpin sexual offending by males. In particular, this research highlighted the existence of a Directed-Coerced Pathway (i.e. women whose sexual abuse is directed specifically by males and maintained via coercion and intimidation). The model also identified another pathway, which was not male coerced, termed the Implicit Disorganised Pathway. The women on this pathway did not appear to set out specifically to sexually offend, but upon making contact with a victim and experiencing sexual arousal or emotional loneliness offended impulsively. Those pathways that did not involve men coercing women to offend are most difficult for society to accept, as the popular conception of female sexual abuse is that it could only take place under male coercion.

Other classifications of female sexual offenders include the following:

- Male Coercion;
- Teacher Lover;
- Adolescent Girls;
- Incestuous Abuse within the Family;
- Female Pedophiles – acting alone or with partners;
- Sexual Violence within Intimate Partner Relationships.

(Saradjian, 1996)

Clinical illustration 2: Aliyah

Aliyah was a 62-year-old woman with a mild learning disability, who had been convicted for sexual offences against two young girls, aged seven and five, some 20 years ago. She was referred to the forensic psychotherapy service because she herself was worried about her capacity to offend sexually, rather than because of known current offences. She was an unusual referral to the service, as a female with sexual interest in children, with a learning disability and no known offences. After an initial assessment, when I felt we made real therapeutic contact, we agreed to meet weekly for psychotherapy, which continued for two years.

As a child Aliyah had been sexually abused in a children's home. She had been diagnosed with a learning disability, although it was not clear to me that her delayed development reflected cognitive impairment, rather than the sequelae of trauma. The depths of her helplessness at the time were extreme, as she had no way to communicate to others what was happening to her. The abuser was a middle-aged teacher, a woman whom she adored and trusted. The teacher had introduced sexual touching into ordinary care, such as brushing her hair and bathing her. This made the abuse even more confusing for Aliyah, a scared little girl, who had been given up by her family at age three and taken into the children's home following a short but severe illness, a form of meningitis, that had left her with some difficulties in speech and coordination. She struggled to speak, and the few words she was reported to have before age three were hard for others to understand. She was slowly able to develop more language but had clear speech impediments. The abuse began before she could express herself verbally so she had no one she could 'tell' about what was happening when she started to feel troubled by the intimate touching, which involved mutual masturbation. She had no voice with which to speak and associated the abuse with care and affection.

She wept as she described this to me, saying how much she had trusted the teacher at first, and how she had longed for her touch when she washed and brushed her hair.

As an adult she found herself sexually attracted to pre-pubescent girls and was employed in positions where she could abuse them as she herself had been abused, confusing sexual touching and masturbation with affection. She used her role as a childminder to cultivate, groom and abuse these girls, many of whom had learning difficulties.

During the sexual activity with children she felt powerful, loved and sexually satisfied, but afterwards she would feel disgusted and ashamed, and self-harmed to expiate her guilt. She described herself as being in a constant state of torture, either filled up with sexual fantasies and urges that excited and enlivened her, or depressed and hopeless. She found it almost impossible to form intimate relationships with adults.

Through psychotherapy we gathered a picture of how sexual abuse of children accompanied these intoxicating states of mind, leading to short lived bursts of euphoria quickly followed by periods of self-loathing, guilt and shame. She also worried about discovery of her abuse and the shame this would create for her family. Although she wanted, at one level, to disclose all the facts of her offending to me, she was also scared to and so she would never reveal the names of her current victims, and would only describe past abuses of nameless children and describe current longings and opportunities. Aliyah initially struggled to trust me, but eventually allowed some intermittent emotional contact that intensified as the work continued.

Part of the work was to enable her to identify the various states of mind that preceded, accompanied and followed the abuse, and to allow her to contain her sexual impulses and modify them through her awareness of her wish not to act and the growing anticipation of the short-lived nature of the pleasure she would achieve. We established therapeutic intimacy but at times she felt persecuted by what she perceived to be my attempt to prevent her from her primary form of release from depression and sense of helplessness and inadequacy. When she became truly despairing she was suicidal and required short periods of hospital admission in order to prevent serious suicide attempts. Aliyah's capacity for internal containment of her impulses was impoverished, and one of the aims of therapy was to enable her to strengthen this through our relationship and the development of ego strengths rather relying on the safety and restriction of external constraints, like a hospital, to act as a container.

Through this psychotherapeutic work, we made some progress, to the extent that Aliyah could use me as an auxiliary superego (Strachey, 1934), as her own harsh conscience constantly scolded her, leading her to despair, and then to seek comfort. She eventually learned how to manage and reflect on her own dangerous, excited and predatory states of mind, in which children were objects to be used for her own gratification. She was then able to resist converting these fantasies into action, but still felt aroused by the presence of small children, especially girls. Despite wanting to return to work as a child minder she realised this would be risky and so she chose alternative, clerical work, where she had only adult clients. Her appearance and manner were so unthreatening that, had she chosen to, she could easily have obtained work with children. Like her trauma, her degree of risk to others was hidden. The difference that marked her out was her learning disability, but this seemed to draw attention away from invisible pain and taboo longings.

The intense transference was somewhat diluted by her reliance on a carer to bring her to the sessions, and who would often remain in the room and ensure that Aliyah understood what was being said to her. Although this was a new experience for me, I grew to understand that this carer presented an important protective figure for Aliyah who was frightened to be alone with adult women, quickly feeling that she was in a vulnerable and child-like role and could be hurt. I was aware of the intensity of my countertransference, which was at times quite hateful and fearful. Initially I was shocked that a woman who appeared so 'safe' with her maternal appearance, and the vulnerability conveyed by her cognitive impairment could act as a sexual predator to young children. She shattered my preconceptions about what a female sex abuser would look and act like, although I had already worked with other middle-aged women who had been charged with sexual offences against children. Through holding in mind her status as victim and perpetrator I could think about her inner world and feel empathic towards her. I could see Aliyah as a victim of serious abuse herself, who was frightened by her potential to perpetrate harm on others. I had to retain a neutral, non-judgemental stance, taking care not to shame or humiliate her, as she expressed strong feelings of self-loathing and suicidal wishes.

Aliyah exemplified Welldon's (2009) notion of 'dancing with death', keeping her suicidal feelings at bay through the use of her perverse and manic defence. She gradually became able to bear her sadder and more depressed states of mind without enacting her sexual wishes. She was increasingly able to tolerate her feelings of shame and guilt without discharging them onto her body through self-harm or through the abuse of children's bodies, though she continued to have urges to do so. The work of Valerie Sinason and Alan Corbett (2014) describing the value of psychotherapeutic work with offenders with learning disability was an invaluable source of help. Being able to place less primacy on the use of language, and attend more closely to the intense emotions in the room, significant features of the therapeutic relationship, including my countertransference feelings towards her allowed me to make contact with a woman with a largely hidden disability, a history of trauma and a wish to sexually abuse children. At times she was silent, but gradually became more able to use her voice and gestures to communicate the pain she felt, and the intensity of her urges to abuse. Aliyah's ability to articulate her wishes and fears seemed to increase in relation to her growing sense that she could trust me to accept her without judgement and to bear both her shame and her pain.

Female child abusers and their treatment

As discussed in Chapter 2, women who commit crimes against their own or other people's children face harsh treatment within the criminal justice system. Their vulnerability as victims and their risk as perpetrators are often seen in opposition, rather than as coexisting aspects of disturbed personalities in which aggressive impulses remain unintegrated, with explosive potential.

Deeply entrenched taboos relating to female sexual abuse of children make such abuse difficult for victims and perpetrators to acknowledge. Practitioners working with female sex offenders may feel angry, punitive or frightened when asked to work with women who harm children sexually, especially if they have acted alone, without male coercion. In order to offer effective, gender-specific therapy it is invaluable to have an understanding of the unconscious forces that lead to women enacting impulses they would rather suppress. Workers need to retain an awareness of the co-existence of victim and perpetrator in the same woman. This requires specialist training, supervision and support, alongside regular reflective practice, preferably offered by a psychotherapist.

Both the clinical illustrations in this chapter describe serious levels of harm to children, creating emotional stress for workers who empathise and identify with them. Here more than ever the practitioner must retain awareness and control of their strong countertransference feelings to work effectively with the women. Their agency and their trauma histories must both be borne in mind so that the woman is perceived accurately as both victim and perpetrator, to be understood and enabled to identify, modify and process her aggression.

In this chapter, I have suggested that the notion of a transient 'psychopathic' state of mind, in which cruelty and abuse, including sexual abuse, can flourish, is a more helpful and accurate concept for understanding female violence than is the static, stigmatising and unitary notion of 'psychopathic personality'. Where race intersects with gender, and black, Asian and other minority ethnic women express these psychopathic states of mind, perceptions of their danger-ousness increase disproportionately as conscious and unconscious biases combine, creating terror and hatred towards them (see Chapter 4).

There are cases where women have entrenched levels of disturbance and repeatedly enact traumatic experiences in which they are now the aggressor such that the term 'psychopathic' is used in relation to them. As this is a loaded term and refers to a nihilistic diagnosis I would suggest it has value more as an expression of moral reprehension than as a clinical or explanatory concept. The idea of the 'female psychopath' gathers greatest momentum in the popular press, where the notion of 'pure evil' and a 'femme fatale' generates excitement; the female psychopath is thought to use her sexual wiles to lure men to an untimely death, often involving sadism. This harks back to the notion of the sirens, calling men to their destruction, and retains a strong hold on the popular imagination, locating woman's power in the misuse of her sexuality, her capacity to deceive and her attraction to destruction.

References

Bateman, A. & Fonagy, P. (2004) *Psychotherapy for borderline personality disorder: Mentalization based treatment*. Oxford: Oxford University Press.

Cleckley, H. (1941) *The mask of sanity: An attempt to reinterpret the so-called psychopathic personality*. Missouri, MO: Mosby Press.

Cleckley, H. (1976) *The mask of sanity*. St. Louis, MO: Mosby.

Cooke D. J. & Michie, C. (2001) Refining the construct of psychopathy: Towards a hierarchical model. *Psychological Assessment, 13*, 171–188.

Cooke, D. J., Hart, S. D., Logan, C., & Michie, C. (2012) Explicating the construct of psychopathy: Development and validation of a conceptual model, the Comprehensive Assessment of Psychopathic Personality (CAPP). *International Journal of Forensic Mental Health, 11*(4), 242–252.

Corbett, A. (2014) *Disabling perversions: Forensic psychotherapy with people with intellectual disabilities* (The Forensic Psychotherapy Monograph Series). London: Karnac.

Cortoni, F., & Hanson, R. K. (2005) A review of the recidivism rates of adult female sexual offenders (Research Rep. No. R-169). Ottawa, Ontario, Canada: Correctional Service Canada. Retrieved from www.csc-scc.gc.ca/text/rsrch/reports/r169/r169_e.pdf.

Cortoni, F., Hanson, R. K., & Coache, M. E. (2009) Les délinquantes sexuelles: Préva-lence et récidive [Female sexual offenders: Prevalence and recidivism]. *Revue inter-nationale de criminologie et de police technique et scientifique*, LXII, 319–336.

Freud, A. (1936) *The ego and the mechanisms of defence*. New York, NY: International Universities Press, 1966.

Gannon, T. A., Rose, M. R., & Ward, T. (2008) A descriptive model of the offense pro-cess for female sexual offenders. *Sexual Abuse*: *A Journal of Research and Treatment*, *20*, 352–374.

Getu, L. (2018) An exploration of complexities of therapeutic work with female-to-female child sexual abuse (unpublished PhD thesis).

Hare, R. D. (1980) A research scale for the assessment of psychopathy in criminal populations. *Personality and Individual Differences, 1*, 111–119.

Hare, R. D. (2003) *Hare psychopathy checklist—Revised (PCL-R)* (2nd ed.). Toronto, ON: Multi-Health System.

Kreis, M. K. F. & Cooke, D. J. (2012) The manifestation of psychopathic traits in women: An exploration using case examples. *International Journal of Forensic Mental Health*, *11*, 267–279.

Kreis, M. K. F. (2009) *Psychopathy in women: A multi-method exploration of the con-struct using the Comprehensive Assessment of Psychopathic Personality (CAPP)* (Unpublished doctoral thesis, Glasgow Caledonian University, Glasgow, Scotland). Available from the British Library EthOS (uk.bl.ethos No. 517968).

Kreis, M. K. F., & Cooke, D. J. (2011) Capturing the psychopathic female: A prototypicality analysis of the Comprehensive Assessment of Psychopathic Personal-ity (CAPP) across gender. *Behavioral Sciences and the Law*, *29*, 634–648.

Logan, C. (2011) La Femme Fatale: The female psychopath in fiction and clinical practice. *Mental Health Review Journal*, *16*, 118–127. doi: 10.1108/13619321111178078.

McKeown, A. (2010). Female offenders: Assessment of risk in forensic settings. *Aggres-sion and Violent Behaviour*, *15*(6), 422–429. doi:10.1016/j.avb.2010.07.004.

Saradjian, J. (2010) 'Understanding the prevalence of female-perpetrated sexual abuse and the impact of that abuse on victims. In T. A. Gannon & F. Cortoni (Eds.), *Female sexual offenders: Theory, assessment and treatment* (pp. 9–30), edited by T. A. Gannon and F. Cortoni. London: John Wiley & Sons Ltd.

Sprague, J. Javdani, S. Sadeh, N. Newman, J. P. & Verona, E. (2012) Borderline personal-ity disorder as a female phenotypic expression of psychopathy? *Personal Disorder*, *3*(2): 127–139. doi: 10.1037/a0024134.

Strachey, J. (1934) The nature of the therapeutic action of psychoanalysis. *International Journal of Psychoanalysis*, *15*, 127–159.

Welldon, E. V. (1988) *Mother Madonna whore: The idealisation and denigration of motherhood*. London: Free Association Books.

Welldon, E. V. (2009) Dancing with death. *British Journal of Psychotherapy*, *25*(2, May 2009), 149–182.

Chapter 8

Extreme violence and female terrorism

Restricted status and indeterminate sentences for public protection

Anna Motz

> Come, you spirits
> That tend on mortal thoughts, unsex me here,
> And fill me from the crown to the toe topful
> Of direst cruelty!
>
> (Macbeth, Act 1, scene 5, 38–43)

Women traditionally commit crimes within the private, domestic realm, harming intimate partners or family members. When they commit acts of violence in the public realm they are considered highly dangerous, if not overtly psychopathic, more like men than women. Like Lady Macbeth, they have been 'unsexed' in the eyes of society.

The rise of female violence in the public realm over recent years is marked, both in the form of adolescent girl gangs and more dramatically through the growing involvement of women in acts of terrorism, particularly in the form of suicide bombing. In this chapter I describe public acts of violence by women and explore how the drive for revenge, and an intoxicating state of mind, combine to enable such acts.

Women who enact extreme violence are often classified as psychopathic, leading to their incarceration for lengthy periods of time, having received a sentence of imprisonment for public protection (IPP) and then placed under the category of restricted status prisoner. An IPP sentence is an indeterminate sentence that was given to men and women convicted for serious offences in the United Kingdom, including murder. Although sentencing to IPPs was abolished in 2012, they still applied to 340 women in 2018. That is, they were not removed for existing IPP prisoners, despite the decision that such sentences were no longer permissible.

In this chapter I discuss the origins and treatment of some of these high risk crimes of murder and terrorism, and explore the significance of being designated either an IPP or a 'restricted status' prisoner, describing how this can create interminable sentences for women, who have few ways to demonstrate that the risk they pose to others has been diminished. The higher profile the crime, the more difficult it becomes for the woman to be released from custody because of the likelihood of a major public backlash and ongoing harassment of her, long after her original sentence has been served. Smart (2019) offers the first qualitative research study of the lived experience of women serving IPP sentences after their abolition and reveals the extent of their hopelessness and despair, as they feel unable to work towards any kind of ending of their sentence and resign themselves to a sense of injustice and futility.

I suggest that there is particular vilification of women who commit certain acts of violence and who have not only broken the law but have contravened precious and deeply held societal beliefs about femininity and motherhood; they are viewed as dangerous morally as well as physically and must be kept in exile.

I outline a model for understanding acts of violence by women within particular social and cultural contexts rather than simply as manifestations of individual psychic imbalance. This chapter further questions the construct of psychopathic personality disorder and its application to women, especially those from an ethnic minority background where issues of difference and unconscious racism can play a significant role in contributing to assessments of 'dangerousness'. (See Chapter 7.) I argue for the need to understand the traumatic roots of the woman's violence in order to develop a psychological formulation that evaluates risk and identifies treatment.

The plight of IPP and restricted status women

These women are often held in custody under 'restricted status'; this designation indicates their dangerousness, and severely impairs their rehabilitative progress through the system, generating hopelessness and despair in the women and the workforce alike. Women considered highly dangerous are at risk of being detained for years over their tariff with limited prospects for being able to lead a prosocial life and manage the challenges of freedom. Like the women on IPP, they experience an overwhelming sense of hopelessness.

Women are classified as belonging in three separate categories of prisons, differently from men:

- Restricted status, the equivalent to Category A male prisoners;
- Closed conditions;
- Open conditions.

I consider it significant that the terms denoting the women's status reflects the buildings in which they are housed, rather than specifying any characteristic of the women themselves. The language used to refer to female prisoners is one of buildings rather than minds, referring to the body of the institutions that enclose these women, unconsciously mirroring the language of slavery. The 'female estate' refers to the prisons in which the women are placed, as though the buildings are themselves gendered. This may reflect the reclassification of women (and men) who are incarcerated as objects, bodies, to be housed, rather than minds to be understood and thought about. Some of the terms appear also to be euphemisms designed to avoid the use of the word 'prison', like 'estate' and 'establishment'. After HMP Holloway closed down, the women were not moved and redistributed, like things, they were 'decanted' into other prisons, like a fine wine, poured into an elegant vessel, in order to improve its taste. This term creates the image of careful and deliberate redistribution of a substance, with the aim of improving its taste, and thus conceals the brutality of transferring human beings between premises without their consultation or consent. They are simply done to.

When women spend too long in prison, years above their tariff, often due in part to their placement on now abolished sentences, they are 'up tariffed', again as though they are commodities who have been priced too highly. The images that underlie these words are important as they reveal the objectification of women in prison serving as defences against emotional contact with their humanity and suffering. (See Chapter 11 for a further discussion of institutional defences.)

The reasons for being classified as 'restricted status' are varied, but the designation refers to 'any female, young person or young adult prisoner convicted or on remand whose escape would present a serious risk to the public and who are required to be held in designated secure accommodation' (Grimwood, 2015: 9). This categorisation only applies to women and young persons, but is equivalent to being a 'Category A' prisoner, namely a prisoner (male) who meets the criteria for being housed in the highest level of security.

An unpublished report conducted by Aiyegbusi (2016) and the third sector organisation, Women in Prison, describes the small subgroup of women with complex needs, within prison, who present particular challenges to the staff and, in turn, can become further entrenched within the system that they are rebelling against. Women with complex needs can be further stigmatised, identified as high risk because of their distressed and distressing behaviour, which then, being designated 'restricted status', further reduces their chances of progressing out of the system. This is a catch-22: women who are restricted status need to demonstrate reduced risk through engaging in accredited treatment programmes but often don't have access to these programmes because their restricted status confines them to prisons that do not offer them. It is difficult to maintain hope in this situation. Aiyegbusi describes this vicious cycle:

> It would appear that this group of women become emotionally overwhelmed by imprisonment. They experience a dramatic and severe form of regression in reaction to the disempowerment that is implicit in the process of incarceration, giving up personal responsibility and locus of behavioural controls to the prison staff, regime and environment. Paradoxically the women are experienced as railing against care, help, rules and authority in attacking,

self-destructive and self-sabotaging ways ... They are typically regarded as 'stuck', often detained long after the end of their individual tariffs, seemingly unable to progress through their sentencing pathways. Because of the immediate and high risks presented to themselves and/or other people, women with complex needs are usually cared for in long-term segregation units and may have restricted status.

(Aiyegbusi, 2016)

For some women, like Enya, in the clinical illustration presented below, having restricted status, while limiting, nonetheless accords a sense of identity that is hard to give up; being seen as dangerous masks her underlying sense of powerlessness, helplessness and invisibility.

Incarceration may seem the only form of safety and the thought of leaving terrifying. This is colloquially known as 'gate fever' and can be a time of great anxiety for women about to be released, who fear that they will be dropped into a void. To get back to safety a woman may engage in apparently 'self-sabotaging behaviour' with the unconscious aim of ruining her chances of moving on. This 'sabotage' is actually a means of protection and communication of fear. It is essential for workers within and outside the prison to hear, and respond to, this communication, without relinquishing hope; this can enable women held on restricted status, for lengthy custodial sentences, to work towards a freedom they can bear. One of the dangers of a criminal justice system that imposes custodial sentences on women, often with non-violent offences, is that the route back into society becomes blocked as the women themselves become reliant on external containment and lose ties in the community.

Enya: 'Guilt that turned my heart black'

Enya is a 39-year-old woman serving a life sentence for an offence of murder that took place when she was 13 years old. She is serving her sentence on an Indefinite Public Protection Order; she was designated 'restricted status' within a high secure prison. Two older, white males were also involved in the murder. The victim was in her early 20s. Despite the absence of forensic evidence Enya was convicted on the basis of her confession, though experts later ruled that this was a false confession by a vulnerable and suggestible suspect. Enya later disclosed that the men she was with committed both the murder and the sexual mutilation of the victim's body, including her genitals. She denied that her part in the offence was sexually motivated in any way.

Enya is a black woman, who was born in the Caribbean. I would come to the conclusion that the colour of her skin, the brutality of her past, her convictions and 'unfeminine' manner all contributed to perceptions of her dangerousness and potential psychopathy.

I met with Enya to prepare a report for the parole board, considering her suitability for either release into the community, following a period of time in an open prison, or for continued detention. Even before seeing her I learned of her reputation and how the prospect of her release from prison created a high level of fear. Although she had shown no violence for over 14 years, a forensic psychological evaluation when she was first transferred to prison from psychiatric hospital described her as 'a high risk psychopath', resulting in her reassignment to the category of restricted status.

This had engendered a sense of hopelessness in her, and limited her options for rehabilitation. The prison therapy team and her personal officers expressed positive feelings about her, seeing her progress since entering the prison a year ago, but were concerned that she had by now stayed within institutions for so long that life outside bars would soon be inconceivable to her. They were anxious to discover whether progression would be possible, and if she could move to a less restrictive prison where she could undertake the accredited therapeutic programmes that would lift her restricted status. This itself presented something of a catch-22 as those prisons where the programmes could be undertaken did not necessarily take a restricted status prisoner.

Although initially apprehensive about meeting me, Enya soon relaxed and described both her present situation and the terrible events that led to her incarceration, including her chaotic upbringing and her offences. She was a strong looking woman, with a direct gaze, conveying both a sense of warmth and child-like confusion at points. She wore a tee shirt revealing a deep labyrinth of scars covering both arms. She told me she had scars covering her legs, breasts and torso, and that for years, self-harm had been her primary source of comfort and release, but that since the first few months in prison it happened only 'once in a blue moon'.

The offences

Enya had been convicted for the murder of a woman in her early 20s, three years after it was committed, based on her self-report. At the time that she 'confessed' to the crime she was in a secure adolescent unit, serving a sentence for grievous bodily harm. She had assaulted another girl at school who had blamed her for starting a fire. The day after the fire she had discovered that this girl, Sophie, had said 'The black girl did it,' although she knew it was, in fact, started by someone else, a white girl. Sophie reminded Enya of a maths teacher, with whom she was infatuated, and who had excluded her from class. This maths teacher was an older woman to whom Enya had been close, but the headmaster was concerned she was becoming 'fixated' on her teacher. On the day of the offence Enya had come into school, learned she was being blamed for the arson and became distraught. She met Sophie coming into the girls' lavatories, and recalled seeing in her eyes 'the same look' that the maths teacher had in hers. She perceived this as a look of fear, noting that her blue eyes were beautiful and seemed to see straight through her. This triggered rage, longing and a profound sense of injustice. As Sophie moved away from her, turning her back, Enya stabbed her in the arm and ribs, using the knife she always carried for protection, ran away and hid. She admitted the assault when found outside the school, shaking and crying.

Enya was subsequently sentenced and sent to a secure adolescent unit for treatment of her mental health issues including anger, impulsivity and depression. There she formed a close relationship with a young female nursing student. When the student was due to move to another placement, Enya, now 15, disclosed that she had something to tell her, and revealed her part in the murder, two years prior to the grievous bodily harm. Later that year she was tried and found guilty, on the basis of her confession, although the older men whom she claimed were present and who had dealt the fatal wounding were never identified nor charged. Enya felt unable to reveal their identities.

She described the murder as unplanned, recalling how she and the men were driving around in the early morning. One of these men was her 'illegal boyfriend', as she was a child and he was an older man who had sex with her. He had known the victim, a young woman whom they encountered on a lonely country road after she had left a party. Being in a car at 3 a.m. was normal for her as her mother didn't care where she was as long as 'she was somewhere and couldn't be seen'. Enya knew that if she were seen it would make her mother look bad, saying 'I knew how to make myself invisible.'

They had been smoking cannabis and drinking before approaching the victim, who was clearly upset and who had been arguing with the man who knew her, who was threatening her with aggression. She was dragged into the car and then held hostage, leading to violent sex. Enya was horrified by this and had not expected to be a witness to a rape. She heard the victim screaming and described how she sounded like

> a wounded animal … it broke my heart, it split my heart, that is what made my heart go black, I could hear it – I could hear them doing it … The wounds went all the way through her, and I had to cut her a little bit so that I would be their accomplice.

Enya expressed her sense of dissociation and despair, recalling her fear and anger that night and the horror of what she imagined the victim had suffered. Although she and the other perpetrators had taken a vow of silence, she found the guilt too much to bear and eventually told a trusted nurse at the adolescent unit about her part in it, the murder in her town. She described how the details of the event made her feel crazy, and how she had tried, unsuccessfully, to erase memories of the rape and murder; she described this as 'the black bit trying to edge itself out of my mind'.

Background

Enya was born in the Caribbean where she spent her first five years, along with her older brother, Dion. She was brought up by her grandmother as her father and mother separated, after both left to live abroad. Enya never knew her father. Her mother had left when Enya was ten months old and moved to France. She married a naval officer, eventually returning to collect her children and bring them to England, to live with her and her new husband. After a settled few years with her grandmother Enya now experienced sustained brutality by her mentally ill mother, including sexualised punishments, neglect and cruelty.

She met her mother again when she was almost five years old. She was kind at first, but never 'tactile' with her. She had a memory of her mother making her and her siblings hot chocolate before bed but did not recollect ever being cuddled by her, describing her first experience of cuddles as coming from her foster carer when she was aged seven.

Enya has a vivid memory of the birth of her sister, Chloe, and of her mother suddenly being absent, without explanation. She described being confused and

> wondering where mum was, then that night, he got us together with my little brother, who was a year old, and we went to hospital, and we walked down the corridor, and there was this tiny little baby, and she was light skinned, sleeping and the softest, prettiest thing I had ever seen … I loved it, thought it was the most amazing thing ever … There were all good things in the beginning, before I was five.

Her mother's fragile mental health deteriorated further after Chloe's birth and she frequently beat the older children, especially Enya. Her mother was also light skinned, in contrast to Enya's darker skin, and this may have played a part in how Enya feels about herself and her mother's particular brutality towards her, the 'blackest' child.

The family lived on a naval base where Chloe and another sister, Liat, were born. However, when Enya was six Social Services received a referral from the lieutenant, reporting that Enya's stepfather had instigated divorce proceedings and stated that his wife was physically abusing the children and incapable of caring for them. Enya and Dion had witnessed serious domestic violence at home and saw her mother throw boiling fat at her stepfather when he announced he was leaving. She received a suspended prison sentence for this assault. They were taken into care, but then returned to their mother. Within weeks her mother was subsequently readmitted to hospital with psychotic symptoms and depression, and all four of the children were returned to local authority care. As before, they were subsequently returned to their mother's care when she was discharged from hospital. This pattern of disruption and chaos was to characterise Enya's life.

Enya described other traumatic events, including experiences of moving country, being racially abused at school for being the only black child there, and being wholly unprotected from her mother's abuse. At points it was difficult to follow her narrative, as it detailed a series of chaotic changes of environment, with her mother's multiple partners introduced to the family, and included episodes where her mother behaved violently. This style of speaking reflected the incoherence and disruption of her early life and was hard for us both to make sense of.

Maternal abuse

Enya disclosed the unpredictable, harsh and profoundly disturbed treatment she received at the hands of her mother, including sexualised punishments. She recalled how once she was home later than her mother expected her to be and her mother 'went mad' accusing her of having had sex with boys. She recalled, 'Mum grabbed me and shouted in my face, screaming at me, "I know what you have been doing." I was shocked, and she pulled me into the bedroom and took off my knickers and clothes, saying, "I will teach you for doing that, you little whore."' Her mother had stinging nettles in the garden, and had used them to punish her, rubbing them between her legs, and then in her nose. This bizarre punishment was painful and distressing but she was 'more scared of her anger than of the burning'. Her mother gave 'punishments that had to do with my sexual parts, on my vagina and she used to accuse me of having sex, with people I didn't know. I became scared of my mum and scared of turning into a big woman, I didn't want to turn into her'. She described the odd feelings she had during her mother's unusual and sexualised punishments, and how this led to confusion and guilt in relation to sex.

The perversion, brutality and humiliation of the punishments was evident in Enya's descriptions and she felt she deserved such treatment, reacting by finding an older group of friends, including sexually exploitative males.

When she was 12, the local authority placed Enya with foster parents, as her mother found it difficult to manage her behaviour, only to be returned to live with her mother later that year. Social Services noted concerns about her mother's increasing inability to manage her behaviour, again removing her to foster care, only to return her shortly thereafter. Enya described leading a wild and unsupervised lifestyle at the time of the index offences, in which she could take friends back to her mother's house and stay up drinking and smoking until the early hours, while her mother was with her new husband at his house. At times Enya was also tasked with the care of her younger siblings and accorded an unrealistic and age-inappropriate degree of responsibility. She carried a knife habitually at this point for her own protection.

Enya now understood that her mother had suffered from severe mental health difficulties, which she believed were a form of paranoia and manic depression. When describing her troubled relationship with her mother, in which she was particularly singled out for punishment, Enya appeared sad and reflective, saying 'I could never understand why my mum hated me. She struggles to love me, ever since I can remember. My beatings, mum could beat me for no reason, she beats the hell out of you, she doesn't hit you slap you.' She would take the punishment for her younger siblings and said 'By the time I was seven or eight I learned not to upset her. I took the punishment for them.' She described being removed to foster care at 11, then at 14, saying that she liked being in care and was happy there. 'Auntie [her foster carer] is like my mum – she never hurt me, seeing what mum did to me.' Enya remembered how her mother would tell her she loved her after beating her, adding to her confusion.

Her childhood and adolescence were characterised by unusual levels of neglect, disruption and exposure to domestic violence and sadistic physical, emotional and sexual abuse, at the hands of the woman she most needed to protect her. Although she had some positive experiences with foster carers, two of whom visit her regularly in prison, her frequent and disastrous return to her mother's 'care' prevented her from achieving a level of stability and consistency in a non-abusive foster placement. Her mother had neither wanted her, nor been able to let her go.

It seems that these intermittent experiences of good foster care gave Enya an experience of attachment figures who offered stable, reliable and protective care, for brief periods of time, before her mother 'reclaimed' her, only to retraumatise her. Enya's repeated removals from a place of safety, back to a situation of abuse and neglect, created profound insecurity and a sense of punishment and rejection. She still craved the reliability, containment and predictability of a restrictive environment that 'wants' and protects her, keeping her *inside* rather than pushing her *outside*, back into the wilderness. This exile was the motif of her early life.

Attacks on the core self: sexual and racial abuse

Enya's experience of disrupted care, multiple episodes of sexual and physical abuse and chronic neglect appear to have contributed to her having sexual intercourse from age 11.

Enya's early life included frequent changes of caregiver, sexualised punishments, brutal physical treatment, movement between locations, sexual abuse by authority figures she trusted, including a pastor in her mother's church when she was eight and a foster sister when she was ten. Though all of these were traumatic, the most significant was her experience of being hated, scapegoated and tormented by her mentally ill mother, who would often tell her she loved her after a beating. Her trust in others, and awareness of sexual boundaries, was deeply disturbed, and her violence often took place in the context of unrequited feelings towards significant women. Her desire for them felt disgusting and wrong; at times she attacked the women in order to obliterate the source of such feelings, and subsequently attacked herself, in penitence and despair.

Racial abuse has played an important part in the development of Enya's identity and she described herself as having a 'black heart'. Her treatment within prison and hospital suggest she was seen as highly dangerous and unpredictable compared to other women. This may be a manifestation of the 'racist gaze' that focusses on her dark skin. Indeed, she assaulted Sophie in response to the 'look' she gave her, through beautiful blue eyes, that saw through her, rendering her both invisible (in her humanity) and yet visible as a monster, the girl falsely accused of starting a fire. This seems the epitome of the racist gaze. (See Chapter 4 for fuller discussion.)

Despite her actual violence against another student when she was 15, the earlier crime of which she was convicted has never been proven by forensic evidence, and she has consistently retracted her confession. The fact that her victim suffered injuries not thought possible for a girl some ten years younger than her to inflict, and the reported presence of males who took the main role in the killing, have largely been ignored; Enya has so neatly fitted into the 'face of evil' stereotype. That she is now some 12 years over tariff can be seen as further indication of racial bias, conscious and unconscious, that she has faced all her life.

Internalised racism

Enya's descriptions of events and feelings reveal her association of blackness with badness,
danger and poison. Guilt 'turned her heart black', and the traumatic constellation of memories of the murder became 'the black bit' lodged in her mind. Unlike Enya, the victim was white, as were her male co-defendants. Enya's own blackness, and the dark feelings of fear, hatred and excitement towards the victim and herself, appear to have become symbolic of danger, wrongness, exile and sin. Her mother's beatings of her, a darker skinned daughter, may also express a form of internalised racism, difficult for either mother or daughter to acknowledge or articulate. She sees herself as embodying these forces, and 'takes the rap' for the actions of the white perpetrators.

As Frantz Fanon describes, so starkly and powerfully in *Black Faces, White Masks*, whiteness becomes the signifier of goodness and purity: 'I am white; in other words, I embody beauty and virtue, which have never been black. I am the color of day' (2019: 27).

It would appear that Enya was unquestioningly accepted as the natural killer, despite her youth, the absence of evidence and her own suggestibility. The 'black girl' became known as the evil one, as if this absolved the white men for their violence, assuaging the fear that society feels about the possibility of an unsolved murder, a criminal still 'on the loose' instead of caged.

The most pernicious, invisible aspect of this process is that Enya herself endorsed this view, identifying with the projections of others that she was bad, dangerous and 'evil'. This phenomenon is well described in Chapters 3 and 4 and by Davids (2011), in his psychoanalytic account of racist projections that become internalised by those who receive them. Both she and wider society unconsciously identified her 'blackness' with animalistic brutality and cruelty.

The danger of desire

In the past, Enya assaulted two women whom she desired, as if by obliterating the objects of desire she could extinguish her own unacceptable urges. This has now changed; as her attractions to women no longer generate unbearable feelings of pain, shame and disgust, she is increasingly able to tolerate them and to recognise them as her own wishes for closeness and care. Despite her mother's brutal treatment and neglect throughout Enya's childhood she maintained that she was a Christian and would not tolerate homosexuality, contributing to her confusion and self-loathing at points when Enya felt attracted to women. This featured in her risk assessment as the clinicians who had previously evaluated her, and determined her to be psychopathic, focussed on the link between violent and sexual feelings, considering her to be aroused by inflicting pain. Enya denied this, and I took her to be confused about her desire; she had wanted, at times, to obliterate its source, and in adolescence had assaulted two women she 'loved' who did not reciprocate this love. She was at greater risk of self-harming, in vicious attacks, at points of perceived abandonment, but this too had subsided in intensity and frequency.

Since her incarceration she has begun to accept her sexual feelings and longings to be close to women; she no longer feels she has to threaten women who are the objects of her desire. She has also ceased to make threats to hurt or kill and found other ways of expressing rage, now realising that any expression of feeling will be taken as a plan of action, a concrete equation. Enya cannot afford to speak figuratively as her violent history colours the interpretation of her expression of anger, desire or fear. This has contributed to a perception that she has made concrete plans to hurt or kill when in fact she may be expressing a feeling that will pass. This is a loss of liberty in the freedom of expression that is rarely imagined when sentencing takes place.

Enya's traumatic early experiences of disruptions of care, neglect and brutality at the hands of her mother has left her with an impaired sense of her own mind and a severe attachment disorder. Her experience of sexualised punishments by her mother, followed by protestations of love, occasional affection and apologies, created profound confusion in relation to Enya's sexual feelings and anger.

Need for external containment in place of internal security

For much of her life Enya sought external containment as she has had little confidence in her own capacity to manage strong feelings, given her repeated experiences of sexual, physical and emotional abuse in early life, such that she has been unable to develop a sense that strong feelings can be borne without resulting in actual violence or sexual brutality. Her own helplessness in the face of what appears to be her mother's unpredictability and cruelty left her with a heightened sensitivity to any changes in the mood or behaviour of those on whom she depends, and she transfers her feelings of infantile dependency onto them.

Exile

Enya's story is one of her exile, from earliest life to the ranks of the untouchables, a pariah who is exiled from ordinary society. Her exiled status marks her out as fit for brutality, abuse and abandonment and, in the end, she finds her home behind bars, and an identity carved out of her 'restricted status'. The cage has become her sanctuary, and both she and those she encounters struggle to see her as 'fit for release'. In the face of this internalised demonisation she becomes as others see her, and is terrified of release. At the point of near-release she has, in the past, retreated into violence, either towards herself or others.

The containment and psychoanalytic understanding of the specialist unit in the prison has enabled Enya to reintegrate previously unacceptable and dis-avowed parts of herself, to speak about things she has hidden and to accept aspects of her sexuality and aggressive feelings. She has used both the psycho-therapeutic sessions and the supportive sessions offered by her offender man-ager to link her thoughts and feelings, establish boundaries in herself and in her behaviour, and to manage her intense wishes to harm herself and others.

When I last met with her, after four intensive consultation and assessment sessions, Enya was finally able to imagine herself in other possible lives, and had developed a richer sense of herself. Her capacity to explore her own strengths grew significantly inside this secure environment; within this highly restricted institution, she finally accepted one aspect of her 'wildness', her sexuality, and had come to view herself as capable of love and of being loved. Enya's 'black' heart had opened up; she recognises that she can refuse to accept other people's projections into her of danger, toxicity and madness.

From victim to perpetrator

The offence of murder was one in which Enya participated, experiencing horror, fear and excitement. This could be understood as her identification with the aggressor, in that she could inhabit the role of the powerful oppressor, rather than being the humiliated and helpless victim, as she had been so often earlier in life. Her feelings of attraction to women might have been activated during this brutal scene of rape, alongside her fear, but she did not kill the victim. Enya acknowledged that she did inflict an injury on her, in an intimate place, signifying allegiance with the killers. She disavowed her own aggression, locating it in the men but then took the blame for the crime, and though she described the 'guilt turning my heart black', it is my belief that this guilt pre-dated the murder, that her 'black heart' and unconscious sense of guilt stemmed from her early trauma, and her participation in this act of murder reflected this guilt and her wish to expiate it. The early trauma, and pervasive sense of guilt, is the starting place for treatment and this was finally recognised in the specialist service for women with complex needs where she was contained through stable relationships with an offender manager, a psychologist and a forensic psychotherapist, as well as taking part in trauma informed groups.

At her last parole board hearing, on the basis of reports of those involved in her care within the prison, including mine, Enya was granted the freedom to move onto a less restrictive environment, where she could be able to develop her sense of herself as an ordinary woman, rather than a demonic one, and eventually to live beyond the prison gates. Whether or not she can do so will depend in part on her developing capacity to resist the projections she attracts, and also on the resources of a trauma informed environment, where her complex needs can be thought about and her violent past understood. This will require a high level of supervision, training and reflective space for staff who work with her and their ability to bear witness to the horror she has both perpetrated and suffered.

Female terrorism: women and jihad

One of the most dramatic expressions of female violence can be found in terrorism, as here the violence generally confined to the domestic realm, targeting intimates, is directed against members of the general public, and can involve the death of the woman herself in the case of suicide bombing.

The rise of female terrorism, including suicide bombing, reveals how women's violence, traditionally confined to the private realm, can also manifest in the public domain in the service of extremism. Historically, women have been a statistically low risk to members of the public or strangers. Their primary victims, when they were violent, far less frequently than men, were their children, their intimate partners and their own bodies – in extreme acts of self-harm.

It was reported in 2017 that ISIS had deployed 38 women to carry out suicide operations in that year, as part of the attempt to hold onto Mosul in Iraq. This was one of the largest cases of women acting as suicide bombers in recent history and revealed the changing roles of females within ISIS, not simply acting as supports to male terrorists, but being enlisted as front line operatives (Moore, 2017).

A deep fear of the other, as embodied in Muslims, the dark-skinned 'foreigner', combined with the unthinking dismissal of women, particularly Muslim women, as oppressed, passive and weak, creates a form of collective blindness in relation to female jihadis. This has been exploited by terrorist organisations, playing on these common expectations and misconceptions of Muslim women. This is crudely portrayed in the 2018 television series, *The Bodyguard*. When convicted these women are likely to receive the classification of restricted status and to be detained for extensive periods of time. Davids (2011) describes the rise of Islamophobia since the 9/11 attacks, using a psychoanalytic lens to view the activation of an inner racist in the face of fear and uncertainty.

A recent report entitled *Muslim Women in Prison* identified the specific challenges faced by many Muslim women, even those with non-violent offences, including isolation and marginalisation within both custody and their own community, and the absence of specialist support. Additionally, their dislocation from their communities makes it harder to access housing or their children on release, as well as difficulties in relation to immigration status (Buncy & Ahmed, 2014).

Denial of female violence and sensationalist reportage of female terrorists

Coverage of these acts often reveals excitement about the fact that these perpetrators of terror are women, as the juxtaposition of womanhood and extreme violence appears particularly shocking, sensational and horrifying.

Since 2000, women have been known to take part in jihads. They have been involved in terrorism since the Second Intifada in Israel and are key players in Boko Haram's reign of terror in Nigeria. Scholars have detected a more nuanced and complex pattern of motivations by females who choose to become suicide bombers, than in the men who do so. Furthermore, the role of shame and stigma in contributing to the women's decisions to join terrorist organisations plays a particular part in the lives of women who become suicide bombers.

The recent case of the 'first all-female terror attack' planned on Westminster in April 2017 configured the women as acting without male involvement, and reports the fact of their gender status in a sensationalistic but somewhat trivialising manner, as if describing a 'girl band', with evident excitement and titillation (*The Independent*, 2017).

Terrorism and psychopathic states of mind

The notion of psychopathic states of mind, described in Chapter 7, is relevant to understanding how acts of such violence can be perpetrated. In this state of great excitement and release, extreme action is possible, with no thought or concern for destructive consequences like pain or injury. The impetus to act is fuelled by religious and political conviction and ideological righteousness, the certainty that violence fulfils a divine commandment and the belief that the victims deserve to die.

This movement from ordinary compassion and fear to psychopathic states of mind and absolute conviction/commitment to violence is a lethal one. The psychopathic state of mind is transient but enables extreme action, remorselessness, sadism and cruelty, even in a personality that is not fundamentally disturbed. Many women who engage in terrorism are not brainwashed by men, nor hapless victims, necessarily, but equally are not character disturbed psychopaths – they are angry, traumatised and ready to kill for what they believe in, expressing the deepest level of hatred against societies that have often rejected, humiliated or offended them or their families. This rage has been crystallised around an ideology of purification through killing, with the promise of an idyllic afterlife and the destruction of the infidels.

The use of violence as a defence against shame often plays a crucial role in the development of terrorism. The case of women who are shamed and oppressed within a racist society is graphically illustrated in radicalised women, who become jihadists. The motivations of female terrorists reflect their experiences of marginalisation, persecution, vulnerability and suggestibility, alongside choices to commit violence, indicative of moral agency. Women's shame has interpersonal roots both in their earliest relationships where they felt unwanted, unworthy, bad and stupid, and in encounters with wider society, for example in the shame caused by poverty, racism and unemployment. One reaction to shame is to enact violence, designed to wreak revenge and to empower an actor who has felt humiliated and hurt.

Violent acts defend against underlying depression both in the perpetrators and those who encounter them. Offenders find that violent action can temporarily lead to exhilarating feelings of conquest and relief, but then fade, leaving them feeling guilty and desperate; so too can those who work with them prefer the intoxicating feelings of anger or excitement to the dreary states of mind that follow. If the reality that is left behind is oppressive, painful and unwelcome then entering another world is fantastic relief.

One of the most 'exciting' and dangerously intoxicating states of mind can be found in the suicidal and homicidal fantasies and actions of terrorism. In such situations all barriers to action are removed and the usual inhibitions wedding a woman to life rather than death are rendered impotent. Here too there is a reciprocal relationship between the violent perpetrator, who enacts a dramatic act of homicide/suicide, and the spectators who watch in excited terror.

Terrorism and motherhood

We know that women are not supposed to blow themselves up; they are expected to stay at home and give birth. Women entering into the realm of terrorism shatters this revered notion of femininity.

I view the particular horror reserved for female terrorism as a dramatic illustration of the idealisation and denigration of womanhood, and motherhood in particular. The myth of women as naturally gentle and passive is shattered, literally and metaphorically, by the recent rise of female suicide bombers, who kill themselves, others and sometimes their own children. I suggest that the idealisation of women has rendered it almost impossible to conceive of them as capable of serious acts of political violence and that they are often seen as passive victims, groomed into taking part in these suicide bombings.

There is evidence that women who are recruited into these roles are those who have already shamed their families, through behaviour that has dishonoured their good name; acts of suicidal terrorism committed in the context of this shame are envisaged as one means of redemption for the woman herself and her family. The romantic images of the afterlife that tempt people into this deathly act can sometimes include the notion that one's soul flies into the heart of a green bird. It is urgent to recognise that women can and do enact destructive impulses, and this may be especially true in particular circumstances, including states of unbearable rage and isolation, faced with a vulnerable creature in their care, or when recruited in the service of a 'noble' or 'just' divinity and cause, requiring the ultimate sacrifice of the woman's own life alongside her murder of others.

The media portrayal reflects the ongoing resistance to acknowledging female violence, and female agency, as it conveys the sense of shock that a mother could commit this act of atrocity. Women convicted of terrorist offences are treated as high risk within the criminal justice system in the United Kingdom. They may be perceived as intrinsically highly dangerous to work with, or viewed as the helpless victims of male coercion. Staff may struggle to understand the political, psychological and personal motivations that drive forward such behaviour and women convicted of these crimes will generally be deemed restricted status prisoners, to be closely monitored and supervised with little chance of release within their tariff. The sensationalist press they attract is a further obstacle to their timely release. There may be strenuous attempts to deradicalise them, or to situate their violence in terms of mental illness rather than as a form of protest and expression of alienation, leading not to psychopathy but to the enactment of a psychopathic state of mind.

References

Aiyegbusi, A. (2016) Unpublished Report for Women in Prison on IPP Prisoners, Women in Prison and Psychological Approaches CIC.

Buncy, S. and Ahmed, I. (2014) *Muslim Women in Prison. Second Chance Fresh Horizons: A study into the needs and experiences of Muslim women at HMP & YOI New Hall & Askham Grange prisons during custody and post-release.* A project of Hudders eld Pakistani Community Alliance (HPCA) in partnership with Khidmat Centres, Bradford: HPCA and Khidmat Centres.

Davids, F. M. (2011) *Internal Racism: A Psychoanalytic Approach to Race and Difference* (The Palgrave Psychotherapy Series). Palgrave Macmillan.

Fanon, F. (2019) *Black Skin: White Masks*. New York: Grove Press / Atlantic Monthly Press (originally published in 1952).

Grimwood, G. G. (2015) Categorisation of prisoners in the UK. Briefing Paper Number 07437, 29 December. London: House of Commons Library.

Independent (2017) Women accused of planning first all-female terror attack in UK appear in court. Lizzie Dearden, Home Affairs Correspondent. https://www.independent.co.uk/news/uk/crime/terror-plot-uk-isis-stabbing-westminster-first-all-female-plot-court-mina-dich-rizlaine-boular-a7889496.html

Moore, J. (2017) Isis Unleashes Dozens of Female Suicide Bombers in Battle for Mosul. *Newsweek*. https://www.newsweek.com/isis-female-suicide-bombers-battle-mosul-631846.

Newsweek (2017) Why Isis Female Suicide Bombers Mean the End of the Celiphate Dream. Elizabeth Pearson. https://www.newsweek.com/why-isis-female-suicide-bombers-mean-end-caliphate-dream-637892

Smart, S. (2019) Too Many Bends in the Tunnel? Women Serving Indeterminate Sentences of IPP – What are the Barriers to Risk Reduction, Release and Resettlement? The Griffins Society. www.thegriffinssociety.org/too-many-bends-tunnel-women-serving-indeterminate-sentences-ipp-what-are-barriers-risk-reduction

Chapter 9

Intoxicating states of mind
Violence and its impact

Anna Motz

Intoxicating states of mind are transient experiences that can lead to acts of serious violence. In this chapter I describe how these experiences enliven and excite women who commit violent crimes. The sense of being filled with destructive energy, like a drug, is central to the experience of the women themselves. I then outline the 'intoxicating' impact that working with the women can have on the minds and bodies of staff, in that they can feel exhilarated or excited, as well as 'poisoned' by their interactions with the women who have committed offences. I explore how the phenomenology of intoxication, and the push to action, can be mirrored in the staff who work with violent women as they take in their projections, absorbing their dangerous energy and its impact on thinking. The chapter explores all these angles.

I use the term 'intoxicating' rather than 'intoxicated' to emphasise the impact that these experiences have on others, as well as on the women themselves. 'Intoxicating' stresses that they are active, agentive states. Herein, intoxication is referred to both figuratively, in relation to certain feelings like rage, sexual excitement and fear, and literally, in relation to the role of drugs and alcohol in contributing to female offending.

The chapter explores the intoxicating qualities of extreme emotional states, commonly experienced by women when they harm their children and intimate partners, start fires, attack themselves through self-mutilation, drug and alcohol misuse, are involved in violent relationships, engage in eating disorders or commit high risk acts of violence, hostage-taking and robbery. These underlying affects include intense anger, excitement, frustration, guilt and desperation – feelings that are often impossible for the women to process, requiring immediate discharge through action. This action offers a sense of release which is, in itself, intoxicating. There is a profound contrast between the state of mind preceding the action and the feeling after it has been performed.

Although being intoxicated can be offered as a mitigating factor in criminal behaviour, this emphasises the sense in which the individual is rendered passive, irresponsible and disabled by what they have taken in. Conversely, in this chapter, I stress that violence, sexual excitement or the use of actual intoxicants can result in heightened activity and a sense of mastery, power and exhilaration.

I discuss the significant role of actual intoxicants, namely drugs and alcohol, in contributing to violence and offending in women with trauma histories.

Intoxicating states of mind: a description

An intoxicating state of mind constitutes a loss of control and heightened sense of emotionality that can be both exhilarating and frightening. This excitement has a toxic quality, obliterating thought and generating actions, sometimes dangerous, often reckless. Being intoxicated is akin to being poisoned, in that something that is taken in, or ingested, disrupts the inner organisation of both mind and body. It is this quality, of destruction, empowerment and release, that is of central significance. Intoxication often arises after a period of anxiety, depression or numbness and serves as a defence against these feelings. This is well described in Wood and Bower's (2013) psychoanalytic model for 'addictive states of mind' characterised by elements of risk-taking and ritual. Certain activities can create these states of mind, in which there is often a longing for oblivion or ecstasy and a loss of inhibitions, leading to enactments of unconscious phantasy. They consider gambling, violence, the use of internet pornography and other perversions to be akin to substance and alcohol use in terms of their functions and addictive qualities, leading to these states of mind. As previously stated, 'intoxicating' is arguably a preferable term because it refers not just to the women 'under the influence' of destructive, frenzied states of mind, but also to the impact of these mental states on those who encounter them. The term captures the sense of wild, mindless activity that intoxication can generate, and how this can sweep others along.

Women in intoxicating states of mind often take reckless and destructive action without consideration of the consequences. This is at the heart of much violent activity. The sense of savagery and release characterise the enactments of unconscious wishes, obliterating ordinary controls. It is as if the id takes the ego hostage and superego prohibitions are temporarily suspended, as the power and thrill of impulsivity wipes out inhibition and control, offering tremendous release from unbearable pressure.

The presence of others can also be intoxicating, as revealed in the extreme violence of gangs and toxic couples engaged in frenzied aggression either towards one another or against a third party (as described in the illustration of Mia and Amber, who tortured Dwayne, in Chapter 6). The presence of one other person, or a group of others, has been shown to contribute to the severity of violence used as individuals feel a sense of release and reduced responsibility in groups and are consequently more likely to indulge in brutal activity (Lantz, 2018).

Ecstatic states: drugs and alcohol

The use of substances to achieve release, escape and euphoria has a long history and is part of religious ceremony dating back to ancient times. The idea of transcendence, of moving beyond the ordinary constraints of daily life to make contact with the divine, is part of the phantasy and function of intoxication. The fundamental principles and wishes established in ecstatic religions persist today, particularly the use of substances to transform one's physical and mental state and enter a higher, more pleasurable realm, to encounter something divine. Many women in the criminal justice system (CJS) have long histories of drug and alcohol abuse, and will readily acknowledge that they rely on these to self-mediate and block out thought, numb feeling and create a sense of bliss (Ministry of Justice, 2018) (see also Chapter 6 in this volume).

While certain drugs like ketamine and opiate-based substances create peaceful, dissociated states of minds that are tranquil, if numb, others have enlivening properties that enhance a sense of power, confidence and energy. These types of drugs include cocaine, ecstasy and amphetamines. In contrast, hallucinogenic substances, like LSD or peyote, enable the user to experience unusual perceptions and profound distortions of reality that can be both fascinating and terrifying. Whatever their specific properties, all substances serve to disinhibit behaviour, increasing the possibility that aggressive drives and wishes are released.

The significant rise in the use of new psychoactive substances (NPS), otherwise known as 'legal highs', 'mamba' or 'spice', has substantially contributed to the problems of addiction in the homeless and prison population, both male and female (O'Connor, 2018). Its legal status is both confusing and misleading, as its properties are variable, often unknown, and its effects can be powerful and destructive, leading to impulsive and dangerous behaviour and harmful physical effects. It is difficult to regulate both its purchase and its use.

Escape into intoxication

Individuals who have been hurt or neglected in early life are at greater risk of being introduced to these substances at an early age and developing strong dependence on them. The literature on adverse childhood experiences (ACEs) confirms (Felitti, 2003) that women are more at risk for multiple ACEs than men. Women who are sexually exploited and exposed to violence by partners describe using drugs and alcohol to block out awareness of these traumatic experiences. Indeed, the multiple risks associated with adversity such as homelessness, intimate partner violence and sexual exploitation include the increased risk of being exposed to addictive substances and relying on them to block out the pain of terrible psychosocial circumstances. Chapter 5 has outlined how substance misuse and alcohol dependence are correlated with prostitution, offering a means of blocking out the pain and also keeping the woman in a state of need and therefore highly vulnerable to sexual and financial exploitation.

The blissful experience of intoxication

The pleasure and unreality of intoxication is beautifully described by Coleridge in his poem, 'Kubla Khan', that reads like a piece of music, otherworldly, insistent and rhythmic.

'Kubla Khan', Samuel Taylor Coleridge (1816)
Or, a vision in a dream. A fragment

> In Xanadu did Kubla Khan
> A stately pleasure-dome decree:
> Where Alph, the sacred river, ran
> Through caverns measureless to man
> Down to a sunless sea
> But oh! that deep romantic chasm which slanted
> Down the green hill athwart a cedarn cover!
> A savage place! as holy and enchanted
> As e'er beneath a waning moon was haunted
> By woman wailing for her demon-lover!
> And from this chasm, with ceaseless turmoil seething,
> As if this earth in fast thick pants were breathing,
> A mighty fountain momently was forced.

The first two stanzas from Coleridge's poem, reputed to have come to him in an opium induced dream, vividly create the sense of ecstasy and timelessness that intoxication brings. The mind is freed and the body released from constraints leading to a sense of wildness and action. The imagery alludes to 'a savage place' and also to sex itself, 'as if this earth in fast thick pants were breathing, a mighty fountain momently was forced'. These are blissful and urgent states, removed from the ordinary world of pain and suffering.

Alcohol serves to release inhibitions and to enable a sense of freedom from the usual constraints of morality, or from the hypervigilant preoccupations that characterise individuals who have experienced trauma. Furthermore, alcohol and substances create psychological as well as physical addictions and are also associated with risk-taking, counter-culture and defiance against the norms of mainstream society.

The intoxicated mind is one in which tomorrow doesn't matter; fears for the future recede into the shadows as the immediate pleasure of 'being high' takes precedence. The wish to maintain this high, or to return to it as soon as possible, is intense and other concerns are often overwhelmed. Sadly, the addiction, with its demands for immediate gratification, can push aside other activities and concerns, including care of children, awareness of physical risk to oneself, or longer term aims like maintaining education or employment and focussing on other means of escaping difficult circumstances. The fog and bliss of intoxication obscures reality.

Another aim of intoxication is to lose oneself in perceived connection with others and the world, to dissolve the sense of selfhood and individuality, a particularly pressing wish for women whose experiences have taught them to hate themselves. This wish is not pathological, as philosopher Jules Evans notes:

> We have always sought ways to 'unself', as the writer Iris Murdoch called it, because the ego is an anxious, claustrophobic, lonely and boring place to be stuck. As the author Aldous Huxley wrote, humans have 'a deep-seated urge to self-transcendence'. However, we can get out of our ordinary selves in good and bad ways – what Huxley called 'healthy and toxic transcendence'. (Evans, 2017)

Alcohol abuse and violent offending

The empirical evidence indicates that while treatment for substance abuse related to Class A drugs was identified as a major need for women in the CJS, it was not linked to violent reoffending. In contrast, binge drinking is. A recent study reported that 'binge drinking is a crucial risk factor for women which has not been identified before, and which predicted both all, and specifically violent, reoffending for women' (Travers and Mann, 2018: 10). This study also identified that the experience of domestic violence in the women's lives also created a risk factor in relation to their own violent offending. Although the authors do not propose a mechanism for this, this chapter suggests that the traumatic experience of bodily violence in domestic violence creates a template for future discharge of emotion, an association between physical violence and release, akin to the sense of wild intoxication I describe. Actual intoxication through drug or alcohol use increases the likelihood of action, but might not, in itself, be enough to trigger the violence without the underlying trauma and the template for violence.

Empirical evidence for substance dependence in female offenders

The link between early trauma and later drug addiction is clear, indicating that the risk of opioid dependence increases dramatically if there is early childhood adversity:

> Evidence indicates that individuals exposed to opioid misuse experience multiple negative consequences, including loss of employment, poor physical and mental health, suicidal behavior, and disrupted family and social relationships. Among those who misuse opioids, the individuals most likely to experience problems with addiction are those who suffered multiple adverse childhood experiences (ACEs). General population surveys have estimated that 75% of individuals with substance use disorders have

experienced trauma at some point in their lives. Rates are even higher among populations seeking treatment for opioid addiction.

(Press et al., 2017: 1)

It is clear that traumatic, unprocessed experiences in early life greatly predispose women to seek the release and anaesthetic of intoxication, including opioid dependence, as the authors above describe and as Covington (2008) stresses in her development of trauma-informed practice for women in the CJS. While detoxification programmes are important for women with substance addiction, they alone will not be able to reduce reliance on substances to combat painful feelings unless the underlying consequences of earlier traumatic experiences are also addressed.

While there are many such states of mind sometimes induced by drugs and alcohol, other times by intense emotions, including fear, rage and lust, they will manifest differently for different women. Each woman is unique in terms of which experiences are intoxicating for her and how she responds 'under the influence'.

In my experience violence most often occurs in such a state of mind rather than in a cold and calculating one, even when the woman who enacts it has been diagnosed as having psychopathic traits. The states of mind that characterise intoxication are distinct from other mental states that deaden the senses, including dissociation, denial and disengagement; these can be understood as defences against these 'hot' and painful feelings. Some narcotics are designed to deaden rather than enliven the senses, and these tend to anaesthetise rather than energise; for example, ketamine was designed for anaesthetic purposes.

Women who are traumatised often begin using drugs and alcohol to manage feelings of depression, shame and anger. Research indicates that women's use of substances differs markedly from men's in the general population, as do the reasons why women may be reluctant to seek help:

There are clear disincentives that deter women from seeking treatment, such as fears about the risk that their children may be taken into care. Intimate partner violence is a further factor that prevents women from seeking treatment, because they worry about aggravating an existing dysfunctional or violent relationship. (Hamilton, 2017)

These concerns are also relevant to the female offender population.

Classifications of intoxicating states of mind

Bearing the complexity and uniqueness of individual experience in mind, the following suggests a possible classification of these states.

Terror

Inducing terror in others can be a great release for a woman who feels scared and powerless herself. Playing with terror can also be exciting if it is carefully controlled. The sense of playing 'Russian Roulette' is resonant here and women who have been subjected to terror at the hands of others in early life, being suddenly hurt or violated, may find solace in inducing these states in themselves as well as others through exposure to risky situations with uncertain outcomes. Through splitting off the frightened feelings into one part of the self, another part can assert power and triumph over fear, embracing it rather than fleeing it. This primitive defence enables the former victim of terror to feel she has now mastered it, through attacking another part of herself, the hated vulnerable and little child self that still cowers inside her.

Being terrified and inducing terror in others are both manifestation of a particular state of mind, evident in the private, hidden violence that mothers inflict on their children, as well as in the public violence of female terrorists.

Mania/excitement

The feeling of mania is one of energy, frenzy, chaos and freedom. When it offers an escape from the confines of depression it can seem a welcome release, a restoration of the sense of oneself as a powerful agent, rather than passive object. Mania that follows a period of depression, or suppression, has even greater force and affords tremendous relief and excitement. In manic states of mind there are no inhibitions, either external or internal, that prevent the fulfilment of desire or expression of impulses. These manic states are often removed from the constraints of reality.

This is a sense of power which is fundamentally enlivening, defending against a much less appealing and unpleasant affect, the sense of shame. Many women with histories of childhood trauma and neglect carry with them a sense of shame about their secrets, their families, their own bodies and their minds. This pervasive sense of shame often drives violent action, as Gilligan (1997) powerfully describes in his work on shame and violence. Exhilaration is found as a concomitant of all intoxicating states of mind. Welldon (2009) uses the image of 'dancing with death' to describe how the manic defence of perverse activity is an attempt to keep depression at bay.

Sexual excitement

A state of heightened sexual arousal can mirror a state of intoxication, generating a sense of urgency, energy, immersion in the moment and the loss of internal inhibitions. Lust can overcome reason, moral constraint and awareness of long term consequences of one's actions. Thought is overwhelmed by desire, the physical urges outweigh the mind's restraint and there can be a sense of 'losing oneself' in the pursuit of satisfaction.

The phenomenology of lust is crucial to the discussion of its intoxicating power and relevant to a later exploration of female sexual offending. One of the finest accounts of the feeling of being in the thrall of unwanted sexual desire and longings comes from the 4th-century-theologian, St Augustine, in his autobiographical account of his journey towards salvation, *The Confessions*. St Augustine describes the power and pleasures of lust and how it overpowers reason and thought. He uses poetic and striking imagery related to sensory experience and the dampening down of reason. His language evokes sensation as he writes of desire as obscuring his reason and his heart, confusing love and lust, the latter like a whirlpool that sweeps him away. He vividly conjures up the feeling of this state of mind, of losing control, taking action without thought, as if being helpless against a force of nature that takes him over:

> Bodily desire, like a morass, and adolescent sex welling up within me exuded mists which clouded over and obscured my heart … Love and lust together seethed within me. In my tender youth they swept me away over the precipice of my body's appetites and plunged me into the whirlpool of sin.
>
> (St Augustine, 2015, Book II, para. 5)

Augustine describes his sense of spiritual emptiness ('a famine of that inward food') that could be filled up with lust, with the craving for the touch of others, 'desiring to be scraped by the touch of objects of sense'. Once this longing has been met he is left feeling guilty, distressed and still unfulfilled, as the love he craves (that of the divine) is not met in the pleasures of the flesh:

> To Carthage I came, where there sang all around me in my ears a cauldron of unholy loves. I loved not yet, yet I loved to love, and out of a deep-seated want, I hated myself for wanting not. I sought what I might love, in love with loving, and safety I hated, and a way without snares. For within me was a famine of that inward food, Thyself, my God; yet, through that famine I was not hungered; but was without all longing for incorruptible sustenance, not because filled therewith, but the more empty, the more I loathed it. For this cause my soul was sickly and full of sores, it miserably cast itself forth, desiring to be scraped by the touch of objects of sense.
>
> (St Augustine, 2015, Book III: paras 1–4)

He reveals the cycle of intoxication, transient pleasure and sensory satisfaction, and then the return of a profound sense of despair. This sadness and guilt is prompted by awareness of a feeling of underlying emptiness and fear of damaging internal objects, as well as another, whom he believes he has defiled through his lust. There is a sense of conflict, and this echoes the sentiments of so many women who find it impossible, at times, to resist overwhelming feelings and excited states of mind, desperate to keep thoughts and memories at bay. This is most true of women with histories of trauma, where thought can lead to disturbing memories, fear and a sense of worthlessness.

While the model of destructive acting out by female sex offenders is not based on a notion of spiritual purity that gets corrupted, there is an analogous process in terms of the intoxicating effects of action, followed by guilt, pain and intensified feelings of self-loathing. Through gratifying their aggressive sexual impulses they temporarily bypass the pain of unmet needs for love, care or intimacy. Guilt and the return of underlying feelings of despair and depression often follow these acts, leaving the perpetrator with a sense of shame that feels intolerable. One means of escape is to re-enter the exciting realm of sexual fantasy, and then to repeat the cycle, to abuse again. This overwhelming state of mind leads to seeking and achieving sexual gratification, and intensifies her sense of shame and guilt, for many reasons.

Survivors of incest and other childhood abuse may feel traumatised by acknowledgement of their sexual wishes, let alone enactments of these, as sexual desire is often fraught with guilt and confusion. Perpetrators of sexual abuse against the vulnerable, including children, often regret what they have done once their sexual desire has been sated, and their intoxication gives way to feelings of remorse and depression.

Without applying moral and religious concepts of 'sin' or 'innocence' to female offenders, there are psychological parallels in terms of splitting of the self into 'good' and 'bad' aspects, and the sense of being overtaken by other, primitive feelings at times of intense sexual excitement, especially when the objects of this desire are taboo. The religious model is salient here as women who suffer from profound feelings of guilt about sexual activity also feel that they have damaged one part of themselves and require both punishment and purification, though they may not use these terms explicitly. Self-harm often follows the 'sin' of sexual activity with a taboo object, and can be seen as a manifestation of these impulses (see the clinical illustration of Aliyah in Chapter 7).

Violence as intoxicant

Defence against shame

These states of mind can be identified as primitive feelings that are responses to other, less bearable emotions related to shame, fear and helplessness. They can be understood as defences against these painful emotions. Violent action offers excitement, an antidote to shame and helplessness. Shame is a pervasive issue for many of the women in the CJS and is a common feature of their early lives where they have often been bullied, abused, ostracised and humiliated. Shame has both interpersonal roots in terms of the earliest relationships where the women may have felt unwanted, unworthy, bad and stupid, and also social causes, for example in the shame caused by poverty, racism and hunger, all states of being caused by and reflecting societal injustice.

Hatred

The violent, hateful state of mind is characterised by the absence of thought and the spontaneous release of rage, misery and frustration. As violence is inflicted on another, physical sensation can take priority over reasoning and any thought that is formed is one accompanying and fuelling the action.

In cases of instrumental aggression, the other person is viewed as an object, a target onto whom poisonous rageful feelings can be directed. In sadistic violence the pain of the other is part of the pleasure; the aim is not to destroy the object, but to keep her alive, to torture her and have her serve as a poison container, affirming the subject's power and strength. Glasser (1979) distinguishes helpfully between the two forms of aggression in his seminal paper on perversions, differentiating self-preservative from sadistic aggression. In the former, the perpetrator would use violence only to defend herself from a perceived threat to her own psychic or physical existence. Violence stemming from shame and humiliation can be experienced as necessary and reflect a sense of profound existential threat – the woman's whole sense of herself in under attack.

Maternal violence

In Slimani's chilling 2016 novel, *Lullaby*, she offers a stark illustration of how a mother's shame about her unattractive, badly behaved daughter leads to a frenzied assault on her. Louise, the 'perfect nanny', tends to the children of the wealthy with dedication and sensitivity, but hates her own daughter, Stéphanie, whose presence shames her, and with whom she narcissistically identifies, seeing her as an image of her own low status, deprivation and humiliation, this clumsy child who disgraces her. Before Stéphanie is expelled from school for poor attendance, unruly behaviour and failure to complete her work, Louise attends a meeting with teachers, explaining how strict and careful she is with her children. She does not mean her own daughter, the unruly Stéphanie of course, but the children of the wealthy, who deserve good care and discipline. Louise and Stéphanie return home following the decision to expel her, and out of Louise's shame and humiliation strong hateful feelings arise and she becomes suffused with hatred and anger towards her. Slimani describes the contrast between her apparent femininity, as conveyed by her tiny hands, and the immense rage that drove her into violent action. 'She wanted to dig her nails into her daughter's soft skin … Again and again her tiny hands slapped Stéphanie's face.' (Slimani, 2018: 164).

Louise converts her sense of humiliation into rage and projects it onto her helpless daughter, attacking her in a frenzy, her 'fragility' belying her underlying ferocity as her 'tiny hands' tear her daughter's face apart. She hits the eyes that have witnessed her disgrace as an unfit mother, unable to mould her daughter into an acceptable shape. Finally, Louise spits on her battered daughter, in an ultimate demonstration of contempt and humiliation. Her husband observes this but does not intervene. Slimani highlights the contrast between the doll-like presentation of this perfect, blonde nanny, with her delicate white skin, and her underlying disturbance, her hidden fury and hatred. The veneer of Louise's beauty and fragility is shattered and she becomes unhinged, wild in her humiliated fury. This graphic description reveals how violence can be intoxicating, offering release.

Manic defences against depression: intoxicating substances

Intoxicating states of mind defend against underlying depression both in the perpetrators and those who encounter them. Offenders find that violent action can temporarily lead to exhilarating feelings of conquest and relief, that quickly fade, leaving them feeling guilty and desperate. So too can those who work with them prefer the intoxicating feelings of anger or excitement to the dreary states of mind that follow. If the reality that is left behind is oppressive, painful and unwelcome, then entering another world offers relief. While these intense emotional responses are exciting, and in this sense welcome, they can prevent thinking and ultimately collapse into states of despair, anger and hopelessness. The circumstances that are either temporarily forgotten or that cease to matter when the woman is intoxicated remain unchanged, and when the euphoric feelings and escape wear off, the return to reality can be experienced as even more brutal.

This creates particular problems for women in settings where the use of substances will result in setbacks or expulsion. Women in approved premises (formerly known as probation hostels) with long histories of trauma and abuse, temporarily find solace in alcohol and drug taking, only to find, when sober, that they are still fearful of the future and regretful of the past. Use of drugs and alcohol is strictly forbidden in approved premises, despite the fact that many women coming into the hostels from custody may have had access to these substances while inside. Furthermore, such breaches of conditions for remaining in approved premises can result in recall to custody.

The rates of recall of female offenders have risen since the Rehabilitation of Offenders Act (2014) and the subsequent requirement that all offenders are supervised for a year post-custody. This has caused much concern and has interfered with women being able to access treatment for alcohol and/or substance misuse either in the community or in custody as their sentences are so short, and being recalled removes them from community provision for addiction. This is a major obstacle to rehabilitation and the recent Female Offenders

Strategy outlines how treatment should be integrated into community based alternatives to custody, including residential centres to which women could be sentenced (MoJ, 2018).

The impact of intoxicating states of mind on staff

Female offenders violate taboos, and this transgression can itself serve as a source of excitement and fear, a perverse pleasure, which can take hold of both the women who commit these crimes and the workers who come into contact with them. The sense of wildness and recklessness can be exhilarating for the women and others, who are vicariously enlivened through their exposure to the forbidden, the repressed. The notion of vicarious traumatisation of workers closely involved with traumatised individuals is more commonly accepted than the concept of vicarious excitement and vicarious transgression. At times the women can take on the role of acting out the forbidden wishes and fantasies of staff, though this will not readily be acknowledged.

The intoxicating impact on workers attacks their capacity to think, leading as it does to emotional responding and action, which can be in the form of attempting either to rescue or punish the women who offend. It is essential to be aware of this phenomenon, which happens at an unconscious level, and for staff to be able to reflect on their responses rather than simply enacting them without thinking, as this will simply lead to traumatic and toxic re-enactments for the women.

The central tenet of forensic psychotherapy, which is to convert action to thought, unconscious fantasy to conscious articulation, applies to the task of the forensic worker, to whom is assigned the arduous task of resisting projections and the wish to take action, either retaliatory or collusive, but to remain still in the eye of the storm.

Working with violent women: re-enactments and repetitions

The therapeutic nihilism associated with treating women with personality disorder is even more pronounced when they are placed within the CJS. These women often have a history of antisocial behaviour, challenging presentations and a high level of disturbance that can take a physical form – including violence towards the self or others. I will describe the emotional impact of the work on practitioners and how institutional practices can mirror, and reinforce, psychological defences against engagement with the women. Within both mental health and the CJS we can still see evidence of a prevailing attitude related to working with women with a personality disorder that constructs the women as impossibly demanding, untreatable and manipulative. In a recent and welcome development, Her Majesty's Prison and Probation Service is now investigating trauma informed, psychological approaches to high-risk offenders with personality disorders, a move that challenges the pervasive pessimism related to treating this group (Covington, 2008; Craissati et al., 2015).

The complex dynamics that characterise the relationships between workers and women within the CJS can be understood as unconscious re-enactments of earlier situations, in which the workers are enlisted to play particular roles in the women's internal dramas. Aiyegbusi (2004) describes this powerfully in her work 'Thinking under Fire'. The intensity and compulsive aspect of these relationships – the women who cannot be left, forgotten about, or tolerated, who get under the skin of workers – reflect the depth of feeling that the woman herself experiences. She is taken over by a particular feeling or mental state that demands action and reaction. The worker, in turn, is faced with an urgent demand and responds, often, intuitively, with a counter-action, often without thought. This will not demonstrate the worker's general state of mind, but can be understood as an immediate response to what the woman has brought, a primitive enactment of her request, without an intermediary level of intellectual understanding of what is being communicated.

Many women in prison suffer from a deep-seated sense of shame that is difficult to bear and can lead to a frantic need to avoid the gaze of the other. The displays of either brazen cruelty and violence (defensively used against these shameful feelings) or hiding away altogether are then mirrored in practitioners, whether in mental health or criminal justice systems. Analogously, practitioners feel shame because either they cannot help, or cannot bear to see the women's suffering and pain. This happens when they look away repeatedly, ignoring suffering, causing suffering to others or naked self-harming, as if the wound that is opened is too deep to be tended to. The only 'polite' response is to turn away. Chapter 6 has further explored self-harming by women in secure environments, within both criminal justice and mental health settings.

Impact on workers

Workers who have to manage the chaos and disappointment of this repeated and destructive cycle can be left with angry, hurt and vengeful feelings towards the woman, and may act on this. For example, deciding to recall her to custody, effectively evicting her, can offer relief. Recalling a woman to custody for breach of her conditions may initially appear a measured decision, and apparently inevitable; with further exploration this can be seen as an enactment of the frustration and anger of the staff, who have some degree of discretion about when to recall women. As the literature demonstrates, women who receive frequent short custodial sentences are at increased risk of reoffending and losing heart, without being able to make any long term progress through, for example, engaging in an accredited programme.

Unsurprisingly, over-worked and under-supervised staff may themselves prefer to take dramatic action, rather than bear the pain of thinking about the despair that underlies these breaches and offering a second chance. Taking action can be exciting and dramatic, involving a sense of crisis, purpose and agency. Sadly, this move around services and between secure environments often echoes the patterns of the woman's early life, as she was moved between foster placements or care homes because she was thought 'too difficult' or 'unmanageable'. A similar situation occurs within the secure mental health system, where women who refuse to 'get better' or who consistently humiliate and frighten staff are moved around between wards, or referred to conditions of greater security even in the absence of an objective escalation of risk. Justifications and reasons for moving the women abound, but the underlying and unconscious wish is to get rid of the destructive patient who defeats the best efforts of staff, despite the conscious and stated wish to work with a challenging woman who is 'difficult to engage'.

Staff working with violent women can unwittingly incite conflict, unconsciously preferring events that 'kick off' to calmer, but more depressed and anxious, interactions with women in which uncertainty prevails. The relief of this action is that it offers a release from unbearable affects and offers a (false) sense of resolution to an underlying difficulty. These enactments between the women and the workers repeat and illustrate what has gone on before in the woman's earliest relationships and in her offences, rather than changing the dynamic and offering her another way of relating to others. Again, this is a manifestation of perverse excitement, or intoxication, rather than of a thoughtful and mutative interaction. The possibility for learning, growth and repair is destroyed through such repetitions. It is essential for staff to recognise their own unwitting contribution to these destructive re-enactments.

Clinical illustration: Candace – rage/hatred in the countertransference

The intoxicating impact of violence is illustrated through the case of Candace, a woman who was suffused with hatred, including thoughts of sexual violence, revenge and murder. She would terrorise the staff through threats and vicious personal insults, provoking violent feelings in them. Some would find it difficult to be distant from her when she was insulting other women on the unit or on the staff team, while others would avoid her altogether, barricading themselves against her onslaughts. She was experienced as so frightening that her own fear was hard to discern, as if it was powerfully projected into others; she was seen as fearsome rather than fearful.

Candace was a 34-year-old woman with a diagnosis of antisocial and borderline personality disorder and a forensic history that included sexual assault on another female, arson with intent to kill and several violent offences against other women. She had been an inpatient within a high security hospital before being transferred to an enhanced medium security unit, where she was considered one of the most frightening and destructive patients on the ward. In childhood she had been sexually assaulted by her mother and her mother's boyfriend before eventually being removed into a local authority placement in a secure adolescent unit. She became estranged from her mother at this point. During her time in the adolescent unit she ran away repeatedly, trying to return to her mother's house, and had begun using crack cocaine. She sometimes smuggled it into the unit. She became infatuated with a female member of staff who appeared to have reciprocated her advances, eventually leading to her suspension from the role. Despite her wildness and the fear she evoked in others, Candace had 'another side' to her that evoked sympathy and care. She was clearly an intelligent and sensitive woman whose volatile moods and sharp tongue left those around her apprehensive and anxious, eager to please and placate her.

On one occasion she encouraged a group of women on the ward to torment another inpatient, Jude, whom she (falsely) believed was a sex offender, in order to get her to leave the unit. There were three other women involved in the gang who entered the woman's room and started to threaten her, to describe the harm to which they would subject her. She was terrified that the women would hurt her and planned to escape from the locked unit. She went out on her unescorted leave but didn't return at the agreed time, leaving staff to alert the police to her whereabouts, and was eventually found, hiding in a bus shelter. She disclosed the threats to staff, who assured her that she would be kept safe and protected from the others in the hate campaign, led by Candace. Eventually, however, she didn't believe the reassurances, and on her return she started to self-harm by inserting glass shards into her vagina, requiring emergency treatment in the general hospital. Her level of self-harm was considered unmanageable and within ten days she was transferred to a more secure unit, leaving Candace and the others pleased that their intimidation and rage had 'worked'.

Although Candace herself had committed acts of violence, including sexual violence, she could forget this when she turned her rage against Jude. She felt temporarily released from her own feelings of shame, guilt or vulnerability and was enlivened, excited and empowered. Candace's state of mind had a contagious effect on others, inviting them to enter her world of cruelty and revenge. The intoxicating impact of her mental state on others was dramatic, and they too felt temporarily released from their usual inhibitions and fears, excited to take part in this group warfare and project their own unacceptable impulses onto Jude, whom they victimised. Candace turned her own fear, rage and shame into a physical attack, an action that enabled her toxic feelings to be evacuated.

Jude, too, felt temporarily freed from unbearable feelings when she was able to enact harm, drawing blood from within to the surface of her body, and alerting the nursing and medical team to the danger she faced on the ward. In one sense, Jude's extreme self-harm was the fulfilment of Candace's wishes, so that she suffered the assault that had been planned for her, inflicting it on herself. Jude had been sexually abused during much of her childhood, so to be accused of being an abuser was particularly awful, and her hatred of her own sexual organs, the site of violation, was illustrated in her self-harm. She inserted glass inside herself in an act of self-punishment, but also self-protection, in that this brutal violence against herself allowed her to not only free herself from the terror of waiting passively to be attacked by Candace and the others, but ultimately allowed her to be cared for by the staff team and moved away from this frightening ward.

Staff felt frightened, hopeless and 'held hostage' to the venomous attacks. They felt they had no choice but to move Jude for her own safety. They took action to deal with the threats by Candace and became preoccupied by her behaviour, to the neglect of other patients. While they feared her, there was also a sense of excitement and dread about her movements, and this mirrored her own internal world, the need for action to relieve underlying anxiety and depression. This reveals the intoxicating impact of violence. The sense of arousal it generates in others, as well as in the perpetrator, masks the empty, powerless feelings that underlie it.

Intoxication and gangs

The gang mentality created another form of mindlessness and intoxication, making it impossible for staff and patients alike to counteract the destructiveness of Candace's murderous wishes. The collective immersion in activity is well known to disinhibit individuals and enable them to suspend the usual ethical judgements and restraint. Belonging to a group or gang clearly adds to the intoxicating aspects of the experience, and encourages brutality and primitive behaviour, as seen so powerfully in riots, football violence, looting and gang warfare. Each of the women felt relieved that she was not the outsider, the hated scapegoat who could be attacked with impunity. This relief added to the pleasure of belonging to the gang and losing a sense of individual responsibility, a common aspect of deindividuation (Zimbardo, 1969).

Managing the intoxicating countertransference

The feelings that women find unbearable, either before or during acts of violence, can have a powerful impact on others. The impact on staff working with extreme violence is intense and can itself be intoxicating, at least for the duration of the actual incidences, in which action is required. The 'burn out' results from the fear, depression, guilt or helplessness that can follow and precede violence, and can leave practitioners feeling useless, or rageful, identifying with the intolerable experiences that the women project into them and to which they bear witness. The meaning of their 'crimes against the body' vary, but often reveal and repeat earlier trauma. Powerful feelings of shame, disgust, fear and rage are conveyed in such acts and can often be viscerally felt by those who encounter self-harm.

Chapters 2 and 8 argued that the concept of a fundamental personality disturbance, along the lines of psychopathic disorder, does not help to elucidate how and why some women commit acts of extreme violence, seemingly without remorse. In this chapter I have linked intoxicating states of mind with extreme violence, against the self and others, and suggest that this may also illuminate the phenomenology of experiencing a psychopathic state of mind, in which violence is exciting, enlivening and freeing.

Throughout this chapter I have argued that the states of mind that violent women experience, and engender in others, are intoxicating, and this perverse excitement inhibits thinking. I suggest that the process of intoxication can be a shared one within institutional settings, with staff and violent perpetrators becoming caught up in violent enactments that are preferable to the amorphous situation of shared anxiety and depression. At times the thought and emotional distance required for real change in relating to women with histories of trauma is impossible to achieve as the psychic pressure to act in response to the woman's violence does not allow space for reflection. Practitioners working with violent women must find a way to remain still in the eye of the storm, and resist the intoxicating impact of their actions, despite their unconscious wishes to rescue or punish the women.

References

Aiyegbusi, A. (2004) Thinking under fire. In N. Jeffcote & T. Watson (Eds.), *Working therapeutically with women in secure mental health settings* (pp. 108–119). London: Jessica Kingsley.

Bower, M., Hale, R., & Wood, H. (Ed.) (2013). *Addictive states of mind.* Tavistock Clinic Series. Abingdon, UK: Routledge.

Coleridge, S.T. (1816) Kubla Kahn. In Arthur Quller-Couch (Ed.), *The Oxford book of English verse 1250–1900.* Oxford: Oxford University Press.

Covington, S. (2008) Women & addiction: A trauma-informed approach. *Journal of Psychoactive Drugs* SARC, Supplement 5, 377–385.

Craissati, J., Joseph, N., & Skett, S. (Eds.) (2015) *Working with offenders with personality disorder: A practitioners' guide.* London: Department of Health.

Evans, J. (2017) Dissolving the ego. *Aeon.* https://aeon.co/essays/religion-has-no-monopoly-on-transcendent-experience

Felitti, V.J. (2003) The origins of addiction: Evidence from the adverse childhood experiences study. *Praxis der Kinderpsychologie und Kinderspychiatrie, 52,* 547–559.

Gilligan, J. (1997) *Violence: Reflections on a national epidemic.* New York: Vintage.

Glasser, M. (1979) Some aspects of the role of aggression in the perversions. In I. Rosen (Ed.), *Sexual deviation.* Oxford: Oxford University Press.

Hamilton, L. (2017) Breaking the silence on women and drug use. *The Pharmaceutical Journal.* www.pharmaceutical-journal.com/opinion/comment/why-women-who-misuse-drugs-have-different-needs/20203081.article.

Lantz, B. & Joonggon, K. (2018) Hate crimes hurt more, but so do co-offenders: Separating the influence of co-offending and bias on hate-motivated physical injury. *Criminal Justice and Behavior, 46*(3), 437–456.

Ministry of Justice (2018) *Female offender strategy.* London: MoJ. https://assets.publish ing.service.gov.uk/government/uploads/system/uploads/attachment_data/le/719819/ female-offender-strategy.pdf.

O'Connor, R. (2018). Public Health Matters. https://publichealthmatters.blog.gov.uk/ 2018/01/31/what-we-learned-about-alcohol-and-drug-treatment-in-prisons-from-the- 2016-17-statistics/

Press, D. et al. (2017) Trauma-informed approaches need to be part of a comprehensive strategy for addressing the opioid epidemic. Campaign for Trauma-Informed Policy and Practice Policy Brief, Number 1, June 2017. https://publichealth.gwu.edu/sites/ default/files/downloads/Redstone-Center/CTIPP_OPB_final.pdf

Slimani, L. (2018) *Lullaby.* London: Faber and Faber.

St Augustine (2015) The confessions of St Augustine. *Bishop of Hippo.* Translated by E. B. Pusey (Edward Bouverie).

Travers, R. & Mann, R.E. (2018) *The dynamic predictors of reconviction for women.* Analytical Summary 2018. HMPPS: London.

Welldon, E.V. (2009) Dancing with death. *British Journal of Psychotherapy, 25,* 149–182.

Zimbardo, P.G. (1969) The human choice: Individuation, reason, and order vs. deindivi- duation, impulse, and chaos. In W.J. Arnold & D. Levine (Eds.), *Nebraska Symposium on Motivation* (pp. 237–307). Lincoln: University of Nebraska Press.

Chapter 10

'What happened?'

An attachment-based understanding of detained women with offending histories, extreme self-harm and diagnoses of personality disorder

Anne Aiyegbusi

Introduction

This chapter is informed by considerable clinical experience of women's forensic services and from the vantage point of multiple roles, including nurse, psychotherapist, teacher, reflective practice group facilitator, supervisor, researcher, manager and leader. In these different roles, I have been able to work alongside, listen to, think with and about and feel overwhelming psychological turbulence with which the women themselves live and front-line colleagues mirror due to the emotional consequences of their roles. Importantly, through collaborative working I have been able to inquire at depth about the clinical phenomena and consider pathways of care that ultimately enable women in secure settings to salvage lives worth living from cycles of chaos, pain and harm. This chapter sets out to articulate and conceptualise some of the complex interpersonal aspects of clinical work on the staff–patient interface in women's forensic services. Suggestions are made as to how understanding this particular complexity can inform subsequent clinical interventions.

I use the term 'front-line staff' as an umbrella, representative of a range of different professional and occupational groups whose roles base them in the social and communal environments of secure services. Included are nurses, health care support staff, housekeeping staff, psychosocial therapists, occupational therapists, social care workers, prison officers and probation staff. Typically, these front-line professionals spend hours at a time with their clients, are required to cover the services 24 hours a day, seven days a week and are unable to retreat to off area offices, for example, that are outside the site of care delivery. Importantly, this staff group can be particularly vulnerable. Despite receiving only cursory training and support, they work closely with clients who have extreme and complex needs.

The quality of services provided for women in secure care has undoubtedly improved exponentially over the three decades of my experience. Despite this there are problematic threads stubbornly woven through the tapestry of care provision regardless of time or place. I believe this reflects the emotional impact the women have on those who care for them and vice versa. As well as shedding light on the complex way early traumatic experiences shape the women's complex needs, I aim to provide insight into the experiences of front-line staff working in these services where traumatised women typically receive diagnoses of personality disorder. Women's impactful risk behaviours can be overwhelming, being frequently and keenly felt by staff. Without an effective framework for understanding their experiences in relation to the women, the staff group will most likely feel solely abused by them, attributing the abuse to sadistic, gratuitous or psychopathic motivations.

My intention is to reframe some of the most complex phenomena encountered, from the perspective of trauma and attachment theory. This is coherent with the relatively recent, and in my opinion, welcome shift in mental health practice towards asking 'What happened to this woman?' rather than 'What is wrong with this woman?' (NIMHE 2008; Johnstone and Boyle 2018), and is in line with current women's mental health strategy highlighting the importance of providing trauma informed care (Department of Health and Social Care 2018).

A way of gaining an understanding of the meaning underlying individual women's behaviours including any deeper communications from the perspective of what happened to her can be offered by a formulation-based rather than a diagnostic approach. Included would be the way she has made sense of her overwhelming emotional experiences and the strategies she developed, probably while unsupported in childhood, to try to survive intolerable feelings on a day-to-day basis. The same strategies are likely to have become immensely problematic in adult life. Furthermore, a formulation-based approach offers a way to work in collaboration with the woman to produce a mutual understanding and narrative of her development and its link with current circumstances in a way that can then be employed to inform care and treatment. This includes identifying triggers to episodes of emotional dysregulation and crisis and establishing what helps to prevent or resolve them (Johnstone and Boyle 2018). An important aim of this type of approach is to work proactively with the aim of avoiding re-enactments of prior traumas within the treatment setting (Department of Health and Social Care 2018), something people with personality disorders have identified as occurring routinely (NIMHE 2003a, 2003b).

'It's behavioural'

The task of front-line workers in services for women offenders diagnosed with personality disorders is rarely experienced as straightforward. Indeed, without specialised training and support, staff whose work bases them in the social environment of services often find themselves feeling bewildered by the perplexing array of behaviours the women engage in. The behaviours can seem so extreme and overwhelming it is possible never to get beyond them to a place of understanding in terms of what they might represent, let alone how the women might be supported towards better health. In forensic settings, as experienced from the perspective of staff members, these behaviours typically include various forms of abuse, self-injury, oscillations between idealising and denigrating staff, rejecting, abusing and sabotaging the care that is offered, 'attention seeking', 'manipulating' and 'demanding'. Additionally, there are roles such as 'the special patient or prisoner' and 'the scapegoat', which seem consistent and add further layers of complexity. These behaviours and roles are often described as 'learnt' in a way that suggests staff perceive the woman or women as coming into the system free from them, only to pick them up by way of contagion from their peers once detained in the institution. Indeed, as if to emphasise this belief system, the term 'it's behavioural' is used as a way to explain, for example, the self-harm, abuse of staff or outbursts of 'demanding' access to items that are deemed prohibited. On the surface this reflects a notion of women developing behaviours that are unconnected to any underlying psychological process, illness or relational context. Actions like self-harm, violence and threats to harm are seen simply as behaviour aiming itself at particular targets such as attention, exploitation or persecution. Perhaps at a slightly deeper level 'it's behavioural' suggests the woman's presentation requires 'consequences' in order to cease engaging in a way staff find difficult to understand. Typically, there is a lingering theme amongst staff expressions of frustration and confusion that concerns the wish to resort to something hard, to retaliate or to punish. The behaviours overwhelm staff and their thinking can come to mirror that of the women whereby sophisticated or thoughtful solutions to difficult-to-bear feelings elude them. Instead, the practical, physical, simple and *behavioural* are sought out.

The picture I've described seems standardised where there has not been considerable investment in psychodynamic, attachment and trauma informed practice. In my experience it reflects the emotional impact the women have on staff, within which the narrative of their individual stories are viscerally communicated. But because of the unexpected and often unfathomable and painful nature of these communications, they go unheard. So the women, lacking alternative strategies, simply escalate the same communications, generating more pain and bewilderment or fervour in staff. The unconscious intention is typically for these communications to make the staff feel something of the women's bodily and emotional experiences in order that they may then understand what is wrong and help. Unfortunately when staff are not trained or supported to decipher these communications, they can be experienced as attacks, which further alienate the women from the help they require (Aiyegbusi and Kelly 2015; McMillan and Aiyegbusi 2009). Nevertheless the behaviours the women engage in and the way front-line staff and the wider team experience and respond to them can potentially go some way towards answering the question 'What happened to these women?'. As we shall see, while the behaviours typically elude conceptual understanding on the part of staff, at the same time they reveal details of previous trauma and the relational context they occurred in which an attachment and trauma informed approach can elucidate.

'What happened to these women?'

In keeping with the wordless narrative of trauma, the woman may not have access to verbal language with which to articulate what happened to her. Her enactments and risk behaviours may be the only form of communication available to her. Along with this non-verbal form of communication, and no matter how abusively she herself behaves, the norm is that she unconsciously wishes to be heard and contained. Hence it is important to ask the question 'What happened?'. Women who find themselves detained in secure settings with diagnoses of personality disorder and who engage in the repertoire of behaviours I have described so far in this chapter often bear a non-verbal imprint of their suffering and the history behind it. Severe attachment traumas feature prominently in their histories, including interpersonal abuse and neglect by those entrusted with their care and wellbeing. Indeed I argue that this factor is at the core of the women's difficulties and is what front-line professionals find themselves on the receiving end of. This argument is in line with Hinshelwood's (2002) thesis about the way those diagnosed with severe personality disorders have usually been traumatised in the context of early care and so go on to identify care with pain and abuse in the future. Because they have come to experience care as abuse, the women may become triggered when professionals approach them, doing their job, communicating in various ways an intention to establish an ongoing interpersonal relationship that is caring, supportive and helpful. What gets triggered is often unprocessed terror and dread associated with the expectation of abuse and betrayal. It is manifest in dissociation, mirroring the flight of the child victim whose fear activated their attachment to the same person abusing them. As such, dissociation was their mind's only available solution to this terrible dilemma.

There may be a number of possible and likely overlapping reasons for the way care and abuse become interrelated. I offer some possible models for how it occurs. None are mutually exclusive. Earlier in life, the repeated dilemma of having to turn for care and protection to abusive or neglectful caregivers happened (Fonagy 1998). Internally, this psychologically irresolvable position is faced again in the budding therapeutic relationship. The offer of care by the professional activates an existing internalised model for intimate relationships with caregivers. During the original trauma, dissociation offered a solution to the irreconcilable position the child was faced with. In this current adult scenario, the dilemma still cannot be logistically or affectively managed with the woman unconsciously perceiving and therefore treating the offer of care as potentially a mask for abuse, rejection or another unbearable attachment experience. The dissociation that now ensues includes behavioural enactments, which unconsciously aim to be rid of the threat while neutralising painful affects that become stirred up. It may be added that these dissociated enactments bring with them something of the rage that could not be expressed to powerful and abusive adults during childhood. They also include elements of repetition compulsion with prior, unprocessed trauma re-enacted in the here and now relationship. Inherent in the repetition compulsion is often the unconscious wish to try to master the trauma in identification with the aggressor (Freud 1936), reliving it now with the affective triumph and power of a perpetrator rather than with the pain and humiliation of a passive victim. Another potential reason for engaging in abusive behaviours, which replicate the abuse she has suffered, is because the woman may at an unconscious level feel the inevitability of pending abuse or pain to be inflicted by this professional just as they have experienced in past attachment relationships. Therefore, it is asking too much for her to be open, trusting and accepting of a relationship with a professional. The stakes involved are too high with the risk of further attachment-related pain felt to be beyond what she can survive. For that reason it unconsciously behoves her to be rid of the threat in her own terms rather than bear the anxiety of waiting passively for what feels like emotionally annihilatory pain to be brought down upon her.

I will describe two case examples of women with complex needs, diagnoses of personality disorders and histories of offending with the aim of clarifying how their extreme behaviours in the treatment setting can be understood from the perspective of what happened to them. I will employ attachment theory as a basis for formulating their needs in a way that can be usefully lent to informing effective plans of care. Both case examples are fictitious but intend to reflect the complexity of the clinical picture women who offend and who are diagnosed with personality disorders typically have in the real world of secure care.

Case example 1: Tara

Tara was born into a family with an extensive history of criminality, domestic violence, excessive substance use and mental health problems. Child sexual abuse had been present in several generations of the family including this one. There were frequent interventions by social services whereby the children, including Tara, were placed into care. They were typically returned to their parents only to be taken into care again, usually a year or so later. By the age of six – and after the third time Tara had been removed from her parents due to neglect, witnessing domestic violence and the strong suspicion that she had been a victim of sexual abuse – she was considered to be unmanageable. She was physically aggressive to foster parents and siblings, ran away from placements, refused to go to school and when she did, bullied other children. As a result, she was frequently moved from placement to placement. By the time she was 11 years old she was regularly stealing alcohol from stores and getting drunk. She also cut herself, always on the same hand. By age 14 Tara seemed unable to mix with other children. Her interactions with her peers were characterised by her dominating and belittling them. Her abuse of alcohol got worse and, though perceived as a bully, she was also considered vulnerable due to repetitively placing herself in unsafe situations while intoxicated. These particular unsafe situations involved a high risk of sexual exploitation. At the age of 15 she was placed in a secure unit, having been convicted of theft numerous times. Her self-harm to her right hand was now regular and severe. And given any opportunity to do so, she drank alcohol until she was comatose. Throughout Tara's life so far, there had been a repeated theme of hope, on the part of the various agencies involved, that she could be cared for well enough to resolve her acting out and destructiveness only for her to overwhelm those looking after her to the point that they requested she be moved on somewhere else.

While in secure care, Tara endeavoured to isolate herself from others. She found her key worker particularly difficult. She did not like what she experienced as 'overtures' that her key worker made in an effort to establish a therapeutic relationship with her. Tara threw hot sugared liquid in the face of her key worker at a time when the latter was kindly but assertively trying to engage her in activities on the unit. The method she used, involving sugar and hot water, is particularly vicious because an intensely hot paste is created that attaches to the skin, maiming the victim. It was felt by her team to be an unprovoked, gratuitous and premeditated assault on a worker who had merely been trying to do her job. Following the assault, Tara was placed in a safe suite, which is a self-contained area within the ward for the segregation of individual patients presenting an immediate risk of harm to themselves or others. She remained under the continuous engagement and observation of three members of staff as she was assessed to be very dangerous. Her team could not understand the assault so did not feel able to predict when she might do it again. Tara initially appeared pleased to be isolated from other young people on the unit but found the intensity of staff presence anxiety-provoking. She tried to avoid them but found nowhere to hide in the relatively small safe suite. She refused activities and as much engagement as she possibly could. Then she began opening old wounds on her right hand and stopped eating. As a result, input from staff revolved around her wound care, self-harm risk, diet and physical health, which was affected by both her poor diet and repeated injuries. Tara remained in the safe suite for a couple of years, physically frail and apparently compulsively harming herself. Attempts to support her to engage with her peer group fell flat. Staff reported that she raised the stakes every time they tried to help her to progress or changed her plan of care. It was also felt that she escalated her risk if there was any suggestion she was improving.

At the age of 16 Tara was transferred to a women's secure mental health setting due to her adjudged risk to others, especially care staff, and her risk to herself as evidenced by her poor diet and self-harm. Surgeons assessed her as being at risk of having her right hand and lower arm amputated. This was because of the severity and repetitiveness of her focussed self-harm. She was considered to be chronic in her presentation and was diagnosed as suffering from emotionally unstable personality disorder and dissocial personality disorder. The team in the secure mental health setting felt her risks could be managed there and discontinued her observations, which were felt to create regression and, as such, for her they were judged to be anti-therapeutic. Her bedroom door was locked while the ward activities programme was underway, when she was encouraged to participate. She was also persuaded by staff to attend the ward community meeting whereby she did sit in the circle but remained passive and silent with her head bowed, hair hiding her face. It was felt to be positive that she managed to remain in communal areas at this stage rather than isolated away. She was praised for this in an attempt to encourage her. Her diet remained poor and it was made clear that if she fell below a certain weight she would be tube fed. It was felt by her team to be important to be clear about boundaries and limits so that Tara knew where she was. She seemed to hover just above the weight at which tube feeding would be initiated.

Despite numerous attempts to immobilise her right arm and observe her continuously, she still managed to pick at old wounds, opening them where she could. As a result, her physical wound was at the centre of clinical thought and interventions. There were periods of a few months at a time when the team felt they were making progress with Tara only for her to regress back to a position where anxieties about her wound and diet overwhelmed the team, who did not know what activated the periods of improvement or regression.

In terms of Tara's life at present, she has remained in the secure unit for four years. Many of the professionals perceive her to be a 'manipulative psychopath'. There are two main reasons for this. The first is because of the way she manages to circumnavigate their plans. The second is because they see her as someone who has no feelings. Nothing is felt to have changed over the four years and she still manages to avoid establishing meaningful relationships with staff or peers.

What happened to Tara?

Tara's early attachment experience can be described as traumatic, involving frequent discontinuities of care with separations back and forth between an abusive family and care placements. This meant she was repeatedly required to develop new relationships only for them to be terminated. A message about herself she internalised as a result of these attachment experiences was that getting close would almost certainly be followed by the pain of separation, rejecting loss and displacement. In terms of internalised models for attachment (Bowlby 1969) she took in that she was not worth caring for, that there was no reliable source of care for her at times of vulnerability and that betrayal and rejection were the inevitabilities of intimate relationships with caregivers. By the age of six and vastly wounded, she had developed an unconscious strategy for these painful interpersonal processes. She took control by behaving in ways that overwhelmed others and whereby she got herself moved from place to place rather than allowing herself to be rejected and moved on by people she had become attached to.

Her sense of herself as fundamentally wounded or ruptured was evident in the form of a persistent, unfathomable but overwhelmingly unbearable emotional experience. The strategies she developed to try to block her internal experiences included numbing by drinking excessive amounts of alcohol and overriding the emotional pain with physical pain through self-harm by cutting. Her stealing likely represented the peace of mind she felt robbed of. The trauma narrative was particularly clear in the nature of her self-harm. She repeatedly cut the hand she'd been persuaded to masturbate her abuser with. Additionally, by way of re-enactment she placed herself in positions where she was vulnerable to sexual exploitation. As well as re-enacting her trauma as victim and non-protecting mother, she also did so as perpetrator in identification with the aggressor where she was experienced as a bully, serving the purpose of keeping familiar people away from her and avoiding intimate contact or vulnerability in relationships where she could then be let down. She destroyed opportunity before it could be destroyed for her. The hope of a different experience in relationships was projected onto professionals who despite their good intentions, could still not manage to contain her and so the repetition of moving on and elsewhere continued.

Tara's pattern of disturbed but also desperate relating persisted. It overwhelmingly emotionally impacted on the professionals working with her. Pushed into a reactive stance, professionals had not completed a clinical formulation. While in secure care, Tara made a very severe assault on a key worker, whose kindness (or metaphoric sweetness) was concretely thrown back in her face. Within the constraints of secure services, Tara went on to establish a life in a kind of suspended animation whereby, dissociated, she existed without intimate relationships within a clinical context ridden with physical pain, discomfort and starvation. Her inner wounds, deprivation and emotional pain were converted and concretely represented as bodily wounds, dietary needs and physical pain. This concretised conversion shaped her interpersonal experience, controlling the nature of interventions she did have with professionals to those she could emotionally manage. Unconsciously it was preferable to churning anxiety and panic elicited by emotional intimacy with people who according to her internalised model, would act in unpredictable ways, inevitably betraying her through rejection or abuse. When relating occurred on her terms she knew the interpersonal terrain, feeling an element of control that she would not have if lost in the wilderness of a healthy relationship. Professionals regarded her as psychopathic, identifying that she was engaging in some form of strategic behaviour to dictate the conditions of her life in detention to spite them but could not recognise the profound distress, trauma and dissociation that lay beneath the manoeuvres, re-enactments and enactments.

Case example 2: Cassie

Cassie was the eighth and youngest child in a large chaotic family. The sibling immediately older than her, a girl, had learning disabilities, epilepsy and congenital heart disease, requiring a lot of care. The message Cassie took in regarding this sister was that she was special. Because Cassie was left maternally deprived and felt this was related to the intense amount of care her sister needed, she took in that she was not special. Indeed, Cassie's mother appeared to her to be preoccupied with the sister with whom she seemed to have a very special bond. This was the opposite of Cassie's relationship with their mother. She was overlooked and considered self-sufficient from early childhood. In fact Cassie was often lonely and under-stimulated. She tried to bond with her older siblings but they were busy with their own lives and did not want to be slowed down by a much younger child. Or this is what Cassie felt. She relied on her older siblings for care however, as their mother was so involved with her sister. It was in this domestic context that Cassie came to be sexually abused by a maternal uncle. This uncle had identified that she was neglected and somewhat isolated and lonely. He groomed her by being emotionally and physically available, making a fuss of her and making *her* feel special. At the same time he justified his presence and additional time spent with her as helping her mother out given she was so busy with the sister. This sexual abuse occurred for a number of years, until Cassie reached puberty. Unbeknown to her, she had reached an age which her paedophile uncle no longer found sexually desirable. Her experience was that she was dropped and forgotten by the only person who appeared dedicated to her. She kept the secret of the uncle's sexual abuse and did not tell her mother or anybody else about it. However, she began to act in a way that suggested something was very wrong with her.

At 14 Cassie began to self-harm, take drugs to block her feelings of inner pain and get into fights with other girls. She seemed depressed and unlike most girls at her school, did not seem remotely interested in her appearance or her future. Although considered intelligent, Cassie lost interest in her studies and showed no evidence of ambition. At home she withdrew from the family, which did not seem to be particularly noticed. Due to depression, she was treated at the local Child and Adolescent Mental Health Service (CAMHS). It was noted by the CAMHS team that her mother seemed to be distracted by her other daughter's needs. By this time, the daughter with special needs was seriously ill and receiving end of life care. When she died, Cassie's mother experienced profound depression and in fact, within the family, her needs were put before Cassie's.

Cassie struggled through adolescence with some support from CAMHS. She attempted further studies a number of times but always gave up before completion, citing depressive relapse as the reason each time. She no longer took illicit drugs but did misuse prescribed anxiolytics and hypnotics, intermittently taking more than prescribed in order to achieve numbness from the inner pain she felt. She became avoidant of contact with peers and therefore had not been in a fight for some considerable time. While still self-harming by cutting, this was less frequent and less severe than had been the case prior to contact with CAMHS. She still had not disclosed the sexual abuse by her uncle to anybody.

Cassie remained directionless until she met an older man. She fell in love with him and for a couple of years her mood and interest in herself and her appearance improved. She blossomed under her boyfriend's loving attention and found her sense of psychological distress diminishing. She moved in with him and became pregnant with a daughter. Cassie was looking forward to the birth of her child but as her pregnancy progressed, she experienced old familiar feelings associated with neglect and loneliness. Her partner was actually far from enamoured by the prospect of having a child. He emotionally withdrew from Cassie, spending his time outside of the home, socialising with others, frequently coming home drunk and belligerent. When Cassie complained about this he became verbally abusive, complaining about her incessant neediness. Cassie felt painfully rejected and as her pregnancy neared its end, she rapidly became depressed and took an overdose. She could not explain why she had done this except that she was overcome with a despair she found intolerable. She was reluctant to say this was related to her partner's withdrawal and rejection of her.

When Cassie's daughter was born, she was receiving care from a perinatal mental health team. The team noted that Cassie seemed to be entirely focused on the baby to the exclusion of all else. She and her partner appeared to be living separate lives, he socialising outside of the home much of the time and Cassie completely enraptured by her baby to the point of enmeshment. Even by the standards of early motherhood, she seemed preoccupied by her baby's every breath. By the time the baby was six months old Cassie was regularly taking her to the doctors and had already taken her to the emergency room twice, appearing fearful for the baby's health. On no occasion was the baby found to be suffering from any health condition. By the time Cassie's daughter was three years old, her partner had left the family and she continued to be engrossed in her daughter's wellbeing, constantly convinced the child was sick despite medical evidence to the contrary. Due to concern about her relationship with her daughter, Cassie was referred to parenting classes. She reluctantly attended. Staff working with her and her daughter expressed concern about her suffocating effect on her daughter. Cassie was not inclined to take up offers of more in-depth psychotherapy.

When Cassie's daughter started school, she developed unusual physical symptoms that required frequent medical attention. She missed a lot of school and Cassie remained preoccupied, seemingly coming to life only when she was able to provide hands-on care for her daughter whether at home or during hospital admissions for exploratory tests. The paediatric team whose care Cassie's daughter was under, in conjunction with the local child protection team, identified that Cassie had induced the symptoms. While Cassie had denied this, her daughter's symptoms ceased after she was removed from Cassie's care. The accusations and her daughter's placement into foster care precipitated a rapid and extreme breakdown in Cassie's mental health. She appeared profoundly depressed and self-harmed seriously. She also took overdoses, attended accident and emergency departments, where she then abused hospital staff when they tried to care for her. On one of these occasions she assaulted a doctor who was attempting to examine her. Importantly, it was when the doctor turned her back on Cassie that she assaulted her.

Due to the assault, Cassie was remanded to prison. In addition to the charge of assault on the doctor, police were investigating the allegations that she had fabricated or induced illness in her daughter. Her distress and self-harm escalated in prison to the point where she was considered to be at high risk of suicide. She was diagnosed with emotionally unstable personality disorder and depression. She was transferred under an emergency section of the Mental Health Act (1983) to an enhanced women's secure unit. Throughout her escalated distress Cassie required high numbers of staff to observe and escort her. Despite this, she was not felt to be amenable to engagement and rarely did the staff input involve anything beyond restraint or providing basic care such as addressing her personal hygiene, serving food and drink or providing strong clothing. The staff felt dominated by her and could not find a way to reduce her distress, extreme behavioural enactments or self-harm through conversation or interpersonal engagement. Her self-harm escalated to including trying to bite and tear at her breasts. Staff felt overwhelmed and completely deskilled. Other patients felt she took up all the staff time and then abused it while leaving them feeling deprived, neglected and unable to have their needs met. Because of her risk of suicide, Cassie had come to the attention of the most senior levels of management in the service. Staff looking after her felt she was able to go over their heads, drawing very senior managers into questioning her care in a way that left those on the front line feeling diminished and humiliated.

What happened to Cassie?

Cassie's early attachment experience was of neglect. This was complicated by her being placed in a position of feeling overlooked whilst witnessing all maternal love and care going elsewhere, to a special sister with whom her mother seemed to her to be besotted. By implication, Cassie internalised a model whereby she was not special enough for love or care. She took in that to secure love and care, one needed to produce a special bond. Without it, one was left with nothing or at best 'cast off care'. Her paedophile uncle's attentions made her feel special while he exploited her vulnerability solely for his own sexual gratification and then rejected her when he was no longer sexually interested. Rejection by this paedophile uncle precipitated depression and self-harm.

Both her rivalry and inability to compete with her sister was evident in her fights and sense of defeat with other girls. Cassie had also internalised her abuse by the paedophile uncle, now abusing herself through self-harm and drug taking. After a few unsuccessful attempts to succeed in mainstream life, Cassie finally came to life when she fell in love, securing a special bond for herself whereby her internal distress fell away under the dedicated care of another. However, when she became pregnant, her partner lost interest and once again she experienced the pain of sudden rejection and consequent depression and self-harmed in the form of an overdose. This relationship paralleled that of her paedophile uncle. Then she was rejected because she reached puberty. Now she was rejected because she was pregnant.

When Cassie's daughter was born she mirrored the maternal care she had seen her mother provide for her sister with special needs. This was also the all-consuming mothering she had craved for herself. Cassie unconsciously redoubled her attempts to secure care by perceiving illness in her child. This would also mirror the narrative of her early attachment experiences, confirming that special children get everything, which includes dedication from professionals as well as parents. It was also a way for her to receive the full enormity of care services that she had witnessed her sister getting.

As her daughter got older, Cassie unconsciously sought to maintain her dependency and therefore amplify the bond between them. She did this by keeping her daughter ill. By inducing illness, Cassie was able to exacerbate her daughter's attachment to her and revel in the role of mother to a completely dependent child. The function of this abuse of her daughter was to keep their special bond active in an intense way. It was to re-enact the relationship she had been kept out of as a small child, the one between her mother and disabled sister. Only this time she was not the passive excluded child but the all-powerful mother. She was also in identification with her paedophile uncle, eliciting attachment from and then abusing her daughter for her own gratification.

When Cassie's abuse of her daughter was discovered and followed by her removal into care, Cassie again experienced severe depression. Her anger towards hospital staff as proxies for her internalised neglectful mother was evident in her abuse of them. When one doctor turned her back on Cassie, she was flooded with previously repressed rage about how her mother had been able to overlook her time and time again. The assault on this doctor led to her admission to secure care. Within the enhanced secure unit, she experienced profound regression. She again unconsciously re-enacted the traumatic attachment scenario of her childhood from a position of control, this time as the 'special needs patient', whereby she was able to project her inner feelings of deprivation and neglect onto other patients (or siblings) on the ward. She acted in a severely disturbed way, which amplified the levels of input staff were required to provide for her. Regardless of how degrading and traumatic this was, at least she was not the one left wanting again. Another layer of insight about her internal world could be seen in her destructive attacks on her breasts, representing rage at her failed womanhood and motherhood with the loss of her daughter as well as the failure of her own mother to provide good enough nurturing. In yet another layer of insight about what happened to Cassie, she was able to behave in a way that drew in senior levels of management. Thus, the frontline staff were left diminished and humiliated, as well as the other patients on the ward. All resented Cassie as she had resented her sister during their childhood.

What might help?

I have provided two case examples of women diagnosed with personality disorders in secure settings. The intention is for the case examples to represent the way early attachment traumas and abuse typically lack verbal narrative but become enacted or re-enacted in the index incident or offence. Importantly these enactments and re-enactments continue in the institutional environment, with professionals on the front line becoming drawn into the trauma script, as victim, perpetrator or non-protecting carer who turned a blind eye. Complicating the picture is the way the women internalise models for attachment relationships that intertwine care with abuse. This has particular relevance to those clinical staff whose role is to establish relationships with the women in order to deliver help and support. The women may attack their offers including by assaulting the professionals themselves because of underlying but unarticulated distrust and fear that the professional may use their role as a guise for perpetrating further abuse, pain or harm. Likewise dissociated rage felt towards original traumatising caregivers, or the responsible adults who failed them, may come to the surface within these new relationships. The narrative of their trauma along with their feelings about it may also be written on the women's bodies through their self-harm (Adshead 1997; Motz 2008, 2009) or on those of their children who may not be experienced as separate (Motz 2008; Welldon 1988).

Davies (1996) captures the unconscious, unarticulated task of professionals working with forensic patients:

> The view is taken that professionals who deal with offenders are not free agents but potential actors who have been assigned roles in the individual offender's own re-enactment of their internal world drama.

The professionals have the choice not to perform but they can only make this choice when they have a good idea what the role is they are trying to avoid. Until they can work this out, they are likely to be drawn into the play, unwittingly and therefore not unwillingly.

(p. 133)

Davies (1996) goes on to explain that if the professional does not know what the role is before they commence their work with the patient, they will believe their subsequent actions to be autonomous. Davies (1996: 133) mentions that the index offence offers a 'preview of the plot ... in the somewhat cryptic form of the offence'. As mentioned, with regard to women diagnosed with personality disorders, previews will also be graphically available in their self-harming behaviours and in their relational patterns. Therefore, it is crucial to ask what happened? It is crucial to begin to build up the picture of what happened from the first contact with the woman.

It is important to involve the woman, her family if possible, and information from professional reports and case notes in the task of building up a picture of her developmental history. This can then be used to inform an understanding of her mental health problems, risk behaviours including offending, and her current relational style. Typically these mirror the early history of attachment trauma and abuse. Once this picture has been established, professionals will be able to be aware of the roles they need to avoid. In order to provide containment and a secure base rather than accelerate insecurity and facilitate re-enactment, the woman herself needs to also be aware of how what happened to her in her early life is replicated in her current distress and dangerousness. In partnership with professionals, she needs to be helped to identify what triggers episodes of emotional dysregulation and risk behaviours, along with strategies for preventing and managing them when they occur. They may take the form of advanced directives whereby a plan of care is developed to address future escalated distress and risk while the woman's mood and mental health are more regulated and stable.

Due to the sensitivity to intense attachment experiences that women requiring secure care typically have, special attention needs to be paid to attachment related events when identifying triggers. These will include those which are routine aspects of institutional care such as when new patients are admitted or discharged from the clinical or residential area, when the woman herself is transferred from one environment to another, changes of key workers, key workers' holidays and use of temporary staff on shift. Likewise, assessment as to how best to begin to establish therapeutic relationships should be thought about.

Some women find the early stages of such relationships intolerable and when unable to employ avoidant strategies, and in the context of dissociation, reflexively attack to put an end to the felt torture of it. This pattern can be seen in the case example of Tara. In such cases, a team-based approach (Clarke-Moore & Barber 2009) may be preferable to the intensity of a one-to-one relationship. This formulation including the risk assessment and care plan would be helpfully shared with the woman and the whole of her care team as the basis of their work together. This approach requires thinking and clinical work to take place proactively in order to avoid the kind of overwhelming reactive work that occurs once the woman and professionals become immersed in full scale re-enactments and concretisations of her trauma.

Even when working in a proactive and integrated way, this clinical work is emotionally difficult. Staff will inevitably experience a surfacing of their own attachment and emotional vulnerabilities. For that reason, training and regular containing structures such as reflective practice groups are essential. In these spaces the work can be thought about and emotional reactions explored and made sense of within the narrative of patient formulations and an awareness of individual staff and team vulnerabilities.

I have attempted in this chapter to operationalise a dimension of complexity that applies to women whose extreme trauma histories leave them vulnerable to becoming 'othered' and hidden within secure mental health settings. I have focused on attachment, trauma and psychodynamic processes in order to present as clear a picture as I can of the phenomena in question. As such, I must acknowledge that because of limited available space, I have made no attempt to address the relevance of intersectional factors. However, it feels important to note the relevance of these factors in regard to individual women's presentations and their impact on others, including staff within interpersonal transactions. Interactions will also have intersectional relevance to members of staff in accordance with their own demographics and this will require consideration and reflection within staff support spaces. For example, frontline staff from Black, Asian and Minority Ethnic backgrounds may be particularly vulnerable to attracting projections that their white colleagues are not, and vice versa. Within the team, this would need to be validated and thought about, with the team able to remain integrated in the face of such differences.

References

Adshead, G. (1997) Written on the Body? Deliberate Self Harm and Violence. In *A Practical Guide to Forensic Psychotherapy*. Eds: E. V. Welldon & C. Van Velsen JKP. London, pp. 110–114.

Aiyegbusi, A. & Kelly, D. (2015) 'This is the Pain I Feel!' Projection and Emotional Pain in the Nurse – Patient Relationship with People Diagnosed with Personality Disorders in Forensic and Specialist Personality Disorder Services: Findings from a Mixed Methods Study. *Psychoanalytic Psychotherapy*. Vol 29 (3), 1–19.

Bowlby, J. (1969) *Attachment and Loss Volume 1: Attachment*. The Tavistock Institute of Human Relations. London.

Clarke-Moore, J. & Barber, M. (2009) A Secure Model of Nursing Care for Women. In *Therapeutic Relationship with Offenders: An Introduction to the Psychodynamics of Forensic Mental Health Nursing*. Eds: A. Aiyegbusi & J. Clarke-Moore. JKP. London, pp. 201–210.

Davies, R. (1996) The Inter-disciplinary Network and the Internal World of the Offender. In *Forensic Psychotherapy: Crime, Psychodynamics and the Offender Patient*. Eds: C. Cordess and M. Cox. JKP. London, pp. 133–144.

Department of Health. (1983) *The Mental Health Act for England and Wales*. HMSO. London.

Department of Health and Social Care. (2018) *Women's Mental Health Taskforce – Final Report*. Crown Copyright. www.gov.uk/dhsc or https://assets.publishing.service.gov.uk/government/uploads/system/uploads/attachment_data/file/765821/The_Womens_Mental_Health_Taskforce_-_final_report1.pdf.

Fonagy, P. (1998) An Attachment Theory Approach to Treatment of the Difficult Patient. *Bulletin of the Menninger Clinic*. Vol 62 (2), 147–169.

Freud A. (1936) *The Ego and the Mechanisms of Defence*. Hogarth Press. London.

Hinshelwood, R. D. (2002) Abusive Help – Helping Abuse: The Psychodynamic Impact of Severe Personality Disorder on Caring Institutions. *Criminal Behaviour and Mental Health*. Vol 12, S20–S30.

Johnstone, L. & Boyle, M. with Cromby, J., Dillon, J., Harper, D., Kinderman, P., Longden, E., Pilgrim, D. & Reid, J. (2018) *The Power Threat Meaning Framework: Towards the Identification of Patterns in Emotional Distress, Unusual Experiences and Troubling or Troubled Behaviour as an Alternative to Functional Diagnosis*. British Psychological Society. Leicester.

McMillan, S. & Aiyegbusi, A. (2009) Crying Out for Care. In *Therapeutic Relationship with Offenders: An Introduction to the Psychodynamics of Forensic Mental Health Nursing*. Eds: A. Aiyegbusi & J. Clarke-Moore. JKP. London, pp. 171–188.

Motz, A. (2008) *The Psychology of Female Violence: Crimes Against the Body*. Brunner-Routledge. East Sussex.

Motz, A. (2009) *Managing Self-Harm: Psychological Perspectives*. Routledge. East Sussex.

National Institute for Mental Health in England. (2003a) *Personality Disorder: No Longer a Diagnosis of Exclusion. Policy Implementation Guidance for the Development of Services for People with Personality Disorder*. Department of Health. England.

National Institute for Mental Health in England. (2003b) *Breaking the Cycle of Rejection: The Personality Disorder Capabilities Framework*. Department of Health. England.

National Institute for Mental Health in England. (2008) *Informed Gender Practice: Mental Health Acute Care that Works for Women*. Department of Health.

Welldon, E. V. (1988) *Mother, Madonna, Whore: The Idealisation and Denigration of Motherhood*. Guildford. London.

Chapter 11

Imprisoned and in prison

Organised defences working against black women and girls

Maxine Dennis

Introduction

In any organisation there are anxieties which need to be managed in order for employees to carry out the primary task or aim of that organisation. I discuss here how the organisational defence against the anxiety of corruption is managed in the criminal justice system. This defence against recognising the complex needs of those who act out by committing an offence can take the form of criminalisation of women or girls when their actual 'offence' may be related to their social class, deprivation or poverty. There is a criminalisation of women and girls more generally when they step out of line, and violate the acceptable norms of 'femininity', but I specifically examine the treatment of black women. There is some evidence that black women and girls are more harshly treated within the criminal justice system and that they receive longer sentences than their white counterparts for the same offence; black and mixed ethnicity women are more than twice as likely as white women to face arrest (Cardale et al., 2017). I am proposing that this phenomenon is caused by the internalised racism, social stereotyping and bias at play, often unconsciously, within the criminal justice system, and that the system perpetuates a process of colonial object relating.

In this way of operating, the objectified 'black' must be treated more harshly so as to be kept in line, and does not need access to psychological health care to address the complex intersectionality of emotional and social presentations. This complexity is also defended against by the woman or girl through their criminal acting out, self-harm or fragile contact with reality. These presentations are aimed at keeping or protecting a more fragile self safe within the non-facilitating environment of the outside world, the context in which many have grown up within the UK. The non-facilitating environment is both external and may have been further supported within their family structures, and thus their internal object relating. The internal object relating is characterised by a sense of guilt for 'badness' which is attributed to blackness and has to be punished.

In any organisation there is an interplay between the area in which the employee works, the organisational factors and the internal factors. Internal factors are played out in the transference and countertransference and require supervision, consultation and reflective practice-case discussions so that good use can be made of the projective data. I propose that there are parallels between the dynamics of the organisation and the type of work undertaken by the organisation. Throughout this book we have made reference to the over-representation of black women in custody and to them being perceived as dangerous and threatening, rather than distressed and traumatised, which is in contrast to their lived experience. I will explore this in relation to the experience of those who work in custodial settings with black girls and women.

The restrictive experience of being black in a white governed environment is captured well by Rankine (2015):

> Though the white liberal imagination likes to feel temporarily bad about the black suffering, there really is no mode of empathy that can replicate the daily strain of knowing that as a black person you can be killed for simply being black: no hands in your pockets, no playing music, no sudden movements, no driving your car, no walking at night, no walking in the day, no turning onto this street, no entering this building, no standing your ground, no standing here, no standing there, no talking back, no playing with toy guns, no living while black.
>
> (p. 1)

The backdrop

Prison staff work in a highly regimented and restrictive environment, tasked with controlling others, which can affect one's capacity to think and feel (Dennis, 2012). The current culture of many UK public services is such that there is a struggle for limited resources. Professionals are invited to compete with each other for these resources and when services fail the failures are attributed to staff (i.e. a lack of resilience). Often staff have to work under conditions which make reasonable service problematic. The cuts in the number of prison officer roles by Chris Grayling, Secretary of State for Justice in 2014,[1] then the drive to train more workers, is a process that seems endemic across prison, mental health and physical health services. Often a consequence is the loss of experienced staff who can have a calming influence on new staff and those with chronic mental health difficulties or seasoned prisoners. One has to be mindful of staff who are burned out or apathetic and themselves in need of career opportunities to enliven their practice and reduce their vicarious traumatisation; both they and the prisoners can become institutionalised and depressed.

In the classic paper by Isabel Menzies-Lyth (1959), she described how nurses working with very sick and dying patients would refer to the patient's condition and bed number rather than the individual, for example 'the liver in bed 11'; this process mitigated against the pain of working with such patients. Menzies-Lyth referred to this as a social defence mechanism which was unconsciously adopted to cope with the anxiety and pain attached to nursing. Such defences were codified within institutional practice, creating depersonalised ways of working and preventing workers from feeling connected to the women or girls behind their 'charges' or really gaining satisfaction from caring work.

I want to make use of this notion of social defences against anxiety in relation to the criminal justice system and prisons in particular, where, in both, the rules of engagement can serve to alienate the 'offenders' (scum, cons)[2] and the 'guards' (screws, cowboys, yobwocs).[3] The prisoners also have a range of terms for each other (including Charlie Big Spuds, Billy Big Bollocks and Jack the Biscuit)[4] to name but a few.[5] The prison system is organised in such a way as to promote a moral imperative whereby there is social control and punishment for wrongdoing. The prison guards and the inmates occupy polarised positions aimed at managing the effects of corruption and violence. I am suggesting that what is defended against are the effects of deprivation, poverty, psychological distress and disturbance, neglect and abuse. When the prisoners are black girls and women, with histories of trauma, poverty and discrimination, the pain of making real contact with them can enhance the unconscious wish to keep them at a distance, with destructive results.

The source anxiety is that of corruption

Rankine captures the basic phantasies highlighted within this book. In Chapter 3, I describe the perceptions of black women as angry and dangerous, and how that terrible caricature and misperception gets widely replicated and even internalised by the women themselves.

The position of the officer is one of both control and care, but when the women are perceived to be wild or unruly, a perception that can unconsciously be triggered by the colour of their skin and resultant stereotypes, the officer may become a persecutory figure who herself feels alienated and afraid. The prisoner may identify with the perception of herself as a frightening and dangerous person, and respond accordingly, as she is faced with a distorted reflection of herself, and feels threatened and unseen. We can see how this dynamic is deeply unhelpful and would reinforce racist stereotypes in staff and feelings of alienation, hurt and grievance in the women who are seen through this lens.

The position of the inmate: black women and girls

The situation for black women has much in common with the experience of Gregor Samsa in Kafka's story, *The Metamorphosis* (1915):

One morning, as Gregor Samsa was waking up from anxious dreams, he discovered that in bed he had been changed into a monstrous verminous bug.
He lay on his amour-hard back and saw, as he lifted his head up a little, his
brown, arched abdomen divided up into rigid bow-like sections. From this
height the blanket, just about ready to slide off completely, could hardly stay
in place. His numerous legs, pitifully thin in comparison to the rest of his
circumference, flickered helplessly before his eyes.

(p. 3)

Kafka's story goes on to describe Gregor being misunderstood, attacked and gro-
tesquely transformed, and whilst he is not actually describing a character in
prison, it brings to life the horrifying experience of becoming an 'othered' creature. The story graphically details how one can be shunned by one's family and
society. I believe this alienation captures something of the process for some black
girls and women who end up in prison. How can the monstrosity that one becomes
(i.e. one's crime) be rehabilitated, and a future where the individual can empower
themselves through the right support and opportunities be realised? Often there
seems little interest in what has led the woman to the position she currently finds
herself in and how imprisonment changes her. The prison system changes
a person. 'Imprisonment is itself a common source of mental distress, embodying
stigma and condemnation and triggering mental health needs relating to loss, fear
and insecurity' (Bradley, 2009, cited in Player, 2017).

Can these girls and women still be loved and cared for, or is this only
within the idealised realm of liberal politics and wistful thinking, especially
when there are limited after care resources for ex-inmates' mental health and
social support needs? The very short sentences that many women accrue mean
that no meaningful work can be undertaken while they are inside or that work
started might not be completed or followed up. Of course the offence and the
circumstances leading to it need to be understood in reference to the particular
girl or woman. And this understanding may be restricted by our bias.

In his unfinished novel, *The Trial* (1925), Kafka writes about a character who
is arrested on charges he cannot determine, but nonetheless has to go through the
process of trying to contest his case. He describes how the main character is
viewed differently by others, no longer seen as a person but as someone who has
committed an offence. He is never formally charged with a crime but continually
harassed, persecuted and finally executed 'like a dog'. This is the fate of count-
less victims of political and legal injustice. Little did Kafka know his unfinished
story would foretell the worry of many and the plight of some black people.

Roots of the organisational dynamics and transgenerational transition of violence

One can view the current organisational dynamics within custodial settings
where predominantly white prison officers work with black prisoners (Moj,

2019) as an expression of the legacy of slavery, unconsciously codified within the prison system, as in so many other institutions where racist practices have developed without the conscious awareness of workers.

> As of 31 March 2018, just over 94% of prison officers in England and Wales for whom ethnicity was known were White (including White ethnic minorities), and just under 6% came from the Asian, Black, Mixed ethnicity and Other ethnic groups combined.

These unconscious practices may affect both inmates and staff.

We can understand something of how this develops through consulting the analysis of Blanco (Levine and Kline, 2007) who developed a five-generation account of the effects of violence on subsequent generations in South America, applied to the indigenous people of Australia, which is also applicable to the African slavery discourse (Alleyne, 2019). This is not meant to be a commentary on the make-up of families, but an assessment of the effects of violence over the generations. The first generation are enslaved, killed and imprisoned and unable to keep the family together or safe (slavery was abolished in Britain in 1833, French colonies 1848 and in the USA in 1865). In the second generation, the devastating effects of human objectification take hold, destroying a sense of healthy family attachments. The black man is used as a studding machine and the black women as mules. Neither own their bodies. The black woman's obedience to white authority is seen as the ultimate good and rebellion is to be punished. We can see this in the high rates of prostitution and subsequent criminalisation of prostituted women, many of whom are from migrant and black communities, as described in Chapter 4.

With the third generation, the impact of 400 years of slavery is evident – a legacy of mental destruction. Black people are still treated as less than human and captured in the aforementioned quote from Rankine (2015), and described by the work of Fanon (1952,1991), Du Bois (1994), Gilroy (1993) and Morrison (2017). They are still dealing with the effects of colonialisation and hatred. For these families, there is often a breakdown in the immediate or extended family unit – in many cases the father is absent. This creates lone-parent families led often by the mother, either on her own or with multiple partners bearing their children, often subject to domestic violence. The violence in these relationships can be related to the earlier treatment of violence in historical enslavement and the legacy that has been internalised and is now re-enacted. Lone mothers who then receive custodial sentences often lose their children into the care system; this then feeds into an intergenerational transmission of trauma, with a particular impact on black families. Fourth generational effects can be seen in parenting styles as well as in intimate partner relating. Here the children are severely impacted on and this relationship pattern is in turn repeated in terms of harsh disciplining of children with the normalisation of beatings, shaming and infantalisation. By the fifth generation we see increasing societal and political distress and divisions, increasing black on black violence. This is evident in gang/youth violence, and particularly in terms of women in the correctional justice system. Here we can also see internalised racism as an impact of the legacy of slavery, leading to identification as 'white',[6] as Fanon (1952,1991) described, and suspicion of other black women. As racism is deeply ingrained in our society the ongoing work of one's life time is how to interrupt it within oneself and within our institutions. This will involve examining the impact of colonisation.

Organisational factors that bear the impact of colonisation

Black, Asian and Minority Ethnic (BAME) women are vastly under-represented on the Women Offenders with Personality Disorder (WOPD) pathway, so they do not become entitled to specialist services. In the United Kingdom prison officers are rarely black, as previously described. So there is an over-representation of black prisoners not 'deserving' of special treatment from personality disorder services, and an under-representation of black authority figures in the form of prison officers. In this way the legacy of slavery/blacks as criminals gets perpetuated. It is also noteworthy that a few token black authority figures will not challenge a system the majority population need to want that system to change for significant shifts in practice to occur.

There is a question about whether someone should be labelled as personality disordered to obtain the mental health care required (Player, 2017). There may be women who do not have access to treatment who could benefit, but the prison staff see their presentation as reflecting 'bad' behaviour that has been freely chosen. In order to be seen as having a personality disorder in the WOPD screening path, their difficulties need to meet certain criteria, but the BAME women are often seen as mentally ill or violent rather than suffering with personality disorders. The notion of personality disorder as defined by problematic, persistent and pervasive difficulties has been criticised in that 'problematic, persistent and pervasive are terms which are not strictly defined and permit a high degree of discretion' (Player, 2017:). We also need to note the co-morbidity between depression, anxiety, alcohol and drug misuse.

In any organisation the relationship between the hierarchical structures, organisational conflict, conflict between the staff's personal values and organisational values need to be recognised, which can be looked at during staff supervision. In a prison setting, the staff's own experiences of trauma and loss, and their attachment history, will affect their responses to the women, which they may not be cognisant of. Ongoing staff development opportunities through continued professional development (CPD), case consultations, staff support and enabling continued learning is important. This will enable them to keep the female prisoners' experiences in mind. The clinical illustration below highlights the psychosocial history and the internal processes.

Psychosocial history and internal processes: Leanne

Leanne was seen following her initial referral for assessment due to the beginning of care proceedings for her son, Jude, then aged two months. She had an older son, Harrison, born when she was 17, who had been placed for adoption under a care order, against her wishes. When I met her, Leanne was a 23-year-old woman of dual heritage background with a long history of trauma, self-harm and eating disorders, who had been released from custody some 18 months previously after serving a sentence for aggravated burglary and several offences of theft. She had a new partner, Del, who was her baby's father, and their relationship was thought to be stable, as he had no criminal history, had not been known to social services in childhood and there was no reported violence in their relationship.

She presented as a slight and well-dressed woman, looking younger than her years, who told me at the first interview that she wanted to prove to the local authority and other child care professionals that she was a fit mother who could put her baby's needs first. Although she was now a grown woman she evoked a protective maternal response in me, as she appeared vulnerable, despite a well made-up, fashionable appearance. She conveyed the impression of wearing a perfect mask that hid underlying sadness and frailty. Her arms were covered with scars from cuts and also what appeared to be burn marks.

Leanne had a long history of deprivation and abuse in her own early life as her mother had been addicted to crack cocaine and alcohol and her father to heroin, leaving her to bring up her younger siblings, a boy and girl who were two and five years younger. Leanne had rarely gone to school, and when she had, she was bullied and teased about her parents being 'junkies' and about her own unkempt appearance. She found it hard to wash and care for her clothes, as there were few resources in the household for the children, and money was spent on feeding her parents' drug habit. Her mother was a black woman and her father white.

Leanne learned to 'go without' and to associate oral satisfaction with alcohol use and smoking, behaviour she saw her parents engage in daily, alongside her father's injections. She would make minimal meals for her younger siblings, mainly feeding them on ready-made food or snacks, and would eat very little herself. She found her hunger pains satisfying, as they allowed her to feel that she was able to deprive herself of something, rather than indulging her cravings as her parents did. She had also experienced her parents as ravenous, eating sugary foods at times when their 'highs' were wearing off, or in her father's case, when he tried to come off the heroin and craved sugar. She sometimes felt too sick and scared to eat, and so this also inhibited her capacity to eat to stop hunger pains and feel sated. She was a tense and unhappy girl, constantly on the look-out for danger signs at home and trying her best to protect her younger siblings from the kind of abuse she received at school, or from witnessing the violent arguments her parents often had when drunk or high.

As Leanne entered adolescence she became increasingly critical of her body and disliked any signs of development, as these were evidence that she was becoming a woman. She loved her thin arms and legs, and wanted her chest to remain flat. The thought of having periods frightened her and she hated pubic hair. Although she didn't consciously choose to delay her sexual development, her heavily restricted diet meant she was well below a healthy weight for a girl of her age and she did not start her periods until she was 16, enjoying looking like a much younger child. Despite her cruelty towards her own body and its appetites, she was devoted to feeding and caring for her three younger siblings and also seemed to take pleasure in watching others eat while she starved, as so often characterises an anorexic disorder.

Although Leanne would not consider her eating habits violent, her anorexia was evident both from her description and from her medical records, documenting her severely restricted food intake to the extent that her menstrual periods had stopped altogether for several months. She subjected her body to violent assaults, a form of ongoing torture, where she kept herself alive in order to test the limits of her own survival. In this sense, her self-harm could be viewed as a sign of hope, as an attempt to find something that would withstand her attacks and contain her aggressive impulses. She did not want to die, but at times she was not sure she wanted to live, as the fear of her home life and the pressure she felt to parent her younger siblings was hard for her to bear. Although an intelligent girl who loved to learn, her school attendance was erratic, and she often stayed home to keep guard over her mother. When her mother's cravings were particularly intense she would turn to prostitution, and Leanne would see men arriving at the house. Although she herself did not make the connection between anorexia and retardation of sexual development, it seemed likely that her fear of sexuality and wish to remain a child was also linked to the traumatic exploitation of her mother's body, to which she was witness. The significance of her mother's ethnic background (Jamaican) was something Leanne put into words, and her feelings about her own dark skin, which she violently assaulted, were hateful and murderous.

Leanne was frightened of men, and kept herself largely apart from her classmates, not wanting them to learn about her home life, as she felt ashamed and distressed about her parents' addiction and the mess and chaos of home. At 16 she was befriended by an older adolescent, Jason, aged 19, who introduced her to sex, alcohol and shoplifting. All of this felt risky and exciting to her, and it coincided with her next youngest sister now being a teenager and able to look after the younger sibling. Leanne felt released from a terrible burden of caregiving, but also guilty about leaving home to spend time with Jason and also troubled by weight gain from alcohol and from eating fast food with her boyfriend. She began to cut herself on her inner thighs in delicate stripes that she thought no one would see, and under her arms. Like the pains of starvation, she found solace in these self-made injuries, and would spend time caring for the scars, rubbing ointment into the wounds and checking on the healing process. She kept these cuts secret, much as she had hidden her secret pleasure in self-starvation.

Eventually Jason became sexually demanding, occasionally physically abusive, and jealous of her with other men. She fell pregnant at 17 with his baby and he threatened to kill her if she even considered having an abortion. Their relationship became increasingly violent and destructive, and Jason started to deal in Class A drugs. By the time their baby, Harrison, arrived, social services were involved in their case and he was immediately placed on the child protection register. Leanne's family were well known to the local authority but she had never been removed into care herself, as both parents were able to cover up the extent of their drug dependence and neglect of all three children, while Leanne's care of her younger siblings served to create the impression that they were relatively well tended to, clean and well presented. Harrison was taken into care shortly after birth on the basis of the violence between the couple and the family history of drug addiction and crime. He was adopted, and Leanne felt that a gross injustice had been done to her as no one had ever monitored the degree to which she was at risk. The pain of losing him remained a central focus for her and she had an elaborate tattoo of his name and birth date imprinted on her arm.

This sense of a cover-up was a powerful theme in Leanne's life, and was also re-enacted in her own, hidden self-harm. Despite her fundamental wish to preserve life, she needed to feel in control of herself and had no internal model of a nurturing carer that helped to sustain her. She had no external container for her aggression and fear in her early life, yet was expected not only to manage her own needs, but also to tend to the needs of her younger siblings. She was left feeling furious with the parents who abandoned her and the younger siblings whose needs she felt compelled to meet, but without acceptable outlets for these feelings, or the maternal containment of negative affect she required, had learned to turn this rage against herself through self-harm and starvation.

Leanne had continued to self-harm in custody and defaced her skin. She maintained the view that she was ugly, that her skin was too dark, like her mother's, as opposed to her father's pink and white skin, now hanging off him as his heroin addiction had left him thin and unkempt. She did not see that she had internalised racism towards herself, but was clearly in conflict about her own identity and frightened of the darkness she concretely located on her skin, but which could be seen to symbolise the darkness of her parent's violence, to which she felt connected. She was in identification with her mother whose body was used and hurt for the pleasure of others. Her offence and her own attacks on herself reflected her aggression and the sense that the only place that this could be contained was in her own body.

She had committed the offences after Harrison was adopted, when she herself was using cocaine and amphetamines, the latter partly because it kept her weight down and gave her energy. Going inside prison at 20 enabled her to come off drugs and, ironically, gave her the opportunity to engage in counselling that had never been offered to her in the community. Once released from prison, she got a job in a local dry cleaning firm, found herself a shared flat and eventually formed a relationship with Del, a man from a stable background and supportive family, with no criminal history. They moved in together and planned to get pregnant, resulting in the birth of baby Jude. Both parents were committed to ensuring they could keep this baby and would do 'whatever it took' to prove this to the local authority.

Del and Leanne were encouraged to engage in a therapeutic programme for parents whose children are considered at risk of harm, and they used this opportunity well. Not only could Leanne explore her own attachment difficulties but she was also able to describe the impulses to self-harm that continued to preoccupy her, and to draw on paper the inner conflicts she faced.

Leanne outlined a terrible conflict she faced when the urges to self-harm arose, and how these originated in the part of her that felt like 'not me', an alien part filled with self-loathing and a wish to act out violently. In these moments her feelings about herself are cruel and she torments herself with insults, as if turning on herself the hateful treatment she has suffered at the hands of others. She drew a picture of her alien self in which her face was depicted as being full of scars, laceration, blood-shot eyes and multiple ear piercings, which all evoke scenes of violation and penetration. On the other side, a clear blue eye gazes serenely. Interestingly, she is a woman with light eyes, made more striking in contrast to her dark skin. On the side of her 'alien self', she writes, amongst other statements, that she finds herself 'in a dark place with no return'. In therapy, she was able to explore more fully the alien self which also housed the violence of her father and her own internalised racism. Some of that racism could be explored with me towards whom she felt the same kind of hatred she felt towards her mother. This could be thought about in addition to her feelings of anger towards the neglectful father who did not provide for or kept the family safe.

It seemed that a therapeutic space enabled Leanne to take in the experience of a containing figure, where another mind reflects on her emotional experience. This in turn enabled her to notice, focus and think about her feelings and phantasies about herself, including her racialised experiences, her identity, her body, being a mother and part of a couple in comparison to the couple she had in her mind from her upbringing. Developing some understanding of her mind enabled her to provide a different containment for her baby.

There are myriads of women presenting like Leanne in prison and youth offenders' institutions and there is some urgency for structures to be in place that enable these women and young girls to connect with their own histories. Here, initial group work could also be a medium, which could be started whilst in prison. In addition to individual work, rehabilitation should be thought about in terms of skills required to be able to make different choices outside of prison. Post-prison, this requires social factors to be addressed and ongoing support, notably via adequate accommodation, benefits and employment, and probation services. For many women it may be post-prison that they wish to access mental health care to address the factors which led to their incarceration.

The Conservative Government announced in May 2019 that the bulk of prison probation services would resume under the auspices of central government. However, the detail of this involves combining government, private and voluntary services. At the time of writing, how these agencies will work together was not clarified. Such an arrangement could mean the necessary level of service will continue to be less than adequate, without clear and concerted coordination. It leaves too much room for a postcode lottery in relation to prisoners' aftercare. As we know, both the rehabilitation that occurs during prison and the follow up by probation services is crucial in preventing re-offending.

I have explored some of the organisational issues for the women prisoners. I will now turn to the organisational factors in relation to staff development to outline how prison staff, as well as any mental health professionals, art therapists or probation staff, could be enabled to identify and tackle the emotional demands of this work, without drawing on primitive defences designed to keep the 'other' at bay.

The relevance of Bion

In thinking about organisations it is important to reflect on how groups function. I will now describe how Wilfred Bion's work informs our understanding of groups and how they function. Then I will describe how group relations conferences (GRCs) can enlighten us about underlying dynamics between group members and within organisations. I will offer examples of unconscious racism and how this gets played out in these temporary organisations (GRCs), and explore how this can easily happen within prison settings and secure hospitals too.

Group functioning

The work of Wilfred Bion (1961) at the Tavistock Clinic after the Second World War was seminal in our understanding of unconscious processes in groups. He saw members of groups as contributing quite unconsciously to the 'group mentality' or 'will' of the group. This occurred in the face of the anxieties that individual members were confronted with at the prospect of joining and becoming part of a group. In this state there is an unconscious collusion or primitive form of organisation that constitutes the group mentality. The group culture develops based on the conflict arising between the individual and the group mentality. Bion is well known for his differentiation between work groups and basic assumption functioning groups; the former able to cooperate to achieve tasks, and the second less functional and operating at a primitive level. These both refer to states of mind which group members occupy and that enable or hinder their primary task. In the criminal justice system this primary task is to keep the public safe and to punish offenders for their crimes by imprisoning them. However, one could say that without a secondary task of treating any mental health problems and helping the prisoners formulate and understand their issues, specifically what might lay behind how they find themselves imprisoned, they are bound to reoffend.

Types of group functioning

In work groups there is some capacity to learn, and group members are seen to cooperate in relation to the primary or main tasks or function of the group. On the whole there is some awareness of the impact of how the internal group functioning and the external world relate and affect each other. However, Bion saw the 'basic assumptions' group as rather more typical of group functioning, these assumptions operating principally as anti-group tasks. This means that the dynamics between individuals operate destructively and prevent achievement of the primary task.

Features of basic assumption groups and racism revealed

It is important to see if the forensic setting is functioning in what Bion thought of as the three basic assumptions: dependency, fight/flight or pairing, and in terms of what Foulkes (1946, 1948) spoke of as 'the means of communicating'.

In the basic assumption 'dependency', the group consultant is seen by the members as possessing all the knowledge, whilst the group are devoid of their own capacities. In 'pairing', the group phantasy is that they might produce a saviour via two members coming together, and thus provide a solution for the group's difficulties. With 'fight/flight', self-preservation in the group is based on fighting with, or taking flight from, a common enemy, a role which the group can encourage the group consultant to take up, or alternatively select a member with a valency towards a more paranoid/individualistic position.

It is thought that individuals have a propensity to take up particular roles within groups, and that this happens unconsciously, and will reveal and repeat patterns from earlier life and societal expectations related to class, gender, culture and so on that have been internalised. It is noteworthy that individual members will come with their particular valency/propensity to follow one of the basic assumptions both within the group and during a GRC. The discovery or confirmations of such valences can be an important process of awareness derived from ongoing group psychotherapy or from the shorter, intense and immersive experiences of GRCs. I will give a brief description of these GRCs.

The development of group relation ideas was through the collaboration of the Tavistock Clinic and the Tavistock Institute (1957). The conference design at the Tavistock Clinic is based on the Leicester Conference of the Tavistock Institute of Human Relations. A GRC is a temporary learning institution where it is possible to explore the organisational dynamics that might typically be observed within institutions. There is a hope that the insights gained can be applied outside the temporary setting and this is a question we aimed to begin to explore. The experiential learning typically referred to as occurring in the 'here and now' focuses on how the individual relates to the group and the organisation as a whole. This emphasis is in order for change to occur – a combination of an awareness of the unconscious processes which are in operation and the more conscious rational understanding of the system. Psychodynamic principles are applied to the study of a group as a social system (Fraher, 2004).

The group relations approach encompasses both the psychoanalytic approach (Bion) and Open Systems Theory (Von Bertalanffy, 1950). The system, which can be thought of as open or closed, has its specific boundaries of time, task and territory which help to differentiate who and what is inside and outside the system. An open system, being more fluid, enables exchange across boundaries in contrast to the rigidity of a closed system. There is an attempt to explore the group unconscious and the organisation in the mind of the members of the GRC. There are further psychoanalytic ideas which aid our understanding of group processes within these conferences, such as Freud on *Group Psychology and the Analysis of the Ego* (1921) and Klein on primitive defence mechanisms (1946). Splitting, being one of the defence mechanisms used in a paranoid-schizoid (PS) state of mind or 'position'. The PS position is an early and more primitive state of functioning which manages anxiety by attempting to hold onto certainties. Here the world is defined in good and bad terms. One is either for or against. There are no shades of grey. Use is made of 'projective identification' where there is an unconscious identification with the projector and there can also be a projected attribute, whether it be of an impulse, feeling, thought, part of the self or internal object (Bott Spillius et al., 2011). The PS position is followed by a more depressive position, where there is depressive guilt and concern for the injuries inflicted in reality and in phantasy on loved ones, including objects inside and outside of the self (Bott Spillius et al., 2011).

Relation to racism and enactments in prison settings

In relation to looking at racism, fear and anxiety can be heightened and become exposed in group settings, in particular in a large group. Here Foulkes's (1975) theory, involving a combination of psychoanalysis, sociology and Gestalt psychology, has led to an understanding of individuals in large groups as nodal points in a network of relationships, and ill health as a disturbance in this network which presented through an individual because of their valency.[7] The anxiety in a large group can often be a paranoid one with manifestations in very concrete and/or suspicious thinking. One way in which the group can deal with this paranoid anxiety is to throw up (or over throw) its own leader. Ultimately, within the wider group there is the fear of its members losing their minds, of violence and of annihilation. In prisons, one see these fears manifest in breakdowns in functioning (e.g. prison riots or prisoners taking charge of a wing) which occur from time to time. It becomes hard to listen to what is being communicated about the lack of staff, time out of cells, meaningful things to do, dealing with drug problems, violence and intimidation. Instead there are greater restrictions and controls put in place. On the other side there may be the struggle and fear being carried by the prison staff of not being able to provide what they would like to because of the lack of resources. One can also see how black members can be a receptacle for hostile projections from other inmates and prison staff.

Staff being reminded of the complexity of how groups function and experiential learning about the positions they can occupy within a group is fruitfully conveyed in a GRC, which provides a unique opportunity for staff development. I will turn to some examples of the learning which can occur.

GRC example: staff development by the use of GRCs

The conference's particular title helps to focus participants on aspects relevant to the organisation. It can examine how the group constructs, for example, its multiple identities, leadership and followership. The impact of discussing identity, class and culture are particularly relevant to the areas we have been examining in this book and the roles members might occupy within a GRC. This would have relevance to a staff member's development. I will turn to two simple examples from GRC conferences.

Example A: an attack on leadership

This specific example shows how racist projections were made, and made use of, as well as how certain members of particular ethnic/cultural groups were assumed to 'go together'. It also shows how they led to attacks on the GRC director, a black woman (of high stature and great competence) by an older white male, who acted behind her back to allow a relative into the group conference, thereby asserting his power and control as if he were the director, finding it impossible to act as an associate.

The conference membership was discussed in directorate planning meetings. These meetings look at the structure and organise the conference, and are appropriate times to mention any connections between membership and staff, so that learning experiences, as far as possible, are unaffected by personal links. However, the relationship between the associate director and a relative did not come to light until raised in the feedback of one of the small groups. This was a shock. There were feelings of exposure, sadness and a sense of betrayal experienced both by the director and the staff team. There was an opportunity to examine, think about and understand whether the membership as a whole enabled this or if their role was to expose an act of wrongdoing. The work of the staff group was to think about how the group would respond to this attack. Was the associate actually sorry or just shamed by his exposure? What was the functioning of the staff team? What might this reflect about the dynamic within the membership?

This example reflects some of the pressure on a leader who is black, who can feel that they are given power but then perhaps expect their authority to be undermined in tacit ways. The failure of an organisation, especially if the black member of staff has been brought in to 'deal with black issues', or 'satisfy the ethnic quota', becomes quite clear. The feeling arises that they can only 'deal with black issues' and have little else to offer. Organisations may present themselves as wanting to address racism within their functioning, but what might be kept quite split off is how black staff can be used as 'window dressing' to maintain the status quo. This is often highlighted by black members of staff being given responsibility without any power to effect change, in addition to being given a staff team who undermine rather than facilitate change. The wish for the director to be just window dressing while the associate was 'really in charge' was part of what had to be explored, along with the group facing their struggles with younger female black leadership.

One's relationship to authority is always something to be negotiated when it comes to the dynamics of leadership and authoritative followership. Both white and BAME staff can find black leadership a challenge; for some white staff they don't feel it's the natural order of things, or it stirs up feelings of intense rivalry, whilst others present a nice liberal attitude which can act as a carapace over more complex feelings. The rivalry may often not be acknowledged and the black leader is left feeling inadequate or incompetent and over time that may become a self-fulfilling prophecy. Alternatively, they end up feeling burned out, as they are working much harder than they need to, both managing their role and racism or micro-aggressions on a daily basis, whilst their white contemporaries in similar roles often, irrespective of how limited their experience is, are afforded the initial respect of authority, goodness and capacity. They are innocent until proven guilty, and for the black leader they are guilty of incompetence and relentlessly have to prove otherwise. One error condemns them and every black person to follow. This is another legacy of colonialisation, where white privilege is assumed and goodness, authority and capacity are accorded, regardless of the actual capabilities of the white staff member. Black or mixed parentage staff can often become jealous of each other, feeling that there is only room for one, especially if one staff member is in a position of authority. The unconscious belief can be that this is the only post the organisation is going to allow, so they have to fight it out. If this conflict is observed it can be misused to confirm a racist bias, for example that it reflects 'black on black violence', rather than being 'set up' by an organisation that unconsciously assigns only one post to a black person, thereby inviting conflict, unhelpful competition and discord.

Example B: they are all the same

Here there is a lack of interest in differences, I think in part because to address difference means addressing too much complexity. One is having to take note of who is actually present rather than responding to what you project onto the person, and acknowledge one's bias or stereotyping. For example, on a GRC, a Hispanic women of middle-class (adopted) background was taken to be a poor Latina woman, here confirming a more ego-syntonic way of relating to her rather than noticing what privileges she may have had access to. In noticing that she did not conform to the stereotypical view generated a more ego-dystonic dynamic between participants. I think similarly all black people in the UK are often seen as foreign, poor and working class. They are a homogeneous group in the eyes of the majority of the population, except for the 'exceptional ones' referred to in Chapter 3. The idea of a more heterogeneous group of people is a challenge.

One GRC member spoke of how her team leader often addresses her by saying 'Yo!' each morning. He seemed to think because she was black this would make her feel comfortable as they were 'talking street'. This instead left her infuriated because that was not how she addressed people within or outside the work setting. It also was not the way a boss addresses his employee in a professional or any other setting. It is also a challenge to some black people who see others as presenting themselves in a way which is 'acting white', that is 'the coconut'. Here the person is seen as betraying their 'race'. This slur seems to deem what is appropriate and is restrictive, limiting designated ways of thinking and relating. It appears to involve a ghettoisation of a way of being, which sets limits upon what is accessible and possible.

In terms of multiple identities, it is what is projected onto members and the impact this has within the institution that is important; specifically, how such constructions are made use of within the temporary institution, this being perhaps in part to manage various anxieties and uncertainties around being accepted, wanted and valued. In the realm of group relations, the primary task is that of learning. What is learnt is dependent on each member. Indeed each member will leave the conference with something slightly different and hopefully unique to their particular needs. Essential to this process is that of being able to explore and investigate organisational life, its dynamics and one's part in this process. In turn, by developing greater awareness of this, an individual may feel more able to take up their roles, in work or otherwise, with more awareness and authority.

When staff within criminal justice settings are given the opportunity to explore the roles they take up and unconsciously accord to black staff and prisoners they may be shocked to see how restrictive, confining and ultimately damaging their unconscious biases are. While such work could ideally be undertaken through GRCs as described above, these are not possible for staff following tight rotas and not yet part of prison culture. However, staff training days, reflective practice groups and organisational consultancy can be integrated into psychologically informed prison environments, on the lines developed below.

(A) Staff attending training and teachings days

Training which could enhance consciousness would be important, on subjects such as unconscious bias, trauma, vicarious traumatisation, burnout, self-harm, mental health and working with women who fear authority figures.

(B) Reflective practice groups

These are helpful in understanding the impact of trauma on individuals and groups and are regular structures in which a facilitator can join the whole staff team to think about the work and its impact on them, reducing the risk of re-enactments. They also provide an opportunity to examine organisational structures and functioning and identify how these impact on staff functioning and the treatment of the women and girls.

(C) Review of organisational structure

Away days and use of external consultation looking at team functioning and the environment provided for women. Such a consultant would need to be aware of the increasing body of work on white identity, for example Frankenberg (1997), DiAngelo (2018) and Ryder (2019), colonial object relations and how these dynamics play out within the institution being consulted.

(D) Self-care

Opportunities for staff to look at their own functioning with staff support and team training days. Often staff teams working both in health and the criminal justice system are referred to as 'being fit for purpose' and 'resilient'. Both terms are often misused to attack staff when there is a lack of adequate resources, or there are cuts which are perversely called 'savings', where the actual reality is not being faced.

A term which is often misused in organisations to criticise rather than enable the women prisoners and staff is 'resilience', leading to the view that mental health difficulties or crises are a personal failing of the staff or woman prisoner. The implication is that if they were more resilient they would be able to cope.

The relevance of social and economic factors in creating adversity can be ignored with this reductive notion. Resilience is the capacity to adapt in the face of challenging circumstances, such as being socially isolated or dealing with stressful workplace conditions, whilst maintaining a stable mental wellbeing. Resilience can be taught and learned but the learning opportunities need to be provided.

When a prison is understaffed and staff lack adequate training, are inadequately resourced and pressured this impacts their well-being and functioning. Equally, women's rehabilitation requires adequate resourcing and thought about how much time women spend outside of the cells, what activities are available for them and the quality of rehabilitation on offer. The confinement being referred to in this chapter and in this book is not just physical confinement but a psychological/emotional one which needs addressing both within and after leaving prison.

Because of the complexity and unconscious nature of institutional and individual racism it is only through such a comprehensive, systemic and holistic approach that these entrenched dynamics can be made manifest and modified. The power of systemic and group relation principles has been developed and researched by the Tavistock Institute and I have shown how it can be used effectively to uncover central issues of racism, bias and disempowerment.

Notes

1 The national audit identified that problems with the part-privatisation of probation services had cost taxpayers nearly £500m. From December 2020 offenders will be monitored by the National Probation Service. Currently, community rehabilitation services have been monitoring low and medium risk offenders; these services were not required to employ professionally qualified staff. Whilst the National Probation Service monitored the high risk prisons, the categorisation of prisoners did not make allowances for changes in their risk level (BBC News, 16 May 2019).
2 Slang terms used for offenders. 'Con' is short for convict.
3 Slang terms used for prison officers. 'Screws' or 'kangas' was first used for prison guards in 1812, which refers to the key they carried. Kanga is an abbreviation of the cockney rhyming slang for screw – 'kangaroo'. 'Cowboy' is a new correctional officer, or (backwards) 'yobwoc'; 'care bear' is a prison officer of a caring nature. 'Fraggle' is used for a therapist dealing with mental health.
4 Terms for an offender who is acting in a superior way or trying to reinvent himself.
5 See www.dissidentreality.com/articles/uk-prison-slang/.
6 What 'white' represents in terms of a relationship with authority or 'superiority'; so racist ideas about hierarchy are internalised and damage one's own self-perception.
7 A member has a vulnerability or receptivity to a particular time of dynamic within a group which may or may not be out of their conscious awareness.

References

Alleyne, A. (2019) Conference presentation: Post slavery syndrome and intergenerational trauma. London.

Bion, W.R. (1961) *Experiences in groups*. London: Tavistock.

Bott Spillius, E., Milton, J., Garvey, P., Couve, C. and Steiner, D. (2011) *The new dictionary of kleinian thought*. London: Routledge.

Cardale, E., Edgar, K., Swaine Williams, K. and Earle, J. (2017) *Counted out: Black, Asian and minority ethnic women in the criminal justice system*. London: Prison Reform Trust.

Dennis, M. (2012) Ordinary differences, different states of mind. *New Associations*. BPC.22 Winter 2016/17.

DiAngelo, R. (2018) *White fragility: Why it is so hard for white people to talk about racism*. Boston: Beacon Press.

Du Bois, W.E.B. (1897) The strivings of Negro People. *Atlantic Monthly*. August 1897.

Du Bois, W.E.B. (1994) *The souls of black folk*. New York; Avenel, NJ: Gramercy Books.

Fanon, F. (1952, 1991) *Black skin, white masks*. London: Pluto Press.

Foulkes, S.H. (1946) On group analysis. *International Journal of Psychoanalysis*, 27, 46–51.

Foulkes, S.H. (1948) *An introduction to group analytic psychotherapy*. London: Heinemann.

Foulkes, S.H. (1975) Problems of the large groups from a group-analytic point of view. In Kreeger, L. (Ed.) *The large group dynamics and therapy*, 33–56. London: Karnac.

Fraher, A.L. (2004) Systems psychodynamics: The formative years of an interdisciplinary field at the Tavistock Institute. *History of Psychology*, 7(1), 65–84.

Freud, S. (1921) *Group psychology and analysis of the ego*. Standard Edition, Vol 18. London: Hogarth Press.

Gilroy, P. (1993) *Black Atlantic – modernity and double consciousness*. London: Verso.

Goffman, E. (1961) *Asylums: Essays on the social situations of mental patients and other inmates*. London: Penguin.

Kafka, F. (1915) *The metamorphosis*. Planet EBook.com.

Kafka, F. (1925) *The trial*. London: Penguin Classics.

Levine, P. and Kline, M. (2007) *Trauma through the child's eyes*. Berkeley, CA: North Atlantic Books.

Menzies-Lyth, I. (1959) The functioning of a social system as a defence against anxiety. *Human Relations*, 13, 95–121.

Minstry of Justice (2019) Prisoner officer workforce. www.ethnicity-facts-figures.service.gov.uk/workforce-and-business/workforce-diversity/prison-officer-workforce/latest.

Morrison, T. (2017). *Playing in the dark: Whiteness and the literary imagination*. New York: Vintage Books.

Player, E. (2017) The offender personality disorder pathway and its implications for women prisoners in England and Wales. *Punishment & Society*, 19(5), 568–589. doi: 10.1177/1462474516672883.

Rankine, C. (2015) On racial violence: The condition of black life is one of mourning. June 22. https://www.nytimes.com/2015/06/22/magazine/the-condition-of-black-life-is-one-of-mourning.html

Ryder, J. (2019) *White privilege unmasked*. London: Jessica Kingsley Publishers.

Von Bertalanffy, L. (1950) The theory of open systems in physics and biology. *Science*, 3, 22–29.

Chapter 12

Conclusion

Why the caged bird sings

Anna Motz, Maxine Dennis and Anne Aiyegbusi

Maya Angelou uses the metaphor of the caged bird in her writings to represent
the plight of the enslaved, oppressed and abused. In her 1983 poem entitled
'Caged Bird' Angelou contrasts the African American caged bird with the
white free bird. Of the caged bird, she writes:

> But a bird that stalks
> down his narrow cage
> can seldom see through
> his bars of rage
> his wings are clipped and
> his feet are tied
> so he opens up his throat to sing.
>
> The caged bird sings
> with a fearful trill
> of things unknown
> but longed for still
> and his tune is heard
> on the distant hill
> for the caged bird
> sings of freedom.

Like the caged bird, the plight of women detained within the criminal justice
system is harrowing, and yet they long for 'things unknown'. Typically, their
traumas have been 'forgotten', secret or hidden and therefore invisible, their
existence only surfacing through the women's violent acts or conspicuous presentations and behaviours. The over-riding theme within each chapter of this
book is the way that even when incarcerated, the women's history of trauma
and of suffering, whether its roots are trans-generational, social, political or
domestic, remains invisible. The women's experience is of being hyper-visible
while their cries and communications go unheard as the focus remains on their
puzzling un-womanliness. They are caught up in systems designed for men,

and face multiple losses when they are imprisoned, feeding into the cycle of deprivation that has brought them into prison in the first place. Black, Asian and Minority Ethnic (BAME) women are overrepresented in the criminal justice system (CJS), yet overlooked. The unintended consequences of custodial sentences are destructive and far-ranging, as the previous chapters have shown, in terms of the impact on children, the creation of a sense of hopelessness in the women themselves, and the lost opportunities to engage and support the women in the community.

In a fundamental sense the women have been 'unsexed', treated as if they were men within a punitive system designed with men in mind. While many acts of female violence are committed behind closed doors, and never come to light, some are detected and enter the public arena. The violence hidden behind domestic tableaux does not require public punishment, though its imprint may be harsh and deep. Through these acts of violence, women have broken taboos, shattered ideals of femininity and motherhood, and often been subjected to a vicious backlash by the press and general public. They are not simply punished for injuries against the victims of their crimes but also for violating societal norms and cherished beliefs about womankind.

In this concluding chapter we identify ways forward to support women, and offer thoughts on how best to ensure they are properly seen, and attended to, rather than overlooked or perceived through a distorting lens. The central paradox that women can both be invisible – in terms of actual trauma histories, cultural identities, strengths and hidden losses – and simultaneously hyper-visible – seen as monstrous and dangerous, particularly if black – creates a complex and urgent challenge for true reform. We will outline some of the initiatives that attempt to address this dilemma, and to both see and respond to the women in their true complexity. For example, female Muslim prisoners, who make up 6% of the women's prison population, are both invisible and hyper-visible:

> Their voices are often unheard, and they are often invisible in policy-making, families and communities. However, there is an additional hyper-visibility in the media and with the public, particularly for those who are visibly Muslim (i.e. those who wear the hijab or have certain surnames).
>
> (Malasha, 2016)

The female offender strategy

In 2018 the UK government announced the Female Offender Strategy (MoJ, 2018) which is a significant commitment to improving outcomes for women who offend, with the result that fewer women will serve custodial sentences and that conditions for those that do will be improved. A key message of this strategy is to reduce or abolish custodial sentences altogether, improving the quality of care for women in custody and establishing community based alternatives, that may include residential women's centres. This strategy argues that sentencing and disposal practices should be altered to address the complex needs and traumatic histories of the women with a greater emphasis placed on community provision. In February 2019 the then Secretary of State for Justice, David Gauke, announced that all short sentences should be abolished. The emphasis on addressing the needs of female offenders, and recognising the low level violence of their offences, is evidence-based and reflects a deepening understanding of the complexity and traumatic roots of women's offending. The Strategy was informed by the views of dedicated third-sector organisations campaigning for prison reform and attention to the needs of criminalised women, who were advising on government policy.

While this is an important development, and sets out a clear basis upon which to build holistic and trauma-informed services for women, it remains to be delivered. Although £50 million had originally been allocated to build new women's prisons this funding has now been diverted to focus on community provision, though the funding has been reduced to £5 million pounds. Other aims of the strategy include workforce development across Her Majesty's Prison and Probation Service (HMPPS) and improvements in pre-sentencing reports prepared by Offender Managers, which will include highly significant information on whether the woman has child care responsibilities, to enable sentencers to consider this carefully before imposing a custodial order, the improvement of conditions in custody and the establishment of a National Concordat for Female Offenders.

Residential women's centres

The Ministry of Justice is committed to funding pilot women's residential units and evaluating their success in terms of enhancing female offenders' treatment, retaining their community ties and diverting them from custody wherever possible. The proposal for at least five pilot residential units across England and Wales is an exciting one, whose results will prove highly informative and offer guidance for the ways forward for women who offend. Another commitment of the Strategy is to identify and address the needs of BAME women offenders, a long overdue objective, and one that is urgently needed.

The use of residential women's centres in place of custody is one of the pillars of the proposal, and is closest to Baroness Corston's vision of women's centres as a 'one stop shop' for women in contact with the criminal justice system. The use of women's centres has been recommended by important voices advocating for the most humane and effective treatment of women who commit crimes, including The Prison Reform Trust, arguing that such centres keep women in communities where they can continue to have regular and meaningful contact with their families. The best model for these centres remains to be seen, as there are already some excellent examples of practice in community-based women's centres where women can remain in their own home but receive support and supervision from a centre, as part of their conviction, but with a clear rehabilitative purpose.

Criticisms of the proposals for these women's centres focus on their residential status; one concern is that centres will simply replace custody and deprive women of their freedom without necessarily addressing the underlying difficulties that have led the women into criminality. The route into independent living will remain circuitous and the risks for the women returning to their communities will not necessarily be reduced. These include the dangerous partners, pimps and other associates who remain in their community and the strong links to criminality that they pose. Furthermore, sentencing bodies, such as magistrates, are not yet aware of these options and would need to be educated fully about the range of sentencing choices available to them.

A further criticism of the government proposals for residential women's centres is that this is a case of reinventing the wheel, as such centres already exist and have to compete for funding at a level that does not sustain them. For example, the radical and far reaching work of the centre in Birmingham, Anawim, was formerly used in place of custodial sentencing, but this stopped when the Transforming Rehabilitation programme was rolled out. Splitting the probation service into a public and private service dramatically impacted on the provision of care for women offenders, with the majority of women being seen by the privately run Community Rehabilitation Centres, who link into local services in vastly different ways. As Glenys Stacey writes in her Inspectorate Report of March 2019, the privatisation of the probation service has resulted in a wholly flawed system. Significantly, the stipulation that women offenders, over 70% of whom are serving short sentences, require supervision for up to a year post-release, within an already fragmented probation service, has resulted in a vast increase in recall rates, as described eloquently and starkly in the recent report by the Prison Reform Trust, *Broken Trust*, as part of its Transforming Lives project. Dr Jenny Earle, Programme Director of Transforming Lives – Reducingwomen's imprisonment, said,

> This research confirms a principle of the Transforming Lives programme: that the solutions to women's offending lie in the community. One of the programme's objectives has been to improve awareness of and support for women's specific needs – for example the links between their experience of abusive and coercive relationships and their offending, unmet mental health needs arising from histories of trauma, and the adverse effects on children due to their mother's imprisonment. The recall of women to prison began to emerge as a serious concern in 2015–2016 and prompted Prison Reform Trust to undertake this research.
>
> (Prison Reform Trust, 2019)

Retaining ties with families: the Farmer review for women

The recommendations made by Lord Farmer, in his 2019 independent review, stress the importance of strengthening family ties and other relationships for women in contact with the criminal justice system, to prevent reoffending and reduce intergenerational crime. This follows his first review, commissioned by the Ministry of Justice into family and other relational ties for men in prison, of which all the recommendations were accepted by government. Justice Minister Edward Agar welcomed this report and emphasised that the aims of the Female Offender Strategy were supported by his findings, with the aim of strengthening community ties for women and reducing rates of imprisonment.

In his report Lord Farmer (2019) states:

> Healthy, supportive relationships are utterly indispensable for every woman in the criminal justice system if they are to turn away from criminality and contribute positively to society.
>
> Yet female offenders have often experienced abuse and trauma which can profoundly impact their ability to develop and sustain healthy, trusting relationships.
>
> The importance of good family and other relationships, which are rehabilitation assets, needs to be a golden thread running through the criminal justice system.

Despite its humane and radical focus, and several innovative recommendations to enable women and their children to maintain contact with one another, the report does not detail particular issues facing BAME women, describing its focus as the entire women's estate, but missing the point that there are additional stresses and complexities in the lives of those women. This is a regrettable omission from an otherwise deeply humane, psychologically rooted and significant report.

The Women's Offenders with Personality Disorder Pathway (WOPD)

Linked to the overall strategy for female offenders, the WOPD is a psychologically informed programme designed for the highest risk women and jointly commissioned and managed by HMPPS and NHS England. This important joint initiative arose out of the crucial findings of Lord Bradley's Report (2009) as part of the Offenders with Personality Disorder Pathway for males, and is designed to identify women deemed to be at high risk of harm to others and themselves, where there is a clear link between their offending and their personality difficulties. Having been 'screened into' the pathway, the women are offered specialist services, in the form of prison and community-based provisions for those with personality difficulties, including residential units like the Rivendell Service in HMP New Hall or psychologically planned environments (PIPES) that can offer pre-treatment engagement, treatment provision or post-treatment environments that support pro-social living. This programme is designed as a pathway in that women are able to move from highest security to community based provision both in residential settings like Women's Approved Premises (formerly known as hostels) and even when released into independent accommodation. Their engagement on the pathway continues through regular meetings with offender managers who have consultations with psychologists who work within the Pathways Services. The premise of the Pathway approach is that the offending is linked to personality issues and that a psychological formulation will inform how probation and other criminal justice workers engage with the women and reduce their risk of re-offending, at times supported by direct psychological input where required.

An example of a specialist personality disorder service for high risk women can be found in the Rivendell Service, part of HMP New Hall, and jointly operated by HMPPS and the NHS who provide psychological supervision, treatment interventions, consultations and service development strategy planning under Dr Caroline Logan, Consultant Clinical and Forensic Psychologist. This service has been described as a psychologically informed environment, and, like the EOS service that is part of HMP Bronzefield, is designed not only to offer treatment both to the highly complex women who are imprisoned there, but also to help the teams around them to gain understanding of the women, how best to work with them and how to manage the impact of the work on them, with the aim of reducing the impact of past trauma.

Key ingredients for an effective psychologically informed service for women offenders include staff training, specialist psychological supervision for the staff both within prison and probation services and in mental health care, reflective practice delivered regularly and reliably, and trauma – informed treatment provision. As outlined in Chapter 10, the impact of this work on staff is immense, and the needs and challenges of the women can only be met through thoughtful exploration, formulation and reflection. Managing intense countertransference feelings is an essential part of this work, and frontline workers should not be left do this alone. As Dennis powerfully argues in Chapter 11, workers within institutions designed for women who offend may find themselves unconsciously enacting dynamics related to the legacy of slavery and other oppressive relations, such that those who are clients of the service are in fact subjected to further stigmatisation, othering and humiliation, defeating the conscious purpose of the organisation which is for rehabilitation.

In order to achieve real understanding and support for complex women within the CJS, both within and outside custody, the system itself needs to be psychologically informed, and have a robust model for understanding the links between trauma and offending. Highlighting the impact of racism, poverty, sexism and cultural stereotyping on individual women and on the workers themselves and their perceptions of the women with whom they work is an integral part of this understanding.

Training for staff on WOPD

Workforce development for staff in the CJS is a key objective of the Knowledge and Understanding Framework. One of us, Motz, was commissioned in 2014 to design training programmes for staff working with women in the CJS and secure mental health service, along with an Expert by Experience and Educational Consultant, Dr Julia Blazdell.[1] This programme offers an introduction to the basis for understanding how women develop personality difficulties and why these link both with past and present trauma, and can be manifested in destructive and violent behaviour, against both themselves and others.

The training is experiential as well as didactic and introduces psychoanalytic concepts to front-line workers, including exploration of the potential for the re-enactment of traumatic relationships with the women, in response to their unconscious wishes and disturbances. It emphasises the need to resist these enactments and remain thoughtful and aware of the attachment disturbances that underlie the challenging behaviour. The principles of such work are illustrated in Chapter 10.

The programmes have been evaluated and demonstrated efficacy in improving understanding of personality complexity and confidence in working with women who present in highly challenging and disturbing ways. The notion of personality disorder is implicit in this model, alongside the central role of attachment and trauma, and recent critiques of the concept of personality disorder indicate that more focus should be placed on complex trauma and the notion of profound difficulties in relating, borne of lived experience and unconscious templates for relationships, rather than on the existence of a nebulous and stigmatising form of disorder. Although the notion of a biopsychosocial model of personality disorder had been at the heart of the Offenders with Personality Disorder Pathway model, the emphasis on psychological formulations and understanding remains valid even if the idea of personality disorder is replaced with concepts that are less rooted in the notion of dysfunction and disease.

The Pathways approach is helpful in terms of highlighting the significance of attachment in the lives of women and particularly in describing how traumatic early attachments and disruptions in care create profound difficulties that impact across the lifespan. Criminal justice staff, including probation staff, report finding the 'top tips' for working with female offenders helpful and easy to follow (Craissati, Joseph & Skett, 2015). The link between early trauma and later offending is explicit in this model and it can be used to inform the nature of services designed to engage and assist women whose experiences have led to criminality and high levels of risk. It allows practitioners to identify the significance of their own roles in relation to women with whom they work and to recognise that they are important attachment figures, who can easily be drawn into destructive re-enactments with the women, or, alternatively, offer new ways of relating. The experiences of marginalised women can be addressed using a pathways model, and the significance of continuity of care is highlighted as being even greater for those women who have consistently been placed outside of the line of vision of mainstream society, unseen, unheard and unheld.

The lack of attention paid thus far to BAME women has, rightly, generated criticism of the WOPD. This is clearly outlined in the paper by Dr Elaine Player (2017), in which she argues that:

> whilst emphasis is placed upon the need for services to be gender-responsive, there remains a significant lack of attention to the intersection of gender with race and ethnicity, as well as other sources of oppression and inequality. Given the critical history of black and ethnic minority engagement with criminal justice and mental health services, most notably evidence of how risk and race are interrelated in correctional risk and therapeutic discourses, issues arising from these intersectional dynamics should be at the forefront of OPD Pathway development and evaluation (Bernard 2013; Goddard and Myers 2016; Russell and Carlton 2013).
>
> (Player, 2017:573)

Aspects of the traumatic experiences of women from BAME backgrounds and foreign nationals are mirrored by their treatment within the CJS and mental health services, and there is evidence that BAME women are not being screened onto the pathway. This is a major problem and one that the Ministry of Justice and Women's OPD are anxious to address, as it highlights how, even when specialist provision is made available within the CJS, women of colour are somehow overlooked and remain on the edges of this service too. We can hypothesise that this relates to their being perceived as dangerous and intrinsically violent rather than traumatised and in need of understanding, psychological support and holistic, trauma-informed care.

The concrete recommendations made by the Women In Prison 'Open Up' campaign to reform criminal justice within the United Kingdom include: a trauma-informed diversion from the custody scheme, the reduction of use of remand to custody for women with children, a general reduction in custodial sentencing, particularly for short sentences, the greater use of treatment in community orders, the creation of a release date for Indeterminate Public Protection Order (IPP) prisoners, abolition of the year-long post-release supervision order and for every prison to have women's centre link workers to enable the women to engage after release – all would be important steps to improve the lives of female offenders. The specific issues for BAME women, and those with protected characteristics, will need to be outlined, and the major problem of housing and resettlement, including employment prospects, remain key.

Over years of engagement with women in forensic settings, both within criminal justice and mental health, issues of their perception and misperception have become evident. They are viewed through a lens of gender stereotyping that can blind those who encounter them to trauma and vulnerability. This is most glaring when women have committed violent sexual or terrorist crimes that render them psychopathic, or when they come from BAME backgrounds. The ways that BAME women are sometimes described is not just in terms of their skin colour but also in relation to the sensory impressions they leave, namely the shape of their bodies, textures of their hair, smells on their person, sounds of their voices – this reveals unconscious racism. Sometimes shockingly the language used connotes animals, savages, wildness and terror, while at other times it can be imbued with longing, with a form of forbidden desire that itself reveals perceptions fraught with not really seeing, but being blinded by difference and seeking to subdue this unknown force, by whatever means necessary.

Desistance

For women to 'go straight' they need hope, and a narrative that offers meaning and a life story in which they are viewed as active agents, capable of choosing and living meaningful and pro-social lives. In order for this sense of hope to develop it is urgent that there is a culture shift within the CJS and within forensic mental health services to enable women who offend to be seen in their entirety, not overlooked altogether or seen through a highly distorted lens. The victim and the perpetrator within the individual woman need to be held in mind and brought into a relationship with both individual workers, including therapists and CJS staff, and with the institutional and community structures in which they are placed.

The re-marginalisation of women from BAME backgrounds requires urgent attention, and the focus of all our work must be on making conscious the unconscious biases which have rendered so many women invisible. This will require an investment in external consultations aiming to address the institutionalised culture of white fragility (Diangelo, 2018) underpinning the entrenched blindness to the vulnerability and suffering of BAME women that exists throughout criminal justice and forensic mental health systems.

Those crimes thought most taboo, including sexual abuse, terrorism, killing and sadistic violence, also need to be explored, understood and their traumatic roots uncovered, if real understanding is to occur. Through this understanding the risk of reoffending can be reduced, and the welfare of the woman herself protected. The psychological truth of trauma and its sequelae must be made explicit. The true impact of trauma must be laid bare, seen without the distorting effect of racial bias and prejudice; so too must the beauty and hopefulness of the women's spirit and courage in attempting to survive unspeakable acts of brutality. This violence against the women is transmitted through the generations, as described so powerfully in Chapter 3, in the legacy of racial abuse, in the development of the racist gaze described in Chapter 4, and through the intergenerational repetition of maternal violence and neglect, as explored in

Chapter 2. Having been victimised, the women who come into contact with the CJS are amongst those who re-enact their abuse in the role of perpetrator.

Seeing the unseeable

In order to see the women who come into contact with the CJS in their true complexity, practitioners will need to be prepared to confront harsh realities about the nature of female agency and aggression, and to suspend judgement, as they seek to understand rather than condemn them. Learning about the underlying trauma in the women's histories is an essential part of the process. Understanding how victims and perpetrators coexist within the same woman and the dynamics that drive the transition from abused to abuser helps to hold the position of understanding and working with the woman, without becoming rescuer or judge.

How do we address blind spots? The fact of unconscious bias means that there will be aspects of the women that will, inevitably, be overlooked, while other features will assume undue levels of attention. Only through identifying this bias can there be the hope of modifying it. This is a slow and painful process for all, as practitioners will struggle to own their unconscious racism and other defences that come into play as they encounter women who engender fear, hopelessness and frustration. It is tempting to locate these countertransference responses in fixed features of the women themselves, rather than to subject these feelings to interrogation and process them, along the lines identified in Chapter 11. These defences are codified and embedded within institutional practice, and can become rigid, destructive and powerful forces that prevent 'seeing' the women in their pain and complexity.

Attending to, caring for and bearing witness

Having described the plight of women in the CJS, we finally turn to the complexities of professionals' roles in their progress and/or recovery. As we have suggested in previous chapters, the tasks of the professionals working with women whose traumas have gone unseen is by no means simple, requiring understanding and skills not typically availed by mainstream training. Furthermore, aspects of professionals' taken-for-granted socialisation are likely to be challenged in the process of learning to bear witness to the harm done to the women and the way in which this harm manifested in their crimes. Women's needs that may not be visible include their histories of domestic abuse and how this was re-enacted in their offending behaviour and now risks being further re-enacted within the criminal justice or forensic mental health system once detained.

Women who have seriously offended or behaved in ways that seem unfathomable because when viewed through the lens of the (white) feminine myth they are unwomanly, require their stories to be heard, understood and validated. Women whose trauma has been profound, early and extensive often exist as hidden populations, in systems within systems, detained indefinitely. These women are typically experienced as controlling and highly agentive while their desperation and helplessness are masked by behaviours that overwhelm the professionals working with them. The question 'What happened?' is especially relevant to these women whose trauma narratives are often clearly represented in their presentations. Their very cries for care (McMillan and Aiyegbusi, 2009) keep them alienated from it. Professionals working with them require a way to understand this, validate it and negotiate a way to make the invisible visible in the form of a shared narrative which in turn informs an agreed plan of care.

As we have described in this and preceding chapters, black women's visibility in terms of their over-representation in the CJS belies the invisibility of their underlying vulnerability. This includes the intergenerational impact of slavery and colonisation in contributing to their being perceived as having heightened dangerousness and anti- (white) feminine qualities that are denigrated. The consequences of projections loaded with devaluation and debasement add to the particular visibility afforded black women. To date, the CJS has shown no sign of addressing this position or its interplay with the treatment black women receive once detained. The task of bearing witness to the impact of racism is a challenging one for white professionals and flies in the face of the norm, which is to dismiss it, further distressing its victims. The work required to support professionals to take account of the role of racism including generational trauma and its perpetuation within the CJS needs to be undertaken. Other forms of discrimination and 'invisibility' must be brought out of the shadows.

While this book has largely focused on the work of mental health and criminal justice professionals it is important to highlight the powerful impact and strong voice of several remarkable third-sector organisations devoted to prison reform and improving the lives of vulnerable women. The political force of these organisations and their creativity, dedication and passion has been responsible for shaping some of the most important policy decisions relating to women in the CJS and the community and through the gate work has offered hope as well as practical support to thousands of women in the UK, whose traumatic experiences would otherwise have gone unnoticed, and whose voices would never have been heard. These organisations include the Prison Reform Trust, Southall Black Sisters, Women in Prison, Changing Lives, Inquest, Agenda, Clinks, Criminal Justice Alliance, Revolving Doors and Together Women, whose research and publications have informed this book and we would encourage readers to go to their websites and download these highly informative and enlightening documents for themselves. We pay tribute too to the tremendous support, creativity and 'holding' provided by residential women's centres like Anawim, Trevi House and Willodene House, which offer the 'one stop shop', or by community-based women's centres that Baroness Corston envisaged (Corston, 2007, 2017).

Professionals working in the CJS require support themselves if they are not to suffer vicarious trauma and burn out. In addition to education, reflective spaces are required that enable staff to process their experiences. Ideally this includes being able to recognise their own position in the workplace and clinical dynamics. It behoves us all to question why we choose to work in these highly charged, sometimes brutal and always trauma-ridden, settings. Doing so takes us some way towards recognising how we might help or hinder the progress of the women we work with and locate our strengths and vulnerabilities within the team context. Through self-awareness and effective teamwork where feedback is helpfully provided, we learn how to avoid perilous re-enactments of trauma and instead place ourselves in a better position to offer the women something different that helps to discontinue their assumptions about what entrusted authority figures can offer.

If we, as workers, can bear to see beyond what is immediately visible, and are receptive to learning what remains hidden, it may become possible for the women in the CJS to trust us, and themselves. Our hope is that then the cage bars, both visible and invisible, can finally be broken.

Note

1 These programmes were commissioned by the National Offender Management Service, now Her Majesty's Prison and Probation Service, and rolled out to over 600 staff across the United Kingdom and Wales, both in the form of an MSc module, standalone BSc modules and in a four-day enhanced awareness training package.

References

Angelou, M. (1983) Caged Bird. In *Shaker Why Don't You Sing*. New York: Random House.

Bernard, A. (2012) The intersectional alternative: Explaining female criminality. *Feminst Criminology*, 8(1), 3–19. doi: 10.1177/1557085112445304.

Bradley, K.J. (2009) *The Bradley Report: Lord Bradley's Review of People with Mental Health Problems or Learning Disabilities in the Criminal Justice System*. London: Department of Health.

Craissati, J., Joseph, N., & Skett, S. (Eds.) (2015) *Working with Offenders with Personality Disorder: A Practitioner's Guide*. London: Department of Health.

Corston, J. (2007) *A Review of Women with Particular Difficulties in the Criminal Justice System*. London: HMSO.

Corston, J. (2017) *The Corston Report: 10 Years on*. London: The Barrow Cadbury Trust.

Diangelo, R. (2018) *White Fragility: Why It's So Hard for White People to Talk about Racism*. Boston: Beacon Press.

Farmer, M. (2019) *The Importance of Strengthening Female Offenders' Family and other Relationships to Prevent Reoffending and Reduce Intergenerational Crime*. London: Ministry of Justice.

Goddard, T. & Myers, R. R. (2016) Against evidence-based oppression: Marginalized youth and the politics of risk-based assessment and intervention. *Theoretical Criminology*, 21(2), 151–167. https://doi.org/10.1177/1362480616645172.

Maslaha. (2016) *Young Muslims on Trial*. London: Maslaha.

McMillan, S. & Aiyegbusi, A. (2009) Crying out for care. In *Therapeutic Relationship with Offenders: An Introduction to the Psychodynamics of Forensic Mental Health Nursing*. Eds: A. Aiyegbusi & J. Clarke-Moore. London: JKP 171–186.

Ministry of Justice (2018) *Female Offender Strategy*. London: Stationery Office.

Player, E. (2017) The offender personality disorder pathway and its implications for women prisoners in England and Wales. *Punishment and Society*, 19(5), 568–589. doi: 10.1177/1462474516672883.

Prison Reform Trust (2019) *Broken Trust: The Rising Numbers of Women Recalled to Prison*. London: Prison Reform Trust.

Russell, E., Carlton, B. (2013) Pathways, race and gender responsive reform: Through an abolitionist lens. *Theoretical Criminology*, 17(4), 474–492. doi: 10.1177/1362480613497777.

Index

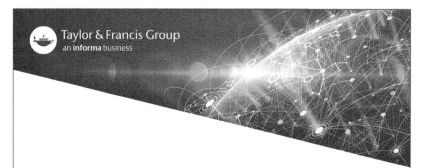